Podcasting For Dummies

Cheat Sheet

iTunes Podcast Catalog: Artwork Parameters

- 300 x 300 pixels, both in width and height
- 8-bit channel, RGB Mode
- JPEG (`.jpg`) format

ID3 Tags Defined and Implemented

- **Name:** The name or number of this particular podcasting episode. Example: Area 51: Show #15 — *Heir Check.*
- **Artist:** Your name or the name of your podcasting team. Example: Area 51, Michael & Evo, Scott Sigler.
- **Album:** The name of your show or your show's Web site. Example: Area51show.com, The Dragon Page, *EarthCore.*
- **Track Number:** (Optional) The sequential order of the podcast. For Scott Sigler's *EarthCore* and the *MOREVI* podcast, the track numbers coincide with the chapters.
- **Year:** The year of your podcast.
- **Genre:** Podcast, if offered. If not, list your podcast as Spoken Word or Comedy.
- **Comments:** A quick two or three lines of show notes for your podcasts. Similar to comments you leave in your XML.

Tips for Preparing for an Interview

- Know who you're talking to and what you want to talk about. It's a good idea to visit guests' Web sites for research. You don't have to be an expert on their subject matter, but you should be familiar with it.
- Have your questions follow a logical progression.
- Prepare twice as many questions than you'll need. Then if your guest gives brief answers, you have a stockpile of questions to call upon.
- Never worry about asking a stupid question. Chances are, your audience has never heard it *answered* before.

Suggested Settings for MP3 compression

- 64 Kbps
- 22.050 kHz / 22,050 Hz
- Stereo

BESTSELLING
BOOK SERIES

Podcasting For Dummies®

Cheat Sheet

Popular Audio-Editing and Recording Software

Program	Where to Find More Info	Mac or PC
Audacity	audacity.sourceforge.net	PC, Mac
Audio Hijack Pro	www.rogueamoeba.com/audiohijackpro/	Mac
Audition	www.adobe.com/products/audition/	PC
Cakewalk	www.cakewalk.com	PC
GarageBand	www.apple.com/ilife/garageband/	Mac

Popular Blogging Software

Program	Where to Download
Movable Type	www.sixapart.com/movabletype
WordPress	wordpress.org
Blogger	www.blogger.com

Finding a Podcast

Site Name	Address
iPodder.org	ipodder.org
Podcast Alley	podcastalley.com
Podcast Pickle	podcastpickle.com
Podcast.Net	www.podcast.net
Yahoo! audio search	audiosearch.yahoo.com

For Dummies: Bestselling Book Series for Beginners

Podcasting FOR DUMMIES®

Tee Morris and Evo Terra

Foreword by Dawn Miceli and Drew Domkus

WILEY

Wiley Publishing, Inc.

Podcasting For Dummies®

Published by
Wiley Publishing, Inc.
111 River Street
Hoboken, NJ 07030-5774
www.wiley.com

WILEY

About the Authors

Tee Morris: Tee Morris is an instructor at EEI Communications, based out of the Washington DC/Virginia/Maryland metro area, and teaches various applications in graphic design and video editing; he also teaches Podcasting for Government and Corporate Business. When he is not working as a freelance artist and instructor, Tee writes science fiction and fantasy; his writing career began with his 2002 historical epic fantasy, *MOREVI The Chronicles of Rafe & Askana,* published by Dragon Moon Press. His other works include *MOREVI's* highly anticipated sequel *Legacy of MOREVI: Book One of the Arathellean Wars* and *Billibub Baddings and The Case of The Singing Sword*, a spoof of both fantasy and hard-boiled detective novels that received an Honorable Mention for *ForeWord Magazine's* Book of the Year and was a finalist for the Independent Publisher's Best Science Fiction and Fantasy book. It was the podcast of his debut novel that led to this team-up with Evo Terra in *Podcasting For Dummies*.

Find out more about Tee Morris at www.teemorris.com.

Evo Terra: Evo is the poster child for Type A personalities the world over. Washed-up musician, tree-hugging herbalist, heretical-but-ordained minister, talk-radio personality, advertising executive and technology innovator, all wrapped up in one single-serving package. In the podcasting world, Evo tends to infect others with the podcasting bug, from budding show hosts to the people behind the scenes finding new uses for podcast technologies.

He hosts three different podcasts, Slice of Scifi (sliceofscifi.com), the Dragon Page Cover to Cover, and Wingin' It! (dragonpage.com) and is helping authors podcast their works to the masses at Podiobooks.com.

He currently resides in Cottonwood, Arizona, with his wife Sheila and his son NJ. Neither of which have a podcast. Yet.

Authors' Acknowledgments

Due to the complexity of the issue and the incredible growth in the community, it will be impossible to properly express our thanks to all the parties who were of great help with this book. So with that . . .

To our editors Steve and Kim: Thanks for letting our own voices shine through while making both of us better writers in the end. And as for the multitude of other editors and proofers on this project: thanks. We hope we entertained you along the way.

To our wives, Sheila and Natalie: Thanks for not strangling us for our constant "Oh! We've got to add that to the book!" moments. We both deeply appreciate the averted gazes of death when we answered that no, unfortunately we would not be coming to bed and that yes we did realize it was three o'clock in the morning.

To the podcasters that provided not only inspiration, but also camaraderie and friendship along the way. Through listening to you all and talking to many, you served as a constant reminder of why we were pouring our hearts and souls into this text.

Evo would like to personally express his gratitude to the TSFPN podcasters for their continued encouragement. Also, he'd like to personally recommend Cake and Soul Coughing, which provided external energy and drive when it was in low supply.

Tee suggests The Anime Radio Nook on Live 365.com, Paul Oakenfold, and the *Battlestar Galactica* soundtracks by Richard Gibbs and Bear McCreary for reserve power during all-night rewrites. And a big thank you to his coauthor, Evo Terra, for covering his back, challenging his opinions, keeping him honest, and still being a best friend, even at the end of this project. (See . . . I told you we wouldn't kill each other!)

Finally, a special nod to Michael R. Mennenga for passing along that e-mail on October 12, 2004, that opened a door to a world of time-shifting, kick ass mystic ninjas, and science fiction and fantasy geeks around the world interested in what we have to offer.

Publisher's Acknowledgments

We're proud of this book; please send us your comments through our online registration form located at `www.dummies.com/register/`.

Some of the people who helped bring this book to market include the following:

Acquisitions, Editorial, and Media Development

Project Editor: Kim Darosett

Senior Acquisitions Editor: Steven Hayes

Senior Copy Editor: Barry Childs-Helton

Copy Editor: Rebecca Senninger

Technical Editor: Dave Slusher

Editorial Manager: Leah Cameron

Editorial Assistant: Amanda Foxworth

Cartoons: Rich Tennant (`www.the5thwave.com`)

Composition Services

Project Coordinator: Jennifer Theriot

Layout and Graphics: Andrea Dahl, Lauren Goddard, Barbara Moore, Barry Offringa, Erin Zeltner

Proofreaders: Leeann Harney

Indexer: TECHBOOKS Production Services

Publishing and Editorial for Technology Dummies

    Richard Swadley, Vice President and Executive Group Publisher

    Andy Cummings, Vice President and Publisher

    Mary Bednarek, Executive Acquisitions Director

    Mary C. Corder, Editorial Director

Publishing for Consumer Dummies

    Diane Graves Steele, Vice President and Publisher

    Joyce Pepple, Acquisitions Director

Composition Services

    Gerry Fahey, Vice President of Production Services

    Debbie Stailey, Director of Composition Services

Contents at a Glance

Table of Contents

Foreword

· ·

A year ago we were just like you . . . and then we became podcasting superstars!

Drew came home in August of 2004 in a full-blown nerd frenzy, raving about how audio blogs and RSS were going to change communication as we know it. I pretended to understand and feigned interest as he spoke on and on, but when I listened to his first audio blog post, it finally clicked — he was onto something. I quickly jumped on board to prevent him from nerding it up too much and thus the *Dawn and Drew Show!* was born.

The term "podcasting" wasn't coined until a short while later, but the idea remains the same: If you have a message, record it using simple software and inexpensive equipment and then publish it to the Web for the world to hear. We have listeners on every continent and get feedback from around the globe, and we do it all from the living room of our Wisconsin farmhouse — sometimes in our pajamas. We're still using the same $20 USB microphone and GarageBand software from Apple, so we're a perfect example that you don't need a lot of money to get started in podcasting. But the very best thing about podcasting is that anyone can do it! When we started, there weren't any how-to books on the subject, but now *Podcasting For Dummies* has made it easy for you to get your own podcast started. There is no censorship, no FCC, and no radio executives to tell you what to say — there are no rules. Podcasting is all about self-expression. So start podcasting now — fame and fortune may await you.

We've always had a great time making the *Dawn and Drew Show!* and now we're able to do it full time. It's the great podcasting dream come true, and if we can do it, so can you!

Dawn Miceli and Drew Domkus

www.dawnanddrew.com

Introduction

Maybe you've been casually surfing the Web or perusing your newspaper when the word "podcasting" has popped up. Steadily, like a building wave that would make champion surfers salivate with delight, the term has popped up again and again — and your curiosity continues to pique as the word "podcasting" echoes in your ears and remains in the back of your mind as a riddle wrapped in an enigma, super-sized with a side of fries and a diet soda to go.

Podcasting For Dummies is the answer to that super-sized riddle-enigma combo, and it even comes complete with a special prize. Beginning with the question at the forefront of your mind — *What is podcasting?* — this book takes you through the fastest-growing technological movement on the Internet. By the time you reach the end of this book, the basics will be in place to get you, your voice, and your message heard around the world — and you can even have a bit of fun along the way.

About This Book

> *"So what are you up to, Tee?"*
>
> *"I'm currently podcasting my first novel, a swashbuckling tale that carries our heroes . . ."*
>
> *"Uh . . . what is a podcast?"*

Asked by best friends and lifetime technologists, this question continues to crop up over and over again, immediately after the word "podcast" lands in a casual conversation. Just the word "podcasting" carries an air of geekiness about it — and behold, the habitual technophobes suddenly clasp their hands to their ears and run away screaming in horror lest they confront yet another technical matter. Too bad. If they only knew how technical it really isn't. When you peel back the covers and fancy-schmancy tech-talk, it's a pretty simple process to make your own podcast. You just need someone pointing the way and illuminating your path.

This is why we are here: to be that candle in the dark, helping you navigate a world where anyone can do anything, provided they have the tools, the drive, and the passion. You don't need to be a techno-wizard or a super-geek — you need no wad of tape holding your glasses together; your shirt tail need not stick out from your fly. Anyone can do what we show you in this book. Anyone can take a thought or an opinion, make an audio file expressing that opinion, and distribute this idea worldwide. Anyone can capture the attention of a few hundred — or a few thousand — people around the world through MP3 players hiding in computers, strapped around biceps, jouncing in pockets, or hooked up to car stereos.

Anyone can podcast.

Podcasting, from recording to online hosting, can be done on a variety of budgets, ranging from frugal to Fortune 500. You can podcast about literally anything — including podcasting for its own sake. As blogging gave the anonymous, the famous, the "almost-famous," and the "used-to-be famous" a voice in politics, religion, and everyday life, podcasting adds volume and tone to that voice. Words on a page are often misconstrued because it's difficult to catch the subtle meanings and innuendos hidden within text. But when those words are actually spoken aloud, the sender's interpretation is clear, concise, and leaves little room for doubt when the message is delivered.

Podcasting is many things to many people — but at its most basic, it's a surprisingly simple and powerful technology. What it means boils down to a single person: you. Some liken it to radio (at least online radio), but it can do — and be — so much more. Podcasting is a new method of communication, transmitting your voice and its message around the world without using public airwaves, connecting the Global Village in ways that the creators of the Internet, RSS, and MP3 compression would probably never have dreamed. It is the unique and the hard-to-find content that can't find a place on commercial, college, or public access radio.

You are about to embark on an exciting adventure into undiscovered territory, and here you will find out that podcasting is all these things, and so much more.

How to Use This Book

Podcasting For Dummies should be these things to all who pick up and read it (whether straight through or by jumping around in the chapters):

- ✔ A user-friendly guide in how to listen, produce, and distribute podcasts
- ✔ A terrific reference for choosing the right hardware and software to put together a sharp-sounding podcast

✔ The starting point for the person who knows nothing about audio editing, recording, creating RSS feeds, hosting blogs, or turning a computer
into a recording studio

✔ A handy go-to "think tank" for any beginning podcaster who's hungry for
new ideas on what goes into a good podcast and fresh points of view

✔ A really fun read

There will be plenty of answers in these pages, and if you find our answers too
elementary, we give you plenty of points-of-reference to research on your own
time. We don't claim to have all the solutions, quick fixes, and resolutions to
all possible podcasting queries, but we do present to you the basic building
blocks and first steps for beginning a podcast. As with any *For Dummies* book,
our responsibility is to give you the foundation on which to build. That's what
we have done our level best to accomplish: Bestow upon you the enchanted
stuff that makes a podcast happen.

This book was written as a linear path from the conceptualization stages to the
final publication of your work. However, not everyone needs to read the book
from page one. If you've already gotten your feet wet with the various aspects
of podcasting, jump around from section to section and read the parts that you
need. We provide plenty of guides back to other relevant chapters for when the
going gets murky.

Conventions Used in This Book

When you go through this book, you're going to see a few ⌘ symbols, the
occasional ⇨, and even a few things typed `in a completely different
style`.

There is a method to this madness, and those methods are conventions
found throughout this book and other *For Dummies* titles.

When we refer to keyboard shortcuts for Macintosh or Windows, we designate them with (Mac) or (Windows). For Macintosh shortcuts, instead of
using that funky cloverleaf symbol, we use the Apple symbol (found on the
Command key) and the corresponding letter. For Windows shortcuts, we
use the abbreviation for the Control key and the corresponding letter. So
the shortcut for Select All looks like this: ⌘+A (Mac) / Ctrl+A (Windows).

If keyboard shortcuts are not your thing and you want to know where the
commands reside on menus, we use a command arrow (⇨) to help guide
you through menus and submenus. So, going back to the earlier example,
the command for Select All in the application's menu is Edit⇨Select All.

When we offer up URLs (Web site addresses) of various podcasts, resources, and audio equipment vendors, or when we have you creating RSS feeds for podcatchers such as iTunes, iPodder, or iPodderX, we use `this particular typeface`.

Bold Assumptions

We assume that you have a computer, a lot of curiosity, and a desire to podcast. We could care less about whether you're using a Mac, a PC, Linux, Unix, or two Dixie cups connected with string. In podcasting, the operating system just makes the computer go. We're here to provide the tools for creating a podcast, regardless of what OS you're running.

Okay, maybe the two Dixie cups connected with string would be a challenge. We both recommend that if you don't have a computer for podcasting, get one. That's an essential.

If you know nothing about audio production, this book will also serve as a fine primer in how to record, edit, and produce audio on your computer, as well as accessorize your Mac or Windows PC with mixing boards, professional-grade microphones, and audio-engineering software that will give you a basic look at this creative field. You can hang on to this title as a handy reference, geared for audio _in podcasting_. Again, our book is a starting point, and (ahem) a fine starting point at that.

With everything that goes into podcasting, there are some things this book is not now, nor will ever be, about. Here's the short list:

- ✔ We're not out to make you into an übergeek in RSS or XML (but we give you all you need to make things work — even get you iTunes-ready).
- ✔ We figure that if you get ahold of Audacity, GarageBand, Audio Hijack Pro, Soundtrack, or Audition, you can take it from there (but we give you overviews of those programs and a few basic editing examples).
- ✔ We're not out to teach you how to use an MP3 player such as an iPod, an iRiver, or a Zen Micro product.

For that matter — to dispel one of the biggest misconceptions of podcasting — you will not be told to run out and get an iPod. _You do not need an iPod to podcast._

If you are looking for a resource that will teach you RSS, take a look at _Syndicating Web Sites with RSS Feeds For Dummies_ by Ellen Finkelstein (published by Wiley).

If you are looking for a resource that will teach you audio editing on your computer, take a look at *PC Recording Studios For Dummies* by Jeff Strong. While the title does refer to "PC" by name, the book opens with the statement *"Whether you use a Windows or Macintosh computer for your home recording studio, your system of choice employs much of the same basic technology . . ."* and carries on its dual-platform attitude from beginning to end. That's our kind of approach.

If you are looking for a terrific start to the podcasting experience, then — in the words of the last knight guarding the Holy Grail in *Indiana Jones and the Last Crusade* — "You have chosen wisely."

How This Book Is Organized

Now that we've told exactly what this book is not, we give you a quick overview as to what this book exactly *is*. And yeah, we're going to keep the overview brief because we figure you're anxious to get started. But the fact that you're reading this passage also tells us you don't want to miss a detail, so here's a quick bird's-eye view of what we do in *Podcasting For Dummies*.

Part I: Podcasting on a Worldwide Frequency

This is a great part for both kinds of podcasters — those who want to participate, and those who just want to listen. We pay heed to the evolution of podcasting from the blogging movement, and then try to explain, in the simplest terms (as if to someone completely unfamiliar with all things technical), exactly what podcasting is.

In other words, we use pop-culture references.

Part I also goes into the bare-bones basics of how a podcast happens, how to get podcasts from the Internet to your computer, and how to host a podcast yourself — ending up with a few places online that offer podcast feeds you can visit to sample the experience — and (later on) let the world know "Hey, I've got a podcast, too!"

Part II: The Hills Are Alive with the Sound of Podcasting

Consider this section of the book part-*Inside the Actor's Studio,* part-Tech TV, part-*WKRP* (with your host, Dr. Johnny Fever . . . *boooouuugaaar!!!*). But instead of (pod)casting you into the wilderness to stumble through personal rants and raves, verbally trip over yourself in interviews, and post podcasts so raw that your listeners' ears bleed, we offer up some techniques the pros use in broadcasting. Podcasting may be the grass-roots movement of home-spun telecommunications, but that doesn't mean it has to sound that way (unless, of course, you *want* it to sound that way). From preshow prep to setting your volume levels to the basics of audio editing, this is the part that polishes your podcast.

Part III: So You've Got This Great Recording of Your Voice. Now What?

The audio file you've just created is now silently staring back at you from your monitor (unless you're listening to it on your computer's music player, in which case it's just defiantly talking back at you!), and you haven't a clue what your next step is. We cover the last-minute details, and then walk you through the process of getting your podcast online, finding the right Web-hosting packages for podcasts, and getting a good working handle on the RSS and XML used in podcast feeds.

Part IV: Start Spreadin' the News about Your Podcast

> *"I wanna beeee a part of it. Podcasting, babeeeee . . .*
> *If I can get on Daily Source,*
> *Then I'll have no remorse for pod—cast—in . . . podcasting . . ."*

Sorry. Sinatra moment.

Anyway, you've got the podcast recorded, edited, and online, now you need to let people know you've got this great podcast just waiting for them — and that is what we explore in Part IV. With the power of publicity — from free-of-charge word-of-mouth (arguably the most effective) to investment in Google Adwords (arguably the most coverage for your dollar), you have a wide array of options to choose from when you're ready to announce your presence to the podcasting community.

Part V: Pod-sibilities to Consider for Your Show

The question of *why* one should podcast is as important as *how* to podcast. We cover some basic rationales that many folks have for sitting behind a microphone, pouring heart, soul, and pocket change into their craft each and every day, week, or month. These questions have no right or wrong answers, but our hope is that this section offers pointers to guide you safely through the thought process behind podcasting.

Part VI: The Part of Tens

Perhaps the toughest chapters to write were these: the *For Dummies* trademark Part of Tens chapters. So don't skip them because we'll be über-miffed if you fail to appreciate how hard we busted our humps to get these chapters done!

Right — so what do we give you in our Part of Tens? We give you a list of the ten people who made (and/or currently make) podcasting the hottest communications trend to come down the pike since the invention of the Internet. We also offer suggestions for the beginning podcaster — such as what kind of podcasts should be on your MP3 player, just to give you an idea of what's out there, how they sound, and how you can benefit from them. Finally, our Part of Tens closes with the great debate: Podcasting versus Radio. Is radio dead? Is podcasting just another fad? Read . . . and then *you* decide.

About the Companion Podcast

In some cases, a *For Dummies* book comes with a companion Web site hosted by the good people at www.dummies.com. *Podcasting For Dummies* is the first book in the *For Dummies* series (and could be the world's first do-it-yourself book) to come with a companion *podcast*. Go to your browser and surf to www.dummies.com/go/podcastingfd and follow the instructions there to get free weekly audio commentary from Tee Morris (and maybe Evo Terra, if time and podcasting schedules allow) about concepts in this book explored in greater detail, from the difference between good and bad edits, when too much reverb is too much, and the variety of methods you can use to record a podcast.

Icons Used in This Book

So you're trekking through the book, making some real progress with developing your podcast when suddenly these little icons leap out, grab you by the throat, and wrestle you to the ground. (Who would have thought podcasting was so action-packed, like a Connery-Bond movie, huh?) What do all these little drawings mean? Glad you asked . . .

When we're in the middle of a discussion and suddenly we have one of those *"Say, that reminds me . . ."* moments, we give you one of these tips. They're handy little extras that are good to know and might even make your podcast sound a little tighter than average.

If that *"Say, that reminds me . . ."* moment is more than a handy little nugget of information and closer to a *"Seriously, you can't forget this part!"* factoid, we mark it with a Remember icon. You're going to want to play close attention to these puppies. They will save you a lot of grief in the future.

Sometimes we interrupt our train of thought with a *"Time out, Sparky . . ."* moment — and this is where we ask for your completely undivided attention. The Warnings are exactly that: flashing lights, ah-ooga horns, dire portents. They're reminders not to try this at home, disclaimers that if you do this we can't be held responsible, and advice for avoiding situations where that earlier-mentioned knight from *The Last Crusade* looks at you and says, "You chose poorly."

These icons can illuminate those *"So how does this widget really work . . . ?"* moments you may have as you read *Podcasting For Dummies.* You can regard them as cool trivia to impress friends with at parties, or surprise the techno-geeks at the Help Desk who believe they know everything already. The Technical Stuff icons can give you a deeper understanding of what the wizard is doing behind the curtain, making you all the more apt as a podcaster.

Where to Go from Here

At this point, many *For Dummies* authors say something snappy, clever, or even a bit snarky. We save our best tongue-and-cheek material for the pages inside, so let's take a more serious approach . . .

We suggest heading to where you're planning to record your podcast or just plant yourself in front of a computer where you plan to download podcasts for listening. Start with Chapter 1 where you're given a few links to check out, some suggestions on applications for downloading podcasts, and directories to look up where you can find Tee's podcast, Evo's (many) podcasts, and other podcasts that can educate, inspire, and enlighten your ears with original content.

Where do we go from here? Up and out, my friends. Up and out . . .

Part I

Podcasting on a Worldwide Frequency

The 5th Wave By Rich Tennant

"This is number 271 of the podcast show, 'Help! Get Me Off This Stinking Island!'"

In this part . . .

Podcasting is (depending on who's describing it) either taking the world by storm or providing an interesting diversion. If neither of those, it falls somewhere in between. Whatever it is, we like it, and we think you will too. In this first part, we peel back the covers and go beyond the hype to talk about what this technology is and exactly what you need to do to become involved with it — from soup to nuts.

Chapter 1

Getting the Scoop on Podcasting

In This Chapter

▶ Finding out what podcasting is

▶ Creating a podcast

▶ Finding and subscribing to podcasts

Sometimes the invention that makes the biggest impact on our daily lives isn't an invention at all, but the convergence of existing technologies, processes, and ideas. Podcasting may be the perfect example of that principle — and it's changing the relationship people have with their radios, music collections, books, education, and more.

The podcasting movement is actually a spin-off of another communications boom: personal Weblogs, commonly referred to as *blogs*. Blogs sprang up right and left, providing non-programmers and designers a clean, elegant interface that left many on the technology side wondering why they hadn't thought of it sooner. Everyday people could now chronicle their lives, hopes, dreams, and fears, and show them to anyone who cared to read. And oddly enough, people did care to read — and still do.

Podcasting combines the instant information exchange of blogging with audio files that can be played on a computer or MP3 player. When you make your podcast publicly available on the World Wide Web, you are exposing your craft to anyone with a personal computer and a broadband Internet connection. To put that in perspective, the Computer Industry Almanac predicts the global online population will top 1.2 billion users by 2006. In the United States, broadband connections are now more popular than dial-up. And to top it all off, portable players are surging in popularity, with over 22 million adult owners.

This chapter is for *podcasters* (those making the content) and *podcatchers* (those listening to the content) alike. We cover the basic steps to record a podcast and lay out the basics of what you need to do to tune in a podcast.

Deciding Whether Podcasting Is for You

Technically speaking, *podcasting* is the distribution of specially encoded multimedia content to subscribed personal computers via the RSS 2.0 protocol. Whew! Allow us to translate that into common-speak:

> Podcasting allows you to listen to stuff you want to hear, whenever and wherever you want.

Podcasting turns the tables on broadcast schedules, allowing the listener to choose not only what to listen to, but also when. And because podcasts are transferred via the Internet, the power to create an audio program isn't limited to those with access to a radio transmitter. This section covers other reasons podcasting is probably for you.

You want to deliver audio content on a regular basis

Sure, you can post your audio content on a blog if you have one. Many bloggers who do that (called *audiobloggers*) record audio segments and insert them as links into the text of their blog posts. Readers of the blog then download the files at their leisure. However, audio blogs require the readers to manually select the content they wish to download. What sets podcasting apart from blogging is that podcasting automates that process. A listener who subscribes to your podcast is subscribed to all of your content, whenever it's available. No need to go back to the site to see what's new!

You want to reach beyond the boundaries of radio

In radio, the number of people who can listen to a show is limited by the power of the transmitter pumping out the signal. Podcasting doesn't use radio signals, transmitters, or receivers — at least not in the classic sense. Podcasts use the World Wide Web as a delivery system, opening up a potential audience that could extend to the entire planet.

No rules exist (yet, anyway) to regulate the creation of podcast content. In fact, neither the FCC nor any other regulatory body for any other government holds jurisdiction over podcasts. If that seems astounding, remember that podcasters are not using the public airwaves to deliver the message.

What's in a name, when the name is podcasting?

As with most items that make their way into the conventional lexicon of speech, the precise origins and meaning behind *podcasting* are somewhat clouded. While the domain podcast.com was originally registered back in 2002 (nothing was ever done with it, as far as we know), and Ben Hammersley suggested that and many other terms in February 2004 (www.guardian.co.uk/online/story/0,3605,1145689,00.html), it's generally accepted in the podosphere that the first person to use the term as a reference to the activity we now know as podcasting was Dannie Gregoire on September 15, 2004 (groups.yahoo.com/group/ipodder-dev/message/41). While some assert the name has connotations to the popular iPod device created by Apple, Dannie didn't have that in mind when the phrase was coined. Regardless of the intentions, the term has been *backronymed* (that is, treated like an acronym and applied to a variety of plausible existing meanings). Of all the possibilities, we prefer *Personal On-Demand narrowcasting* (not *broadcasting*), which shortens nicely to *podcasting*. But of course, you can choose whichever one makes sense to you.

Granted, the podcasting phenomenon was in part fueled by the wildly popular iPod portable audio device, but no evidence suggests that the two were related when the name was coined. And (as one of your authors, Evo, stoutly maintains), "Because I don't even own an iPod, yet am quite obviously a podcaster, I see no reason for the association to continue to be made." Harrumph.

Just because the FCC doesn't have jurisdiction, you're not exempt from the law or — perhaps more importantly — immune to lawsuits. *You're personally responsible for anything you say, do, or condone on your show.* Additionally, the rules concerning airplay of licensed music, the distribution of copyrighted material, and the legalities of recording telephone conversations all apply. Pay close attention to the relevant sections in Chapter 5 to avoid some serious consequences. When it comes to the legalities, ignorance is not bliss.

Narrowcasting (the practice of delivering content to a select group) distinguishes podcasting from traditional forms of broadcast communication, such as radio. Where a radio station *broadly* casts its signal to anyone who happens to be within the radius of the signal, podcasts *narrowly* cast content to people who have made the overt decision to listen.

You have something to say

Podcasters as a general rule produce content that likely holds appeal for only a select group of listeners. Podcasts start with an idea, something that you have the desire and knowledge, either real or imaginary, to talk about. Add to that a bit of drive, a do-it-yourself-ishness, and an inability to take no for an answer. The point is to say what you want to say, to those who want to hear it.

Podcasts can be about anything and be enjoyed by just about anyone. The topics covered don't have to be earth-shattering or life-changing. You have to follow a few rules, but even then you can break most of them.

Some of the most popular podcasts are created by everyday people who sit in front of their computers for a few nights a week and just speak their minds, hearts, and souls. Some are focused on niche topics; others are more broad-based. Quite a few are seemingly put together at random, perhaps moments before the recording started.

You want to hear from your listeners

I've heard more than one podcaster comment on the fact that they get, well . . . comments. For some reason (which we'll let the social anthropologists of the future puzzle out), podcast listeners are more likely to provide feedback to the podcasts they listen to than radio show listeners are likely to e-mail their thoughts to the show host. That's probably traceable to the personal nature of selecting a podcast. Podcasts offer their listeners — and makers — more control, options, and intimacy than traditional broadcast media can. Of course, the radio is much harder to talk back to than a computer with an Internet connection and e-mail (which remains the *killer app*).

When you ask for feedback, you're likely to get it — and from unusual places. Because geography doesn't limit the distance your podcast can travel, you may find yourself with listeners in faraway and exotic places. And this feedback isn't always going to be "Wow, great podcast!" Listeners will be honest with you when you invite feedback.

If you're starting to get the idea that podcasting is revolutionary, groundbreaking, and possibly a major component of social upheaval, great. But not all podcasts are so deep. In fact, many of them are just plain fun!

Creating a Podcast

There are two schools of thought when it comes to creating a podcast: The *"I need the latest and greatest equipment in order to capture that crisp, clear sound of the broadcasting industry"* school of thought, and the *"Hey, my computer came with a microphone, and I've got this cool recording software already installed"* school of thought. Both are equally valid positions, and there are a lot of secondary schools in-between. The question is how far you're willing to go.

But let's dispel something right off the bat about podcasting: You're not reprogramming your operating system, you're not hacking into the Internal Revenue Service's database, and you're not setting up a wireless computer network with tinfoil from a chewing gum wrapper, a shoestring, and your belt — regardless if MacGyver showed you how. Podcasting, as mentioned earlier, is not rocket science. In fact, here's a quick rundown of how you podcast:

1. Record audio and convert it to a download-friendly format.
2. Create a simple but specialized text file that describes your audio file.
3. Upload everything to the Web.

Yes, yes, yes, if it were that simple, then why is this book so thick? Well, we admit that this list does gloss over a few details, but a podcast — in its most streamlined, raw presentation — *is* that simple. The details of putting together a podcast start in Chapter 2 and wrap up in Chapter 5; then Chapters 6 and 9 walk you through all the geek-speak you need to accomplish the podcast.

Looking for the bare necessities

You need a few things before starting your first podcast, many of which you can probably find on your own computer:

- ✔ **A microphone:** Take a look at your computer. Right now, regardless of whether you have a laptop or desktop model, Windows or Macintosh, your computer probably has a microphone built into it — or a jack for plugging in an external mic, and maybe even an included external mic packaged somewhere with the manuals, cables, and such.

  Position the microphone to a comfortable spot on your desk or table. If you're using a laptop, position the laptop to a comfortable spot on your desk or table (make sure you know where the built-in microphone is in the laptop's housing).

  Usually the built-in microphone in a laptop is located close to the edge of the keyboard or near the laptop's speakers. Some models tuck it in at the center point of the monitor's base. Consult your user's manual to find out where the microphone is hidden on your machine.

- ✔ **Recording software:** Check out the software that came with your computer. You know, all those extra CDs that you filed away, thinking, "I'll check those out sometime." Well, the time has arrived to flip through them. You probably have some sort of audio-recording software loaded on your computer, such as RecordIt (Windows) or iMovie (which comes pre-installed with many new Macs and can record voice as well as video).

  If you don't already have the appropriate software, here's a fast way to get it: Download the version of Audacity that fits your operating system (at `audacity.sourceforge.net`), shown in Figure 1-1. (Oh, yeah . . . it's free.)

✔ **An audio card:** Make sure your computer has the hardware it needs to handle audio recording and the drivers to run the hardware.

TIP

Some desktop computers come with a very elementary audio card built into the motherboard. Before you run out to your local computer vendor and spring for an audio card, check your computer to see whether it can already handle basic voice recording.

For tips on choosing the right mic, software, and audio card, be sure to check out Chapter 2.

Getting and setting up the hardware and software needed to record is a start. The next step is using it.

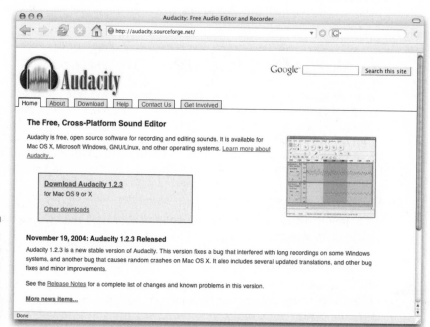

Figure 1-1: Audacity allows you to edit audio and create MP3 files.

Recording your first podcast

When you have your computer set up and your microphone working, it's time to start recording. Take a deep breath and then follow these steps:

1. **Jot down a few notes on what you want to talk about.**

   Nothing too fancy — just make an outline that includes remarks about who you are and what you want to talk about. Use these notes to keep yourself on track.

All this — the checking of your computer, jotting down notes, and setting up your recording area — is called *preshow prep,* discussed in depth in Chapter 3 by other podcasters who have their own ways of approaching pre-show prep (all of which can give you some starting points).

2. **Click the Record button in your recording software and go for as long as it takes for you to get through your notes.**

   We recommend keeping your first recording to no more than 20 minutes. That may seem like a lot of time, but it *will* fly by.

3. **Give a nice little sign-off (like "Take care of yourselves! See you next month.") and click the Stop button.**

4. **Choose File⇨Save As and give your project a name.**

   Now bask in the warmth of creative accomplishment.

Compressing your audio files

If you're using an application other than Audacity, you may need to make your recording into an MP3 file. Many audio players that come with computers offer the capability to create MP3 files, but if your audio player doesn't read or compress audio recordings to MP3 files, you can keep it fed by downloading iTunes from www.apple.com/itunes. Check out iTunes in Figure 1-2. (Even though it's an Apple product, a Windows version is available as well.)

Figure 1-2: Apple iTunes, available for both Mac and Windows platforms, can create MP3 files from a variety of audio formats.

After you install iTunes, follow these steps to convert your audio file:

1. **Choose File⇨Add File to Library.**

   Or you can press ⌘+O (Mac) or Ctrl+O (Windows).

2. **Browse for the audio file you want to convert and then click Open.**

   Your file is now in the iTunes Library.

3. **Find the audio file in the iTunes Library and click to select it.**

4. **Choose Advanced⇨Convert Selection to MP3.**

   Your file is converted to the MP3 format (see Figure 1-3).

Congratulations — you just recorded your first podcast. At least the audio part of it.

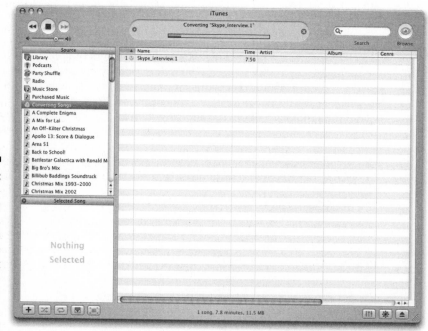

Figure 1-3:
While com-
pressing
audio files,
Apple gives
a progress
report
on the
conversion
process.

Transferring your audio to the Web

An audio file sitting on your desktop, regardless of how earth-shattering the contents may be, is not a podcast. Nope, not by a long shot. You have to get it up on the World Wide Web and provide a way for listeners' podcatchers to grab that tasty file for later consumption.

If you already have a Web server for your blog, company Web site, or personal site, this process can be as easy as creating a new folder and transferring your newly created audio file to your server via your FTP client of choice.

If that last paragraph left you puzzled and you're wondering what kind of mess you've gotten yourself into . . . relax. We don't leave you hanging out in the wind. Chapter 7 covers everything you need to know about choosing a Web host for your podcast media files.

Note that we called your audio a podcast *media* file. Podcasting isn't just about audio. On the contrary, you can podcast any sort of media file you like, even video. Although this book focuses on audio files, you could use all the tips we give here to handle other types of media files.

After you post the media file, you need to create a specially formatted text file, usually *XML* (Extensible Markup Language, explained in detail in Chapter 9), and move it up to your Web server. This file describes where to find the media file you just placed on your Web server. This is your *podcast feed,* and the special format you use for your text is called *RSS 2.0.* Listeners to your podcast can subscribe to your show by placing a link to this podcast feed in their podcatching client.

Yes, we know . . . this sounds really complicated. But we assure you it's not. Some hosting companies such as Libsyn (www.libsyn.com) specialize in taking the technological "bite" out of podcasting so you can focus on creating your best-sounding show. With Libsyn (shown in Figure 1-4), moving your audio files to the Web server is as simple as pushing a few buttons, and the creation of the RSS 2.0 podcast feed and even the accompanying Web page are automatic.

If you want to take more control over your Web site, podcast media files, and their corresponding RSS 2.0 feed, turn to the latter chapters of Part III. In those pages, we walk you through some essentials — not only how to upload a file but also how to easily generate your RSS 2.0 file using a variety of tools.

Grabbing listeners

With media files in place and an RSS 2.0 feed ready for podcatcher consumption, you're officially a podcaster. Of course, that doesn't mean a lot if you're the only person who knows about your podcast. You need to spread the word to let others know that you exist and that you have something pretty darn important to say.

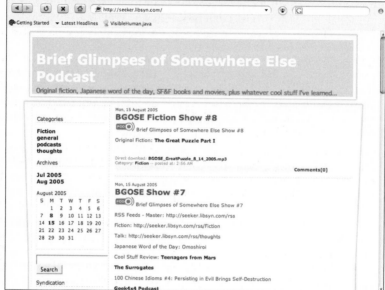

Figure 1-4:
A podcast
hosted by
Libsyn
handles
many of the
technical
details.

Creating show notes

Before you pick up a bullhorn, slap a sandwich board over yourself, and start walking down the street (virtually, anyway), you have to make sure you're descriptive enough to captivate those who reach your Web site. First, you're going to want to describe the contents of your show to casual online passers-by in hopes of getting them to listen to what you have to say.

You can easily glance at a blog and get the gist of a conversation, but an audio file requires active listening to understand, and it's quite difficult to skim. In effect, you're asking people to make an investment of their time in listening to you talk, read a story, or play music. You need some compelling text on a Web page to hook them.

Descriptions of podcast episodes are called *show notes,* and they are designed to quickly showcase or highlight the relevant and pertinent contents of the audio file itself. A verbatim transcript of your show isn't a good idea, but we do recommend more than simply saying "a show about my day." Chapter 8 discusses ways to create your show notes and offers tips and tricks to give them some punch. (Refer to Figure 1-4 for an example of what show notes look like on a Web browser.)

Getting listed in directories

When you have a ready media file and a solid set of show notes, you're ready to take your podcast message to the masses. You can get listed on some directories and podcast-listing sites, such as Podcast Pickle and iPodder.org (explained later in this chapter). Potential listeners visit literally dozens of Web sites as they seek out new content, and getting yourself listed on as many as possible can help bring in more new listeners to your program.

A huge listener base is a double-edged sword: More demand for your product means more of a demand on you and the resources necessary to keep your podcast up and running. We recommend working on your craft and your skills, as well as getting a good handle on the personal and technological requirements of podcasting, *before* you embark on a huge marketing campaign. Part IV has more details about marketing.

Part IV spends a lot of time talking about the various ways you can attract more listeners to your show and ways to respond to the ideas and feedback that your listeners inevitably provide. Many podcasters are surprised at the sheer volume of comments they receive from their listeners — but when you consider how personal podcasting is (compared to traditional forms of media distribution), that's really not surprising at all.

Now that we've finally busted pesky myths about podcasting and given you an honest warning about listener demand, we're going to give a quick overview of various applications that get MP3 files from Web servers to personal players.

Catching a Cast with Your Podcatching Client

So you have the MP3 file, some XML, and accompanying show notes. You're all set, but ask yourself, "How do podcasts get from the Web to my computer?" To access all this great, new content, you need a *podcatcher,* an application that looks at various RSS feeds, finds the new stuff, and transfers it from the Internet to your computer automatically. Take a look at some of the different podcatching clients available for your podcasting needs.

You may think you need an iPod for all kinds of reasons, but you really don't need one to podcast. Allow us to state that again: *You do not need an iPod to listen to or create a podcast.* As long as you have an MP3 player — be it an application on a Mac, an application on a PC, or a portable device you can unplug and take with you — you possess the capability to listen to podcasts. Depending on the MP3 player, you may even be able to create your podcast on the device as well — but to listen, all you need is a device that can play audio files.

The catcher that started it all: iPodder

iPodder (shown in Figure 1-5) was created by Adam Curry (yes, the former MTV VJ and no, we're not kidding). It promotes itself as an *open-source* (free to use) application that downloads audio files from RSS feeds of your choice directly to your Mac or PC. You can then sync your portable player with your computer's media player, and now you're podcasting-on-the-go.

Download iPodder from `ipodder.sourceforge.net`. After you install it, subscribing to feeds is a simple process. Follow these steps if you don't have a specific podcast in mind:

1. **Click the Podcast Directory tab.**

   iPodder comes preloaded with a variety of the more popular directories of podcasts.

2. **Navigate through the directory structure.**

   Click the name of the directory to see the choices offered. In some cases, you may need to click a subdirectory to see additional podcasts.

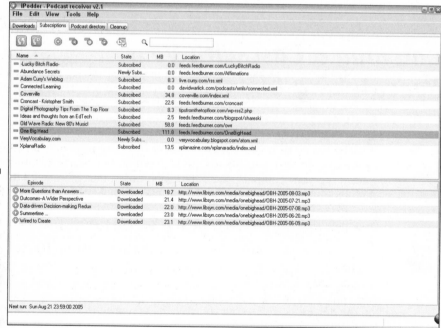

Figure 1-5:
The ground-breaking, trendsetting, and all-around-first podcatching client — iPodder.

3. **Double-click the name of a podcast.**

   You can also single-click the name of the podcast and then click the Add button near the top.

4. **Click Save.**

That's it! You've just subscribed to your first podcast with iPodder.

Of course, you don't have to navigate through the list of podcasts. Follow these steps if you have a specific podcast in mind:

1. **Click the little green button with a plus symbol on it.**

   You find this button on the Subscriptions panel.

2. **Type the URL of the feed in the Add a Feed window.**

   Hopefully, you copied the URL and can simply paste it in. If not, be very careful with your typing!

Congrats! You now know how to use iPodder to subscribe to any podcasts you happen to come across in the future.

Stepping up your game with iPodderX

Shortly after iPodder came on the scene, developers August Trometer and Ray Slakinski raised the bar for podcatching clients across both platforms with their own creation iPodderX (shown in Figure 1-6), a podcatching client (also known by its more geeky name, an *aggregator*) that promised to do a lot more than just download audio files. And it delivers.

iPodderX (available for download at www.ipodderx.com) began modestly enough as a simple aggregator but now offers the following features:

✔ Accesses and displays all HTML, links, and images that accompany the podcast post (called *show notes*).

✔ Retrieves any enclosed media file, not just MP3 files.

✔ Manages files for both iTunes and iPhoto, via Playlist Builder.

✔ Offers SmartSpace, a feature that deletes old podcasts from your hard drive according to the parameters you set. (It also has a safeguard feature that allows you to recover any deleted podcasts you want to archive.)

Add a Subscription Feed

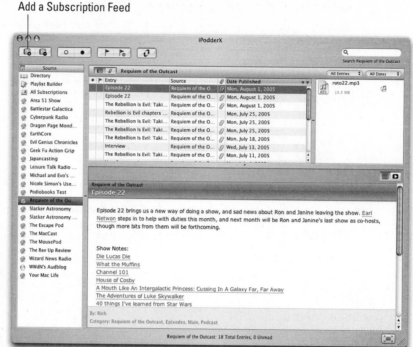

Figure 1-6:
iPodderX
is more
than just a
podcatching
client; it's
also an RSS
reader and
offers file
manage-
ment
capabilities.

Though originally this aggregator was available only to Mac users, iPodderX is now available for Windows users as well, making it an affordable option for people looking for a podcatcher that goes above and beyond the simple downloading of MP3 files.

To subscribe to a podcast using iPodderX, simply follow these steps when you've identified a podcast you want to subscribe to:

1. **In your browser, Control+click (Mac) or right-click (Windows) the podcast link and choose Options⇨Copy Link.**

2. **In iPodderX, click the Add a Subscription Feed icon.**

   This icon looks like a newspaper with a plus sign and is located in the top-left corner of the iPodder interface, as shown in Figure 1-6.

   The Subscription window appears, showing the link you copied (in Step 1) filled in the Subscription Feed URL box.

3. **Click the Downloads tab.**

4. **Choose to download the most recent podcast or all available files from the File Catch Up drop-down menu.**

5. **Enter the name of the show in the Custom Folder/Playlist text box.**

   Dragon Page Cover to Cover, as well as *Area 51* and *EarthCore* by Scott Sigler, are examples.

6. **Click the Add button.**

   iPodderX automatically checks the feed and begins downloading content.

The 800-pound gorilla called iTunes

With the launch of iTunes v4.9, podcasting went from what the geeks were doing in the basement of the Science Building to the next wave of innovation on the Internet (which was, of course, developed by the geeks in the basement of the Science Building). As always, a step into the mainstream market brought some dismay; the hardcore, independent podcasters considered this a sad day for podcasting as corporate entities (sponsored by Disney, ESPN, BBC, and so on) dominated the iTunes Music Store podcast directory (shown in Figure 1-7). What about the indie podcasts — the ones that started it all? Would they be forgotten? Go unnoticed? Languish unsubscribed? Well, at first, it seemed that many of the original groundbreakers that the podcasting community knew and loved (*The Dawn and Drew Show, Tokyo Calling, Catholic Insider, Slice of Scifi*) might get lost in the stampede. But not yet, as it turns out.

Apple's iTunes (available for download at www.itunes.com) works as a pod-catching client. It lends an automatic hand to those who don't know where to find aggregators, where to find blogs that host podcasts, and which podcast directories list the shows that fit their needs and desires — now they too can enjoy a wide range of podcast choices.

With iTunes, podcasting reached into the mainstream markets around the world. (And if that doesn't make you go "Wow!" consider this: On August 4, 2005, iTunes launched in Japan. Within four days, the iTunes Music Store had *1 million downloads.* Sony's own MP3 download service averages under 500,000 downloads a month.) Instead of dealing with third-party applications, Apple iTunes is a one-stop shop for all your podcasting needs.

It gets even better: Subscribing to a podcast with iTunes is just as easy as with the iPodder and iPodderX methods. Follow these steps to do so:

1. **In the iTunes Music Store, click the Podcasts link located in the top section of the left column.**

   You can also click the Podcast icon located in the center of the Featured Artists section.

Figure 1-7:
The new
Apple
iTunes
Music
Store's
podcast
feature.

2. **Find the podcast of your choice.**

   You can do that by clicking its name in the iTunes Music Store or by performing a search using the iTunes Music/Podcast search engine in the top-right corner of the iTunes screen.

3. **When you get to the podcast page (and available podcasts) in iTunes, click the Subscribe button.**

   If you're using iTunes for the first time to subscribe to a feed, you get a confirmation message. You can select the Do Not Ask About Subscribing Again option to avoid this message.

   iTunes immediately takes you from the Music Store to your Podcasts list and gives you the progress of the download.

After your podcast has finished downloading, you can create a playlist for your podcast and organize your downloads accordingly.

Options, options, and more options

Of course, everyone's tastes and styles are different, and there are plenty more options for podcatching clients. Maybe you're using Mac, Windows, or an entirely different operating system. Maybe you don't want to install any new software on your system, or maybe you just like to be different. Hey, that's okay! You too can be a podcast listener:

- ✔ **Doppler:** Designed exclusively for the Windows platform, Doppler (`dopplerradio.net`) has a strong contingent of dedicated users who are perfectly happy with the features it offers. Additionally, it seems to be a pretty rock-solid piece of software, and it's available for free.

- ✔ **Nimiq:** Nimiq (`nimiq.nl`) has been described as an exercise in simplicity. It does what it does (that is, download podcast media files) very well. Some folks looking for advanced features (such as downloading BitTorrent files) are switching from iPodder to this little jewel.

- ✔ **Odeo:** But what if you can't (or don't want to) install podcatching software on your system? Odeo (`odeo.com`) allows you to subscribe to any podcast in its directory without putting any software on your desktop. Instead, podcast media files are assembled and made available so you can listen to them at the click of a button.

- ✔ **Podnova:** Podnova (`podnova.com`) is another service that tracks podcast content, yet doesn't require you to download any software to your desktop. As with Odeo, you have the option to download some software so files can be transferred to your MP3 player, but it's nice to know that some services don't require this step.

We've glossed over quite a few advanced features of Odeo and Podnova, and probably have not done justice to Nimiq or Doppler. And of course, additional clients and services provide similar-yet-distinct capabilities. But an attempt at a comprehensive list would be instantly obsolete, so this quick list simply offers a rough idea of how far the limits of podcasting currently extend. Bottom line: At this point, you should easily be able to subscribe to the podcasts of your choice.

Now that you've got your podcatching client, it's now time to take a good listen as to what is happening in the podcasting community. Many podcatching clients have internal directories of podcasts, accessing their listings from another directory or listing site maintained elsewhere on the Internet. Other aggregators maintain their own lists based on how many listeners have used their podcatcher to subscribe to particular shows.

So where are these directories? Fire up your browser and, as Edgar Winter says, "Come on and take a free ride. . . ."

As you can see, it's pretty darn easy to find podcasts — and to fill up your player of choice pretty quickly. Listen to some shows for inspiration. When you find one that makes you think, "I can do a podcast at least that good," consider it an invitation to do just that. (Good thing you've got this book.)

Quest for Podcasts

If you're going to podcast (and with you picking up this book, it's a safe assumption that the interest is strong), it's a good idea to take a look around the podcasting community and see what other podcasters are doing. We give you a few places to get started in this section — directories, podcast-listing services, and even podcast-specific search engines. (Check out the various sources mentioned in Chapter 10 as well.)

iPodder.org

The directory that started it all, iPodder.org (`ipodder.org`), is a volunteer-supported directory of podcasts. It consists of various categories managed by individuals with particular interests in given categories.

iPodder.org is a bare-bones site. You won't find detailed descriptions about the podcasts, sample episodes, or any sort of ratings. Instead, you find many direct links to podcast feeds — and those can easily be fed to your pod-catcher of choice. Find the category you like, start subscribing, and then listen.

iPodder is very much an open directory. Not only can anyone contribute shows, but also programmers with OPML experience can repurpose the contents of the directory into applications and other directory services. Because of this capability, most of the podcaster directories use the information in iPodder.org to help build (at least in part) their own directories of podcasts.

Podcast Alley

If iPodder.org was the first place to hang your podcasting hat, Podcast Alley (`podcastalley.com`) is the first place to boast, brand, and generally beat your chest about it. With incredibly active forums, detailed descriptions of podcasts, and individual episodes — plus the majority of all podcasters clamoring to get their listeners to "VOTE FOR ME ON PODCAST ALLEY THIS MONTH!" — it's no wonder that Podcast Alley is the most active podcast listing and ratings service to date.

Along with iPodder.org, Podcast Alley is owned by PodShow, the family of podcasts and services produced by Adam Curry and crew. This close affiliation with podcasting services and the podcasts themselves has some podcaster pundits crying foul. While we agree this provides fertile ground for some less-than-ethical activities when it comes to promoting podcasts, we honestly haven't seen that sort of thing going on.

Podcast Pickle

Gary Leland and the crew at Podcast Pickle (podcastpickle.com) take a slightly different approach for listeners to find the podcasts they're looking for. Their best innovation, in our opinion, is the Favorites listing. Rather than rely on voting as a measure of popularity, the Pickle allows registered members to mark as many shows as they like as their favorites. The more people who have marked a show as Favorite, the higher up on the Favorites list a podcast is. A neat idea!

But that's a lot like a popularity contest; you have no way to judge how well *you* might like a show just because a bunch of other people do. That's why Podcast Pickle also allows you to browse by category or search for relevant keywords that mean something to you. Like Podcast Alley, it also has an active forum section where you can see what other folks are saying about a particular podcast before you subscribe.

Yahoo.com Audio search

Browsing through lists and weighing your options, using the relative popularity of shows as a measuring stick, are great starting points — but this is the Internet we're talking about here. When you're looking for something in cyberspace, you likely do one thing first: Run a search.

In late summer 2005, Yahoo! rolled out its audio-specific search engine at audio.search.yahoo.com. While Yahoo! wasn't the first in the space (see Chapter 10 for other options), it certainly has the potential to be the biggest, having been a pioneer in search-based technology for years.

TIP

There are so many directories for podcasts that Rob Walch of podCast411 has put together a "directory of directories" (podcast411.com/page2.html). As of this writing, 66 different directories are listed!

Chapter 2

Getting the Gadgets That Make a Podcast Go

. . . .

In This Chapter

▶ Choosing hardware to lay down sweet sounds

▶ Getting the right software for your podcast

▶ Sending the signal with XML and RSS

▶ Getting a host for your podcast

. . . .

*N*ow that you're effectively hip as to what podcasting is and what it's all about, you need to start building your studio. This studio can come in a variety of shapes, sizes, and price tags. What you're thinking about doing — podcasting — is like any hobby you pursue. If it's something to pass the time and try out to see if you like it, then perhaps you'll want to keep your setup simple. If you find yourself tapping into a passion you did not know was deep inside you, you might want to upgrade to bigger, better, and badder equipment.

If you suddenly decide you — yes, you — are the greatest new sensation to hit the podcasting arena since Adam Curry, you'll quickly find yourself soundproofing the basement and looking at industry-standard equipment that might require some extra homework to master.

This is the beauty of podcasting. In the long run, it doesn't matter if your podcasting studio is an iPod with a plug-in microphone or comprised of the latest mixing boards, audio software, and recording equipment. Both approaches to podcasting work and are successfully implemented on a variety of podcasts.

So which one works best for what you have in mind? That's what we take a look at in this chapter, discussing the options, advantages, and disadvantages of each setup.

Finding the Right Mic

It's surprisingly easy and affordable to make your computer podcast-capable. Your first order of business is to find the right mic. If you already have a microphone built in to your laptop (and you don't mind starting out basic), you can just download Audacity (described later in the chapter) and take advantage of its free cost. That's all there is to it! (For openers, anyway.)

However, if your desktop computer didn't come with a mic (or you're just not happy hunching over your laptop like Quasimodo), you're going to want to shop around for a new microphone. When shopping for a mic, consider the following criteria:

- **What's your price range?** In many cases, especially with "cheap" mics, you get what you pay for in quality of construction and range of capabilities. You want the most affordable model of microphone that will do the job for you and your podcast.

- **Do you plan to use the mic primarily in the studio or on location?** A high-end shockmounted model isn't the best choice for a walk in the park, and a lapel mic might not provide you with the quality of sound expected for an in-studio podcast. Before you purchase your mic, consider your podcasting location needs.

- **What do you want this mic to do?** Record sound? Yeah, okay, but what kind and in what surroundings? Some mics offer ease of handling for interviews. Some are good at snagging specific outdoor sounds. Others may be better at capturing live music. You need to consider multipurpose mics, guest mics, and on-location recording devices, or any kind of condition your podcast provides for you.

The sections that follow give you the lowdown on the mic that's right for your budget.

Mics on the cheap

Most of the economical microphones on the market utilize USB (Universal Serial Bus) hookups. Figure 2-1 shows two types of USB plugs, which you may have used for attaching a digital camera or an MP3 player. You can go online to any of the computer equipment retailers and type **USB microphones** in their respective search engines. Make sure you include **USB**, because a search for microphones can bring up many more alternatives, including video cameras, high-end mics (which we talk about next), and other devices that might be way out of your budget.

High end is relative. Professional recording studios can spend hundreds of dollars on a single microphone. Fortunately, the MP3 format isn't so finicky; as a rule, *high end* for a podcasting mic tops out at less than $100.

Figure 2-1:
The USB ports and connectors on both the computer and the mic.

When shopping for microphones, you'll hear a lot of terminology like *omnidirectional* and *unidirectional.* These multisyllabic words may look cool to type and are impressive to say; but when you read them or they are spoken to you, they can be a little intimidating. We're going to demystify many of these terms and explain how effective these various mic types are for podcasting.

Omnidirectional mics

Most microphones that come preinstalled in laptops are *omnidirectional* — they pick up sounds from all directions at once. The iPod accessory iTalk (from Griffin Technologies, starting at around $32) is an omnidirectional microphone. Omnidirectional mics pick up your voice, along with the television in the background, the traffic outside, the rustling of clothes, the ceiling fan . . . basically if it makes noise and is within range of the mic, it's recorded.

While omnidirectional mics are ideal for *soundseeing tours* such as *Tokyo Calling* (`tokyocalling.org/`) or *Bicyclemark's Communiqué* (`www.bicycle mark.org/`), they may not be ideal for all in-studio podcasting because they don't respond to sound with quality — even when your mouth is so close that your lips brush against the mic's screen. They tend to add a sharp, tinny quality to your voice and cut out on harsh, sudden sounds such as consonants (especially *ps* and *ts*). That's partly because basic omnidirectional mics vary widely in quality and partly because of the limits imposed by their construction. The built-in models, for instance, are sometimes crammed into leftover nooks in their devices, where they are awkward to use and can pick up internal noise. It's no wonder they tend to be tiny and lo-fi.

Unidirectional mics

Unidirectional mics, unlike their omnidirectional brethren, pick up sound from only one direction: the direction they're pointing in. If you want to know exactly what a unidirectional mic is and what it can do, take a look at the Brian DePalma film, *Blow Out.* John Travolta plays a foley artist, a guy who collects random sound effects and then sweetens them for particular moments in whatever film he's working on. One night, he takes a stroll through the park with a "gun microphone," a type of unidirectional mic that only picks up sounds located where it is pointing. This microphone is so particular that it concentrates on recording along the line of sight — so it records not only the sound of a tire blowing out but also the gunshot that causes it to happen.

Blow Out hinges on what a unidirectional microphone does: record sounds from one direction only. And this is what makes the unidirectional mic such an important piece of equipment in your podcast. This type of mic is a good choice for podcasting because surrounding sounds are filtered out and only the sound directed to it is picked up. For in-studio podcasting, interviews, and quality recording, unidirectional microphones are the best option.

One omnidirectional mic that we recommend is the eMic (`www.gembird.us/ html/emic.htm`). It currently retails for about $25.99 and is compatible with both the Mac and Windows platforms. Find a USB port on your Mac or PC, plug in this microphone, and push a button. Your microphone is on and ready for recording.

When shopping for a good unidirectional USB microphone, you'll want to make sure the accessory detail mentions that it has *noise-canceling technology,* which filters out background noise. You'll want your USB microphone to do this, especially if you're planning to do interviews or record on-location commentary. Of course, if you're constantly on the go with your podcast, whether you're using an iPod with iTalk or a digital audio recorder, this type of filter is nonexistent (so far anyway).

You might be tempted to purchase a USB headset when you purchase your new mic. Okay, hands-free convenience is a plus, but having a headset grouped with your microphone isn't all you need to monitor yourself automatically as you record. To self-monitor your own voice, you need software that offers you an on-screen mixer, a mixing board, or the ability to monitor yourself as you record.

Investing in a high-end mic

Remember the opening of *The Blues Brothers?* Jake (John Belushi) turns to Elwood (Dan Aykroyd) after looking over the "new used" car his brother is driving, and asks him what happened to their Cadillac. "I traded it," Elwood replies, "for a microphone." Jake leans forward, a little stunned. "You traded the Bluesmobile . . . *for a microphone?!?*" Then, on reflection, he nods. "All right, I can see that."

Nothing like a movie analogy to drive home a point, but . . . don't offer up your car for trade just yet. There are plenty of high-quality microphones out there that pick up nuances and details that a simple USB microphone doesn't and are still affordable.

What sets these microphones apart from their USB counterparts (described in the previous section) is they are *cardioid* (heart-shaped) in their pickup pattern, as shown in Figure 2-2. They pick up sound from a wider area than the USB unidirectional microphone can but narrower than what an omnidi-rectional mic takes in. They're also the mics most widely used for stage productions. Higher-end versions of these microphones are so sensitive that they come with *shockmounts* — spring-loaded frames that "suspend" the mic when attached to a microphone stand, providing better reception while reducing any noise or vibration from your microphone stand. Think of a shockmount as a shock absorber for your mic.

Figure 2-2:
Various cardioid patterns of different condenser micro-phones.

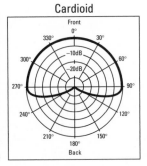
Cardioid

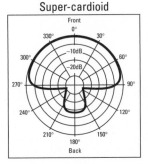
Super-cardioid

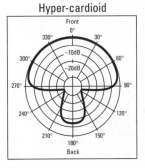
Hyper-cardioid

These shockmounted mics also capture sound better than unidirectional USB mics because they interpret sound in a slightly separate fashion. *Condenser* microphones are constructed with two plates, one fixed and the other vibrated by sound. The distance between the fixed plate and vibrating one changes based on the incoming acoustics, and varying electrical currents become inter-preted as voice. The end result: Condenser mics (because they emulate how human vocal chords work) can reproduce a more genuine representation of vocals, acoustic instruments, and ambiance, making them the ideal micro-phones for in-studio podcasts. Figure 2-3 shows a condenser microphone.

We recommend the MXL 990 Cardioid Condenser Mic with Shockmount (www.mxlmics.com), which retails for around $70.

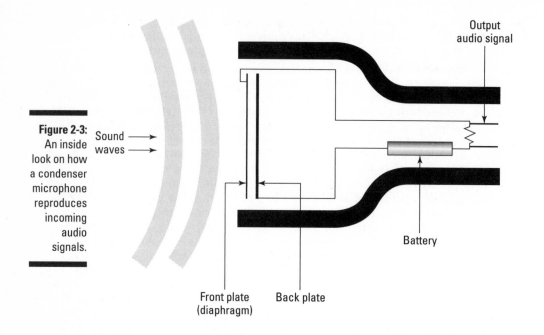

Figure 2-3:
An inside look on how a condenser microphone reproduces incoming audio signals.

Output audio signal

Sound waves

Battery

Front plate (diaphragm)

Back plate

When you purchase a higher-end microphone, keep in mind that you probably will receive no instruction manual, no additional cables for hook up, a jack that does not fit into your computer, and no stand. That's because you're upgrading to professional equipment. The manufacturer is assuming that you already have the tools, bells and whistles, and extra do-dads to make this mic work for you. For the lowdown on what accessories you need to hook up your new mic to your computer, check out the "Accessorize! Accessorize! Accessorize!" section later in this chapter.

The phantom (power) of the podcast

You might notice that some mics (such as the MXL described in this chapter) are *phantom powered* — their connection to the mixer provides them with all the power they need. This is a very good thing and can save you a lot of money and headaches in the future. Condenser mics need an extra little electrical kick to receive audio at their full potential. You can use batteries to power those mics, but when they start to die, so does your recording quality. (A word to the wise: Always check your mic's battery level before you interview and have fresh batteries on hand.) Because phantom power comes from the mixing board through the cable connecting to the mic, it supplies a constant boost — no battery worries.

Expanding Your Studio

If you're podcasting on a shoestring budget, all you really need is a basic microphone and some audio software (several types of which are described in this chapter) to record. But if you have the financial resources and the desire, you can expand your computer's audio setup by making the investment in a mixing board, a new audio card, and additional accessories, as described in the following sections.

Podcasts well with others: Mixing boards

Along with a microphone stand (which can set you back no more than $8 or thereabouts), you need a *mixing board,* such as the Behringer Eurorack UB802 Mixer shown in Figure 2-4. You see mixing boards at rock concerts and in "behind the scenes" documentaries for film and the recording industry. They come in all shapes and sizes, and this section looks at a good typical starter unit that offers features for the podcaster working solo or with friends. What a mixing board does for your podcast is open up the recording options, such as multiple microphones, recording acoustic instruments, and balancing sound to emphasize one voice over another or balance both seamlessly.

Figure 2-4: The Behringer Eurorack UB802 Mixer, a simple mixing board, accommodates two phantom-powered microphones and jacks for live instruments.

First off, let's demystify this contraption called the mixing board. The easiest way to look at a mixing board is you're partitioning your computer into different recording studios, but instead of calling them *studios,* we are calling these partitions *tracks.*

A simple mixing board provides two mono tracks and two stereo tracks, and you can use any of those tracks for input *or* output of audio signals — the unit's outrageously versatile. If you're podcasting solo or with a friend, you can hook up two condenser mics so you won't have to huddle around the same microphone or slide it back and forth as you take turns speaking.

You may also be wondering about all those wacky knobs on a mixing board. These knobs deal with various frequencies in your voice and can deepen, sharpen, or soften the qualities of your voice, and perhaps even help filter out surrounding *white noise* (which is the sound of an empty room and nothing more, unless you're psychic . . .). The knobs on the mixing board that are your primary concern are the white ones that control your volume or *levels,* as the board labels them. The higher the level, the more input signal your voice gains when recording. If one of your tracks is being used for output, the level dictates how loud the playback through your headphones is.

Heavy-metal legends Spinal Tap may prefer sound equipment that "goes to 11," but cranking your mixing board way up and leaving it that way won't do your podcast much good. The best way to handle sound is to set your levels before podcasting. That is what is going on when you see roadies at a concert do a mic check. The oh-so-familiar "Check one, check two, check-check-check . . ." is one way of setting your levels, but a better method is just rambling on as if you were podcasting, and then adjusting your sound levels according to your recording application's volume unit (VU) meter. For more on setting levels, hop to Chapter 4 for all the details.

Accessorize! Accessorize! Accessorize!

A microphone and a mixing board are just the beginning when it comes to putting together your audio suite. You now need, as Martha Stewart would no doubt tell you if she were helping you with this process, to add in the final touches. Now when it comes to accessories, Martha might make suggestions like a doily for the mic stand or a sweet, hand-knitted cover for the mixer. When we talk about accessories, we have something different in mind. Here are some optional add-on's that will help you produce a rock solid podcast:

> ✔ **Headphones:** After shelling out $50 for a mixing board, you might also want to think about purchasing a nice pair of headphones. Headphones help you monitor yourself as you speak. That may seem a little indulgent, but by hearing your voice, you can catch before playback any odd trip-ups, slurred words, or missed pronunciations.

Another advantage with headphones is they have better sound quality than your computer's speakers as well as reduce ambient noise around you. There are those Bose Noise Reduction stereo headphones you see advertised on television, but if you want to keep it simple, pick up a good pair of headphones for around $30. They'll work just as well for a podcast. Make sure the headphone cable ends in a ¼-inch stereo male jack (as shown in Figure 2-5); that's what plugs in to your mixing board.

Figure 2-5:
A ¼-inch male connection, the connection needed to connect headphones to a mixing board.

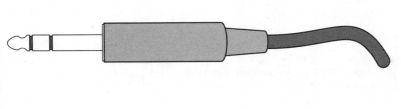

✔ **Cords:** As mentioned in the "Investing in a high-end mic" section earlier in the chapter, your newfangled microphone may arrive without any cords — and buying the wrong cord can be easy if you don't know jack (so to speak). So check the mic's connector before you buy. With high-end condenser mics, the connectors aren't the typical RCA prongs; instead, you use a three-prong connection: a 3-pin XLR male plug. It connects to a 3-pin XLR *female* plug, as shown in Figure 2-6.

To plug a microphone into your mixer, you want to specify a *3-pin XLR-to-XLR male-to-female* cord; the female end connects to the mic, the male end to the mixer. This adds another $9 to $15 to your outlay, depending on the length of the cord. (If your mixer has ¼-inch mic inputs, you can get a 3-pin XLR female-to-¼-inch male, but XLR-to-XLR yields better results — provided your mixer has the needed female XLR jack.)

Figure 2-6:
XLR male and female plugs, standard plugs for phantom-powered microphones.

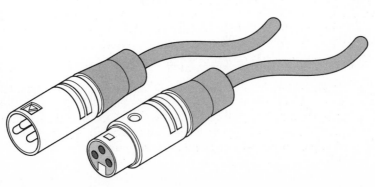

✔ **Microphone windscreens:** Go to Radio Shack or any music store and ask for microphone *windscreens* (shown in Figure 2-7). You may pick up a bag of five (all different colors) for less than $10. Windscreens reduce that amateurish-sounding popping and hissing on consonants, and cut out some ambient noise the microphone would otherwise pick up.

Figure 2-7:
Wind-
screens
help you cut
out the
ambient
noise.

With windscreen　　　　　　　**Without windscreen**

It's in the cards: Purchasing and installing an audio card

At the core of this podcasting recipe is your computer. Apples and Windows, Mac and PCs, there is no bias here. So don't let the screen captures from the sweet Mac Daddy setup throw you. To quote the creepy medium from *Poltergeist,* "All are welcome! ALL ARE WELCOME! Go into the light. . . ."

This audio investment may still need one more ingredient that completes the connection to your Mac or PC: an audio card. Sure, digital audio equipment tends to come with a FireWire or USB port these days, but if your mixing board doesn't have one (and some still don't), and your microphone doesn't look like it'll connect to any ports that look familiar on your computer, you probably need an audio card.

There is a difference between a *sound* card and an *audio* card. A sound card allows your Mac or PC to play and record basic sound. This isn't the highest quality of sound in many cases, and the sound card that came with your Mac or PC is built primarily to play music and those goofy alert sounds. Audio cards, on the other hand, allow you to output to other external devices and provide ports for input such as hi-fi components, mixing boards, and MIDI keyboards. Audio cards also generate higher quality output than default sound cards.

Audio cards are designed to fit into PCI slots (those empty slots inside your computer) and offer red-and-white female jacks similar to the back of stereo components. It's no surprise then that they are *RCA jacks,* as shown in Figure 2-8. These jacks control the left and right channels of sound coming in and out of your hi-fi equipment. After you've installed the audio card in an available PCI slot in your computer, you've given it the same capabilities.

Figure 2-8:
RCA plugs
used for
stereo
component
hook-ups
and audio
cards.

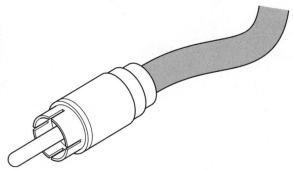

Finding the right PCI audio card

When shopping for a PCI audio card, keep the following points in mind:

✔ Make sure the audio card is compatible with your computer's operating system in the version your machine uses. Just because the card *says* it's Macintosh- or Windows-compatible doesn't make it a shoe-in for Windows XP or Mac OS X Tiger. Check the card manufacturer's Web site and find out whether you need to download the latest *driver* for the card. The driver helps the computer recognize this new card in its PCI slot and set up an interface with it.

✔ Make sure the card offers *at least two sets of analog jacks* (the red-and-white RCA jacks described in the preceding section).

For our money, one cost-effective card for podcasting is the Audiophile 2496 PCI Digital Audio Card from M-Audio (www.m-audio.com); it costs around $99. This simple, basic audio card (shown in Figure 2-9) offers two Analog In and two Analog Out jacks. The M-Audio driver that comes included may need to be upgraded after you purchase the card (new, improved drivers are always coming out). Refer to the manufacturer's Web site for details.

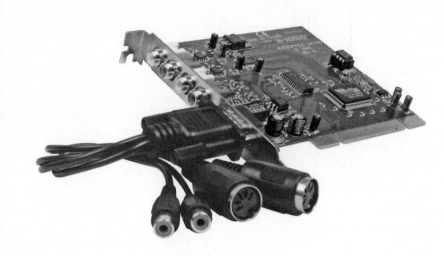

Figure 2-9:
The Audio-
phile 2496
(available
for both PCs
and Macs)
is a good,
basic audio
card,
providing a
connection
between
your mixing
board and
your
computer.

Installing a PCI audio card into your computer

Now, it's a pretty safe bet that some of you out there have opened up your computer and installed a wide variety of stuff — internal hard drives, CD or DVD drives, and of course, audio cards — with never a worry, hardly a concern. Right?

But some of you may imagine confronting the forbidden interior of your computer and suddenly have a tough time reading this page as the book starts shaking in your trembling hands. (Just kidding. Of course we are.) If you worry about doing expensive damage to the innards of your computer (heck, we've known people who won't even *look* in there lest they break something), breathe easy: You're about to find out just how easy (and safe) it is to upgrade your computer. Make sure you have three things handy — this book, a Phillips-head screwdriver, and something metallic to touch — and you can save yourself a few bucks on upgrade fees.

For those of you iMac users who are trying to figure out where your PCI slots are, sorry, but it's no use pulling out your hair in frustration. iMacs don't *have* any PCI slots. While inexpensive and super-sleek in their design, iMacs were built for affordability, not expansion.

To install an audio card into your Mac or PC desktop computer, follow these steps:

1. **Shut down your computer.**

iRiver: The new players in podcasting

The idea of "podcasting to go" had a lot of limits hemming it in at one time, ranging from how mobile the studio could be to figuring out whether the right conditions existed for an iMic to pick up the podcaster's voice clearly. This was before the arrival of the iRiver — a lightweight, unobtrusive, all-in-one solution for portable-podcast recording.

All the products created by iRiver (www.iriveramerica.com) specialize in playback of MP3 files, providing stiff competition for Apple's iPod, but with iRiver's *ultra-portable players,* the company is targeting many of the podcasters who specialize in soundseeing tours. Starting at under $100, the iRiver records up to 16 hours of voice with its built-in microphone, recording directly into an MP3 format, at 32 kHz. (Its latest model, the T-series, offers a full-color display, extended battery life, and faster exchange of music from computer to player. Unfortunately the T-10 operates *only* on the Windows XP operating system. For Mac and other Windows platform users, the iRiver iFP-series pictured here is still the model of choice.)

Weighing no more than a set of car keys and coming with a sport arm band or neck strap, the iRiver has taken the podosphere by storm, becoming the must-have, one-step solution to portable podcasting. Recordings can immediately be imported into Audacity and edited for podcasting purposes, making iRiver a very appealing option if you want to take your show outside your studio or (for first-time podcasters) give your podcasting talents a try before making an investment in a full-blown audio studio.

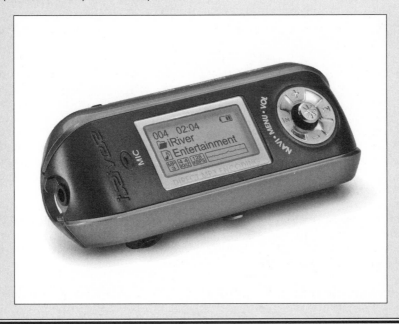

2. **Unplug any peripheral components (power supply, external hard drives, monitors, and so on).**

   Clear a space and pull your computer out into the open so you have room to work.

3. **Open up your computer.**

   On your PC, unscrew the casing from the back and slide it off.

   For the Mac, lift the side-switch and lower the motherboard (Mac G4), or slide the casing away from its housing (Mac G5).

   When the housing is exposed, there is a danger of static electricity jumping between you, your tools, and your computer. A small static spark won't do more to you than sting a little, but it can easily fry your entire hard drive. Now that we've put a Biblical fear into you, calm down. Simply find that grounded metallic item we told you to have on hand and touch it. If possible, try the next few steps with one hand on the metallic item and the other with the Phillips-head screwdriver to ensure you're grounded.

4. **Unscrew from the housing the metal shields located next to the available PCI slot where you're going to install your audio card, as shown in Figure 2-10.**

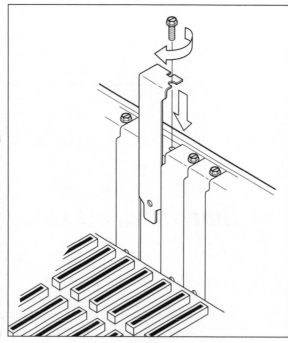

Figure 2-10:
This diagram illustrates how to unscrew one of the metal shields from the unoccupied PCI slot.

Set the screws aside (you'll need them in a few moments), and place the metal shield in whatever box you use to keep the "extra unused parts" of your computer.

5. **Line up the audio card with the PCI slot and push it into the PCI slot until the card snaps into place.**

    You need both hands for this step, so let go of that metallic object we mentioned earlier.

6. **With the screw taken from the slot shield (and another hand on the metallic object used for grounding), secure the audio card into the slot.**

7. **Replace the housing of your computer.**

8. **Put the unit back into its place, reconnect all accessories, and note which audio jacks are In and Out.**

9. **Plug the corresponding RCA cables into your audio card and mixing board.**

10. **Start up your computer.**

Now comes the part where you install or download and install drivers into your computer so it recognizes and activates the card as part of its operations. With your computer seeing the hardware and what it has to work with, all you need now is some software.

The steps depicted here work for a desktop model. For you laptop podcasters who would like to take advantage of a mixing board, your options are not only limited, but also often less cost-effective. One option is to invest in an audio PCMIA card. Some exist, but the majority of them are built for MIDI devices. Another option is to hook up a Canopus Analog-to-DV converter to your FireWire/IEEE-1394 port (you can find out more about these devices at `www.canopus.us/`) and use only the audio jacks for the feed. Griffin and M-Audio accessories can record analog audio through either USB or FireWire ports.

The Audacity of That GarageBand and Its Audio Hijack Pro: Audio-Editing Software

After you have your recording equipment in place, plugged in, and running, it's time to take a look at *audio-editing* software packages. These are the applications that help you take that block of audio marble and chisel the podcast that is hidden within it.

As with digital photo editors, DVD authoring software, and word processors, software for audio comes in all sizes and all costs, ranging from free to roughly an entire paycheck (or three). Like any software package, the lower the cost, the simpler the product and the easier it is to understand, navigate, and use for recording. However, as the software grows more complex (and expensive), the features that offer advantages for pro-level work become abundantly clear. The following sections run down some of the software that might be right for you.

Audacity: Who says you can't get something for nothing?

Audacity (shown in Figure 2-11) is a piece of software that quickly became a podcaster's best friend. It's easy to see why; it's free and simple to use. It's available for downloading at `audacity.sourceforge.net`.

Designed by volunteers who simply wanted to "give back to the Internet" something cool, Audacity was initially designed for a variety of audio capabilities such as importing, mixing, editing, and exporting audio. For podcasters, it provides an optimum tool for recording voice straight off a computer. Another big plus with Audacity is its compatibility with Windows, Macintosh, *and* Linux. (We want to send a big thank you to the volunteers who went out of their way to show that yes, software can be made available for *any* platform, provided the creators are driven enough to make it happen!)

But what can a free piece of software *do?* Well, for openers, Audacity . . .

- ✔ Records live audio through microphones or mixer channels
- ✔ Can record up to 16 channels at once
- ✔ Imports various sound formats for editing and remixing
- ✔ Exports final projects to WAV, AIFF, AU, and MP3s
- ✔ Grants the user unlimited Undo and Redo commands
- ✔ Can create an unlimited number of audio tracks
- ✔ Removes static, hiss, hum, and other constant background noises
- ✔ Offers effects such as Echo, Phaser, Wahwah, Reverse (and these effects are expandable via third-party plug-ins)
- ✔ Records at an audio quality of up to 96 kHz

And then there's a serious bonus: Audacity can digitize analog audio from cassette tapes and vinyl records, a feature found in many commercial audio-editing software packages. For a free piece of software, this is one impressive download.

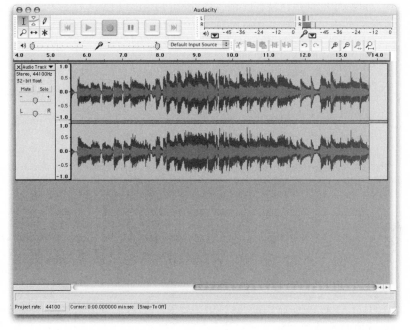

Figure 2-11:
Audacity is
a freeware
application
that allows
you to edit
audio and
create MP3
files.

Make sure you access the right URL. Remember that the Web site for Audacity is `audacity.sourceforge.net` and *not* `www.audacity.com`. If you happen to type in the latter address, you find yourself at Audacity, Inc., a Seattle, Washington–based janitorial service.

Audacity is an excellent piece of software for the basics, but what if you desire more control over the capabilities and features of your audio-editing package? Are you looking for more recording options, additional audio filters, built-in multitrack recording and pre-recorded music loops? (Gads, what some people will do to set a mood or a tone for a podcast.) Coming right up . . .

Cakewalk for the PC: This podcasting stuff is easy!

The Cakewalk application (`www.cakewalk.com`) comes in various shapes and sizes, but the PC podcaster is likely to have two favorite flavors: Cakewalk Home Studio 2 and Home Studio 2XL. Cakewalk Home Studio 2 (which retails for around $99) offers the extra bells and whistles that Audacity doesn't, while Home Studio 2 XL (around $159) offers even more features than Home Studio 2.

Cakewalk (shown in Figure 2-12) offers its users some serious goodies:

- ✔ Support for Project5, Kinetic, Reason, and other ReWire synths
- ✔ Simultaneous recording of unlimited audio and MIDI tracks for multi-channel audio cards
- ✔ Recording up to 24-bit/96 kHz audio
- ✔ Mixing of real-time audio and MIDI effects
- ✔ Support for MP3, WAV, WMA, and MIDI files

The software package includes additional applications for musicians (such as Notation and EDIROL Virtual Sound Canvas DXi) that allow users to compose, print, and produce music loops and original music beds. Of course, if your musical talent doesn't extend much beyond your CD collection or iTunes playlists, then Home Studio 2XL is a better investment, simply for the additional CD: PowerFX Dyad DXi Sampler & Sample Library. Between the easy audio editing and engineering (with Dyad DXi) and the collection of original audio samples, it's a breeze to compose your own themes and music loops.

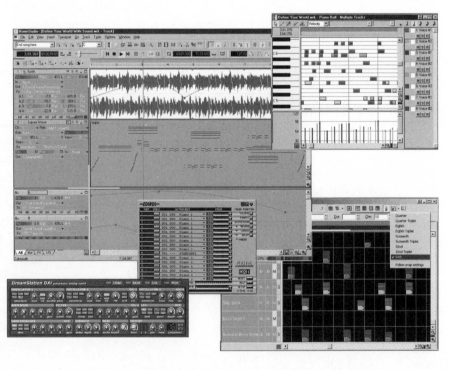

Figure 2-12:
The many palettes in Cakewalk Home Studio provide the Windows podcaster with a slew of engineering and editing options.

Cakewalk is a popular audio package for the PC, but what about Mac users? For those of us in the minority of the computer world, it's always a frustration to hear software developers say, "No, we won't be making this product available for Mac users." Sometimes we seem to be denied the coolest toys and utilities because they just aren't offered for our operating system (maybe a penalty for thinking differently, but still . . .).

Apparently Steve Jobs and his crew heard about this injustice, and shortly after the iPod took off came a gem that made it more-than-cool to be a Mac user — especially one who's into podcasting. We Mac-using podcasters call this gem *GarageBand,* introduced to you in the next section.

GarageBand: Moby in your Mac!

With hundreds of music loops that can easily switch from one instrument to another, GarageBand (shown in Figure 2-13) makes royalty-free music easy-to-compose. Many of the loops are editable and, with a bit of tweaking, can set the right mood for your podcast. With the release of iLife '05, GarageBand is now up to version 2 and has a few new additions (and one blessed repair) to enhance its initial version:

- ✔ The multitrack recording feature can handle eight tracks at once.
- ✔ You can see a display of the music, with actual notation, in real time.
- ✔ You can change the tempo and key of user-recorded instruments at any time during the editing process.
- ✔ You can save the recordings as loops in the GarageBand library.

Perhaps the biggest gripe about GarageBand — shared by those whose podcasts got a bit lengthy (ahem — *hearty*) — is this slick application's refusal to edit and apply dynamic audio effects past the 30-minute (999-measure) mark. For some inexplicable reason, GarageBand editing capabilities stop there, forcing podcasters to break up their extended shows into segments and then reassemble the finished products in another application. (We begrudgingly do this and then mix additional music segues and other recorded segments in Apple's Final Cut Express. We then export only the audio, ending with a dandy AIFF file that's ready for MP3 compression in iTunes. More on compression and final touches in Chapter 6.) For our purposes, however, this time limit on the editing is minor when compared to the convenience of GarageBand's interface and its robust capabilities.

Upgrading from GarageBand to GarageBand 2 means purchasing the complete iLife '05 package, starting at $79.99. There is no separate upgrade for GarageBand, but the good news is that the new GarageBand also includes the latest versions of iPhoto, iTunes, iMovie, and iDVD, each of which is a terrific application in its own right.

Figure 2-13:
GarageBand
is easy to
learn, easy
to use, and
easy to have
a blast with.

GarageBand's most appealing asset is its hundreds of sampled instruments available in loops. You can easily edit and splice together these loops with other loops to create original music beds of whatever length you choose. Pre-recorded beds range from Asian drum ensembles to Norwegian Folk Fiddles to Blues Harmonica; these ensembles are easily incorporated with editable loops of Classic Rock piano, Southern Rock, or Emotional Piano reminiscent of films like *Love Story* and *Sense and Sensibility*.

GarageBand also provides a capability — with many (not all) of the samplings — to create your own musical theme. Sure, some instruments may sound better than others, but you might — with a bit of trial and error — create an original melody that serves as the best royalty-free intro and exit for your podcast.

If you're planning to do a bit of composing in GarageBand, be warned. Much like working with video in Final Cut Express, GarageBand is a lot of fun but can easily soak up your free time that you would normally dedicate to recording. So if you need to get in touch with your inner Mozart, set aside a good-size pocket of time to put together your desired riffs. You have many to choose from; as with podcasting, it's best not to rush the process.

GarageBand's Preferences

We're particularly keen on GarageBand's Preferences, which let you organize your final AIFF files in an iTunes playlist. When you're done with that particular recording session (what GarageBand refers to as a "song" although your podcast probably is primarily spoken-word voice tracks), choose File⇨Export to iTunes. The file is then exported in AIFF and immediately dropped into the playlist you named in GarageBand, where it's tagged with your name (or podcasting ID) and the "album" (which, in the case of the podcaster can be anything from the show title itself to the air date of the show). See Chapter 6 for details on adding ID3 tags.

Following the Apple archetype, GarageBand is easy to tinker with, navigate, and understand within a short span of time. Plenty of terrific books are available for mastering all the nuances of GarageBand, including *GarageBand For Dummies* by "Dr. Mac" himself, Bob LeVitus (Wiley). We cannot praise this application enough — and with expansion packs (called Jam Packs) that add instruments, riffs, and loops to your GarageBand and start at $100 each, this unassuming software offers a lot to the podcaster.

Audio Hijack Pro: Good software with a bad-boy attitude

If you're not interested in the musicality of GarageBand (or any of the other applications offered in iLife), Mac users have another handy application for recording podcasts and it comes with features not found in Audacity. This renegade of audio software is called Audio Hijack Pro (`www.rogueamoeba.com/audiohijackpro`).

What makes Audio Hijack Pro unique is its ability to record audio from nearly any source — not only coming in from microphones and musical instruments, but also from Internet streaming audio of any kind, including live audio chats from Skype and iChat!

Audio Hijack sports the familiar features that Audacity, GarageBand, and Cakewalk possess — such as converting analog music to digital, preparing MP3 files specifically for podcasting (by adding ID3 tags, setting bandwidth, and so on), and supporting audio formats such as WAV, AIFF, and MP3. The latest version of Audio Hijack offers some appealing capabilities:

✔ Record to AAC and Apple Lossless (ALAC) formats

✔ Customize with AppleScript

- ✔ Has built-in CD burning

- ✔ Can record AM/FM radio input sources

- ✔ Supports various radio accessories for your computer such as Griffin's RadioSHARK and D-Link's DSB-R100

- ✔ Can rip and record all audio through AHP's System Audio Input Source

- ✔ Edits and engineers input from multiple applications via the Application Mixer plug-in

- ✔ AHP's New Recording Bin organizes and previews audio files

Retailing for about $32 (less than half the cost of the iLife package), Audio Hijack Pro is quickly becoming a popular application for Macintosh podcasters and prides itself in being a rule-breaker. It's a non-Apple product that can record in Apple's audio-compression formats, burn CDs (so you can skip iTunes), and easily record streaming audio signals that tend to elude other audio-recording-and-editing software. Keep a sharp eye on this new player; it's craving a niche for itself in the podcasting community.

We have a green light, and all systems are go! After you get your software in place, test your set up to make sure everything works. Take a look at your application's preferences so that your sound input and output are going through your audio card, pod up the channel on the mixing board that your microphone is connected to, listen to yourself through your headphones, and you're all set and ready to record your podcast.

The Sky's the Limit: Big-Budget Software

If you're lucky enough to have unlimited funds and resources to build your podcasting studio, this section on software is for you. A majority of podcasts are working on the bare-bones plan, and so far the investment in the equipment we've recommended is for a budget of under $500 — provided you feel like making an investment in a professional microphone, mixing board, or software. Remember, what makes a good podcast is the same whether you're on a budget of $0, $500, or $Ridiculous. The difference is in the sound you can get. For the commercial broadcaster venturing into podcasting, sound quality is crucial as your reputation and experience are now being "socially tested." Do you not bother with the details, or raise the quality bar? Commercial podcasting will demand nothing less than the best in audio quality.

But when shopping online, you see mixing boards, audio cards, and microphones of all shapes, sizes, and sensitivities. You'll also see a wide variety of accessories — including mic stands, windscreens, "popper stoppers," and other add-ons that can improve your quality of recording (or at least look very cool in your office). Depending on your budget, you can purchase and set up the higher-end audio hardware, depending on the future you foresee for your podcast.

Podcasting is still a new field, but if you want to push its envelope and have the bucks, high-end audio software gives you full control over every aspect of the audio you're recording.

At one time, a favorite software application of broadcasting professionals was CoolEdit. But when Adobe Systems purchased it and repackaged the software as Adobe Audition (shown in Figure 2-14), it got even better. Audition is offered as a competitive upgrade at $250.00; a full stand-alone version is available at $299.99, or you can get it as part of the Adobe Video Collection Version 2.5 at $999.99. Audition's features are, at a glance, nothing short of awesome:

✔ 128 tracks available to the user

✔ Can record 32 different sources simultaneously

✔ Offers 50 digital sound effects to enhance your audio tracks

✔ Rips, edits, and saves audio from video and other audio sources

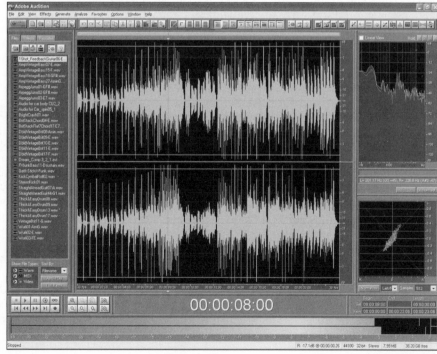

Figure 2-14: Adobe Audition (formerly CoolEdit) is the Windows software for editing and engineering audio that gives the podcaster complete control.

✔ Provides 5,000 royalty-free loops that can be easily edited and compiled to create your own music beds

✔ Offers integrated CD burning for audio

✔ Restores analog audio signals (from vinyl and cassette recordings) for digital playback quality

✔ Can separate vocal and instrumental tracks from imported music sources

What makes Audition so appealing to heavily engineered productions such as *Slice of Scifi* (`sliceofscifi.com`) and *Area 51* (`area51show.com`) is the complete control users have over the audio. Audition gives you dominion over pitch, wavelength, time-stretching, background-noise removal, and Dolby 5.1 stereo output, making it a staple in the digital audio industry.

Audition runs exclusively on the Windows platform, but Mac users have an equal (in cost, features, and control over the audio) called *Soundtrack Pro*.

Gluing It Together with XML and RSS

So far in this chapter we've talked about the hardware (mics and mixers) and the software (GarageBand and Audacity) necessary to record audio and create the podcast media file. That's the fun and creative part for most folks. But to make your recording a podcast, you need to get your hands dirty on the tedious and technical parts, and add two more three-letter acronyms to your vocabulary: *XML* and *RSS*.

RSS is a "flavor" of XML. For all you coding geeks out there, please bear with us; we'll be using RSS and XML as interchangeable terms in this section. Chapter 9 plunges rather deeply into RSS 2.0, but here we give a fast overview of where the RSS 2.0 feed fits into the podcasting equation.

We've helped dozens of non-technical podcasters get started — and in nearly every case, the XML/RSS step is the biggest source of confusion. So rather than serve up technology mumbo-jumbo, we're going to talk about *Star Trek* geeks and trained monkeys. (Say what?)

Consider this: *Star Trek* geeks know everything about their passion in life — *Star Trek*. Perhaps you've seen other forms of geekiness expressed toward other public icons — say, Apple computers or The Beatles. But you know the type of person we're talking about, right?

It's all about the <enclosure>, baby

If you already have a blog, you're probably already generating an XML file — or have the capability to do so. Although podcatching clients can read this existing XML feed, the feed needs to include the <enclosure> tag in order for podcasting to work.

Dave Winer invented the <enclosure> tag in early 2001 for the purpose of embedding links to large audio, video, or other "rich media" elements into an RSS/XML feed. At the time, Dave and Adam Curry were trying to solve the click-and-wait problems inherent in big files such as audio and video. Typically, if a user clicked a link to a 30MB file, several minutes would drag by before the file was completely downloaded to the user's hard drive and was usable. Not a good user experience, regardless of what's in the file.

With the advent of the <enclosure> RSS element, users could subscribe to places where they expected large files as a regular occurrence and move the downloading of those files to the early hours of the morning, when the users were snug in bed and a ten-minute download was no big deal.

Of course, users back then had to be technically savvy to take advantage of this new RSS element. It wasn't until the summer of 2004 that Adam Curry wrote the first iPodder application — a simple, user-friendly desktop program that extracted enclosed media files from RSS 2.0 feeds. And behold! Podcasting was born.

As a podcaster, you need a program that acts like a *Star Trek* geek. Your virtual STG has a single job: To boldly know everything there is to know about your podcast — and to flip happily into data-dump mode every time someone drops by to see what's new.

And the trained monkey? Well, podcast listeners don't have time to drop by and check on each and every podcaster they want to hear. So they employ a trained monkey and tell him exactly which *Star Trek* geeks to check with — and how often. When an STG has something new to say, the trained monkey comes back to his owner with the specifics. (And they said nobody could tie *Star Trek,* monkeys, and podcasting together. Ha!)

Here the role of the STG is filled by the RSS 2.0 file created by the podcaster — and the trained monkey is actually the podcatching client (iPodderX, for example) used by the listener.

As a podcaster, your job is not only to create your RSS 2.0 file, but also to make sure you keep that file updated and current each time you make available a new podcast media file. Lucky for you (and all of us), plenty of software solutions make this step a breeze.

Simplify the process and get a blog!

If you're looking to spend the least amount of time dinking around with your RSS 2.0 feed, look no further than the popular blogging software solutions. Blogs are easy to set up, are often free, and ease the process of generating and updating of RSS 2.0 files (they do it automatically).

You can choose from dozens of blog software packages, each with a variety of bells and whistles that are designed to make your updates (including your RSS 2.0 file) as easy and/or customizable as possible. For a crash course, check out *Syndicating Web Sites with RSS Feeds For Dummies* and *Buzz Marketing with Blogs For Dummies* (both published by Wiley); they can help you choose which blog software might be right for you. Meanwhile, here are a few options to consider:

- **Movable Type** (www.sixapart.com/movabletype): Evo has been using Movable Type, shown in Figure 2-15, for the past three years and has found it to be easy to use, extendable to fit his ever-changing needs, and robust enough to handle significant traffic loads. And with the easy to install MT-Enclosures plug-in, making your RSS 2.0 into a podcast feed is as simple as adding a link to your file.

  Movable Type 3.17 is available as a free download, or you can get the licensed version for $69.95, which entitles you to technical support and other benefits. It's available as a *hosted* model, where Movable Type takes care of the installation, or in a *do-it-yourself* model, where you arrange for hosting and installation on your own servers. Movable Type can boost your show's distribution — and a companion blog is available for show notes and additional postings.

- **WordPress** (wordpress.org): Another popular blogging solution, WordPress has some advantages. Not only is it easy to install and get running, but it also supports podcasting out of the box. Oh, and it's free. (Yeah. Free. Big plus there.) However, WordPress does not have a hosted model. But don't fret; many hosting companies offer packages that have WordPress preinstalled.

- **Blogger** (www.blogger.com): Blogger holds the distinction of being one of the first and most widely used blogging systems on the block. It's only available in a hosted model and is still the de-facto standard for most of the blogging world. Free from cost and any setup confusion, Blogger is also limited in its functionality and customizability. While it does allow you to create an RSS 2.0 template, it won't allow you to include the podcast media file. Several workaround solutions exist, but know that your Blogger account won't allow you to podcast without some work.

- **Libsyn** (libsyn.com): Don't be surprised if Liberated Syndication turns up quite a lot in this book. Libsyn is a combined blog/hosting company specifically designed for podcasting. While it may not address all your needs, its ease of use and all-in-one nature should not be passed up. Turnkey hosting plans start at $4.95 per month.

Figure 2-15:
Movable Type is a popular and user-friendly blog site that helps podcasters get their shows out into the world.

FeedBurner turns any blog into a podcast

Rick Klau and the folks at FeedBurner deserve a nod for their dedication to a podcasting approach that's 100 percent *For Dummies*–friendly. With a free FeedBurner account, any blogger can convert an existing RSS, Atom, or other syndication feed to a podcast-ready feed in three simple steps:

1. **Sign up for a free FeedBurner account at** `www.feedburner.com`.

   Free is good.

2. **Burn your existing feed.**

   Enter the URL of your blog's feed into the easy-to-use interface.

3. **Select Smart Cast from the Additional Services menu.**

FeedBurner then converts podcast media file links into an embedded `<enclosures>` element in a new feed.

That's it! You now have a new podcast-ready RSS 2.0 feed.

FeedBurner is now watching your original blog feed. The next time you make a post and include a link to a media file (MP3, WAV, . . . whatever), your new FeedBurner feed automatically does the behind-the-scenes magic necessary to get the `<enclosure>` tag pointing at the file you referenced in your post. While your original feed (maybe `www.FishingAlaska.com/index.xml`) doesn't change, your new feedburner feed (perhaps `feeds.feedburner.com/FishingAlaska`) is now podcast-friendly and ready to be served to podcatching clients.

Fine. Do it without a blog.

Blogs are great if you want to include text and other information along with your podcast. But if you're enough of a purist that you want your podcast to stand on its own without a supporting Web site, that's okay, too.

A place to put your show notes — and a home for your podcast, where folks can get your e-mail address or other pieces of data they may not catch on the show — is a really good idea. If you're confident that you prefer your podcast to stand on its own and exist only as an RSS 2.0 file, these options may be what you're looking for. If you're not sure, we suggest avoiding this route.

Take a closer look at some of these Web sites to provide a home for your podcast, sans blog. With these services, your podcast is simply an RSS file and an accompanying MP3 file, making show notes, additional comments, and hyperlinks a bit of a challenge; but you can podcast without a blog if you please, and here's where you do that:

✔ **Audioblog.com** (`www.audioblog.com`): For $4.95 per month, Audioblog lets you record, host, and publish MP3 files, generating a custom RSS 2.0 file for you automatically. No blog or hosting company is required. In fact, these folks even came up with a way to record and upload your audio file right in your browser — no recording software required. This is a great option if you want to test the waters of podcasting without making a huge investment of time or money.

✔ **Podcastamatic** (`bradley.chicago.il.us/projects/podcastamatic/`): Podcastamatic automates the creation of an RSS 2.0 file based on the contents of a folder on a Web server. It's not for the technical neophyte, you understand, but if you already have a Web server and don't really want to run blogging software of any flavor, this is a solid option.

Once installed and configured on your server, Podcastamatic watches a particular folder for new MP3 files you upload. When it detects changes to the folder, it generates a new RSS 2.0 file. It even creates or populates an HTML page if you so desire.

✔ **Feeder** (`reinventedsoftware.com/feeder/`): Feeder provides a simple interface that gives a lot of flexibility to podcasters who already maintain an active site. You fill it out, and it cranks out an RSS 2.0 file that's ready to be uploaded to the server. Very easy, full featured, and self-contained, it's popular among many podcasters. It's for Macs only, and it's a steal at $29.95.

Doing it by hand

What? Are you crazy? No, seriously — generating an XML file in RSS 2.0 format isn't overly difficult, but it's extremely easy to mess up! Sure, you could open up Notepad or BBEdit, download a few examples, and generate your own code, but we advise against it.

However, some code warriors — in the same vein of hand-coding HTML, JavaScript, and other markup languages — insist on composing their own code from the ground up (you glutton for punishment, you). You'll want to jump ahead to Chapter 9 for an in-depth look at writing a simple RSS 2.0 feed. We also recommend getting *extremely comfortable* with *Syndicating Web Sites with RSS Feeds For Dummies* (or at least keeping a copy under your pillow); it goes into more detail on these topics.

You can find the full technical specifications for RSS 2.0 (among other places) at feedvalidator.org/docs/rss2.html.

Finding a Host for Your Podcast

Unless you've already got hosting taken care of — either from a pre-existing relationship or from one of the solutions we list earlier — you're going to need a place on the Web to put your stuff. You know — your podcast media files, RSS 2.0 file, and show notes for your podcast. You also need a way to get them up there.

Getting a hosting provider is a breeze, with hundreds of companies all vying for your $9.95 fee each month. The good news is that all this competition has brought down the cost of hosting packages significantly. The bad news is that you have to go through a lot of clutter to reach the right selection.

This section covers the basic needs for most beginning podcasts and mentions a few pitfalls to watch out for. In Chapter 7, we get into the process of actually moving your files to your host.

Don't rush into a hosting agreement just yet. We suggest reading the rest of this chapter as well as Chapter 7 before forking over your credit card. We cover lots of good information that can help you narrow down your choices.

When you're comparing hosting plans, try not to get bogged down in the number of e-mail addresses, MySQL databases, subdomains, and the like. All of those features have their own purposes, but as a podcaster, you have only two worries: how many podcasts the site can hold and how much bandwidth you get.

Size does matter

Podcast media files are big. Unlike bloggers, podcasters eat up server space. Where simple text files and a few images take up a relatively small space, podcast media files tend to be in the 3MB to 30MB range.

Here some suggestions for zeroing in on what you need storage-space-wise:

- ✔ Think about how many podcasts you want to keep online, and plan accordingly.
- ✔ Consider the amount of server space you'll need to host your blogging software, databases, text, and image files. For example, Evo is using 315MB of space for just one of his podcasts, and he doesn't even host the podcast media files on that server! Of course, he's been building his Web site for three years and didn't get to that level overnight.

Podcasters should look for hosting plans that include at least 1000MB of storage space. As of this writing, several host providers charge less than $10 per month for that much space, and more.

Bandwidth demystified

Of equal importance to storage space is bandwidth, an elusive and often-misunderstood attribute of Web hosting that is critical to podcasters. *Bandwidth* refers to the online space needed to handle the amount of stuff you push out of your Web site every month. The bigger the files, the more bandwidth consumed. Compounding the problem, the more requests for the files, the more bandwidth consumed.

For instance, take a look at the bandwidth for Evo's podcast, *Slice of Scifi*. The graphic representation in Figure 2-16 shows not only the amount of information exchanged (read: downloads) but also the rising demands on bandwidth. After a while, the Web host will have to consider when it's time to allocate a larger bandwidth package to handle your show — and that means more cash outlay for you.

And therein lies the trouble for podcasters. Most podcasters want more listeners — and that means more podcatching clients requesting the podcast media files. Bottom line: The more popular your show gets, the more bandwidth being consumed every month.

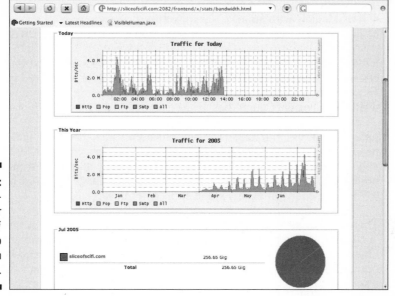

Figure 2-16: The band-width for *Slice of Scifi* continues to grow each month.

To simplify, pretend that you produce one show each week, and your show requires 10MB of bandwidth. You publish the show on Monday, and your 100 subscribers receive your show that evening. You've just consumed 1000MB of bandwidth (100 × 10MB) for that week. But next week, more people have found out about your incredibly amazing show, and now you have 200 sub-scribers. Next Monday, your bandwidth increases to 2000MB, which gets added to your previous week's total to bring you up to 3000MB.

Yep, you're up to a larger scheme of things — where you have to start think-ing in GB (gigs). And to streamline the math, we used 1000MB per GB, as opposed to the more correct 1024.

But those extra 100 subscribers? They weren't satisfied with just the last show. They also download the previous week's show, tacking on an extra 1GB of bandwidth. Now you're at 4GB for the month.

Next week, you're even more popular. Now you have 500 subscribers. Everyone gets the first file (which costs you 5GB), and 300 of them are getting the previ-ous two weeks' files (300 × 2 × 10MB), which rings you up for and extra 6GB. You're now at (4 + 5 + 6) 15GB for the month. See how things stack up?

It's not uncommon for Evo's podcasts to pull down over 250GB of transfer —
and that is only with about 1,500 subscribers. For shows with *tens* of thousands
of subscribers, the bandwidth consumption is in the *terabytes* of data.

It's difficult to estimate how much bandwidth you'll need for your podcast
because it's hard to guess how many people might be interested in your
show. Chapter 7 offers some real-world tips on figuring out what your bandwidth requirements might be.

As a general rule, the longer your podcast episodes, the more bandwidth you
need. If you plan on a five-minute bi-weekly podcast, you have less to worry
about than someone contemplating a thrice-weekly hour long show. The latter
podcaster will be quite concerned with how to manage bandwidth because it
will be an issue with even a small subscriber base.

There are ways to avoid the issue of bandwidth, or at least make it less of
a concern for even the podcaster with large ambitions — as well as files.
Chapter 7 talks about some podcast-specific and some advanced hosting
options. Even if you don't think you'll have to worry about bandwidth, it's
a section to pay close attention to because you'll likely be more popular —
and perhaps more wordy — than you think.

Part II

The Hills Are Alive with the Sound of Podcasting

In this part . . .

A podcast starts with a simple audio recording. Whether you are recording your voice or splicing together various audio clips to create a show, every podcaster needs to know the ins and outs of the recording process. In this part, we help you figure out what to record, how to record it, and how to avoid some pitfalls along the way.

Chapter 3

Before You Hit the Record Button

*T*une to a classical radio station (and when we refer to "classics" here, we mean Beethoven and Haydn, not the Beatles and Hendrix) and listen to the DJs — oh, sorry, the *on-air personalities* — featured there. You'll notice that they're all speaking slowly and articulately, mellowed and obviously relaxed by the melodic creations of greats such as Mozart, Wagner, and Joel. (Yes, Billy Joel's got a classical album — a pretty good one, too!) While the on-air personalities of your local classical music station all sound alike, they sound dramatically different from the wacky Morning Zoo guys on your contemporary hits radio station who sound as if they are on their eighth cup of espresso.

When you hear people talk about *finding your voice* in broadcasting, that is what they mean. You come to an understanding of what your average audience wants (and to some degree, expects), and then you meet that need. This chapter helps you determine what voice and personality you want to come across when podcasting.

Then you find out what you need to do to get ready for the show. This chapter shows you what to do to prepare for smooth and easy podcasts that (one can hope) will be glitch-free during the recording process. Preshow prep is not only important, but also essential in making a feed worth catching. Even the most spontaneous of podcasts follows a logical progression and general direction and remains focused on the podcast's intent.

Choosing a Unique Topic for Your Podcast

Before you can think about putting together a podcast, you need to decide on what topic you want to cover. At the time of this writing, a sample of what people were podcasting (according to PodcastAlley.com) — listed by genre (topic area) from most to least common — looked like this:

- 1,534 Music/Radio
- 1,135 General
- 921 Technology
- 491 Comedy
- 483 Religion/Inspiration
- 486 Cultural/Political
- 240 News
- 207 Business
- 253 Sports
- 209 Education
- 157 Movies/Films
- 114 Health/Fitness
- 57 Food and Drink
- 60 Video Podcasts
- 3 Travel
- 37 Environment

That's a total of 6,388 podcasts — an increase of 4,082 over a six-month period. This averages out to roughly 41 new podcasts going online every day. And these numbers don't include shows registered with Podcast.net, Podcastpickle.com, or other popular podcast directories.

The first thing to understand about podcasts is that this activity isn't all about being "number one" in your chosen podcast genre. Granted, some podcasts (and podcasting personalities) do vie for top honors on various polls and top ten lists. But instead of worrying about garnering ratings (a topic that's covered in Chapter 11), think about what will make your podcast uniquely worth your effort and your listeners' time. Here are some ways you can create a unique podcast:

✔ **Study other podcasts.** Before you can figure out what will make your podcast unique, you may want to check out some other podcasts. The best way to find out what makes a podcast worthwhile is to sign up for a few feeds that pique your curiosity.

Listen to these feeds for a few weeks (provided they're weekly) and jot down what you like and don't like about them. From the notes you take, you might find your angle. Keep in mind that downloading and listening to other podcasts should be educational and constructive, not a raid-for-fodder for your own show.

Don't openly steal content, SFX, or content structure from another podcast. (Approach it as you would someone's Web site. It's okay to be inspired, as long as you don't openly and outwardly make your podcast a carbon copy of your inspiration's work.) Also try to avoid open criticism of another podcast in your own; degrading someone else's work is no way to better yours. Try to stay on the pod-sitive side.

✔ **Pick a topic you know.** Whether you have decided to take on the topic of music, religion, or technology, the best way to make your podcast unique is to find an angle you're comfortable with (Polka: The Misunderstood Music, Great Travesties of Sports History, Forgotten Greats of Science Fiction). There is also the possibility that your initial show may inspire an additional angle so unique that you will have to start another podcast specifically to address that audience.

✔ **Speak with confidence.** A trick in making a podcast work is to speak *confidently* about your topic. No one is going to believe in what you have to say if you don't believe in yourself. It may take a few podcasts to find a groove, or you might hit the ground running and have a podcast that immediately takes off. Just speak with conviction. This is your podcast. Allow yourself to shine.

The content you bring to the Internet — regardless of what genre it falls under — is unique because it is *your* podcast. It is your voice, your angle, and your approach to whatever intent you pursue. Provided you maintain a high confidence level and, above all else, genuinely enjoy what you're doing, people will tune in and talk to other listeners about what you're podcasting.

Finding Your Voice

The broadcasting industry might not want to admit to this, but podcasting and commercial radio share a lot in common. In the early days of what is now a major radio genre, talk shows were reserved for National Public Radio and news stations. In general, they were pretty dry and lackluster, bringing their listeners the news, weather, and daily topics that affected the world — but nothing particularly unusual or exciting.

Then a guy named Howard Stern came along and changed everything in this once-tiny niche! You can love him, you can hate him — you can claim to hate him when secretly you love him — but Stern completely turned around what was considered AM-only programming. Now talk radio is big business. Some of its personalities are just out to entertain (Don & Mike, Ron & Fez), others are using it to voice their own political viewpoints (Rush Limbaugh leaning to the right stereo channel while Al Franken favors the left), and then we have the bottom-of-the-barrel personalities (insert your least favorite on-air loud-mouths here) who turn you off talk radio and on to podcasting!

A majority of podcasting is just that: talk radio. Actually, a more accurate description would be "*homespun* talk audio" because radio is *broad*cast while podcasting is *narrow*cast. Each podcast has a different personality and appeals to a different market. Finding your voice is one of the most challenging obstacles that you (as a once-and-future podcaster) must clear.

Even if your podcast's aim is entertainment, you have a message you want to convey. That message will influence the voice you adopt for your podcast. If you're podcasting an audio blog about life, its challenges, and the ups and downs that one encounters, then maybe a soft tone — relaxed and somewhat pensive — would be appropriate. But if you decide to go political — and let's say you are the Angry Young Man who is fed up with the current state of bureaucracy — then it's time to fine-tune the edginess of your voice. That's what you need for a podcast of this nature.

After you discover the passion your podcast is centered around (see the preceding section for tips on how to do that), here are some ways to *find your voice:*

✔ **Record your voice and then listen to what it sounds like.** It astounds me how many people hate listening to their recorded voice. It's a fear and abhorrence akin to getting up in front of people and speaking. When finding your voice, though, you need to hear what your current voice sounds like first. Write a paragraph on your show's subject. Then read it aloud a few times and find a rhythm in your words. Expect the following:

- Talking too fast

- Swallowing words like *to, in,* and small, one-syllable words

- Ignoring commas, thereby creating one long, run-on thought

- Lip-smacking, heavy breathing, and the unavoidable *ahs* and *ums*

Some of these problems can be edited out (see Chapter 5), but you should grow accustomed to hearing your own voice because you will hear yourself again and again . . . and again . . . during the editing process. The more familiar you are with how your voice sounds, the easier you can edit your podcasts and evaluate them before going online.

✔ **Play around with the rhythm of your speech.** You don't have to be an actor to podcast, but you can apply some basics of acting when you're recording. One of these basics, as one of Tee's acting professors told him, is to "Make a meal of your words." This means to play around with the rhythm of your speech. When you want to make a point, slow down. If you're feeling a tad smarmy, then pick up the pace. Above all, be relaxed and make sure you don't sound too contrived or melodramatic.

✔ **Develop your podcasting personality.** After you know what you sound like when you record, here is where you develop your podcasting personality. Is your persona going to be light, fun, and informal, or something a little edgy and jaded? Is your message taking an angle of marketing, politics, or religion? Or are you podcasting a love of music, science, or your Macintosh?

Deciding Whether You Need an Outline or Script

What method works best for you? A full script and hours of prep time, or a single note card and two clicks of the mouse — one for *Record* and another for *Stop?* Both approaches work, depending on the podcaster's personality. It could be said that there's little difference between a writer and a podcaster. Some writers prefer to use an outline when putting together a short story or novel; others merely take an idea, a few points, and a direction, and then let their fingers work across the keyboard.

If you decide to work with a script, it's a good idea to invest some time into *preshow prep* (simple preparation for what you're going to say *and* how you're going to deliver it). Depending on your podcast, though, prep time may vary. Here are a few examples of how dramatically different prep time can be for different podcasting situations:

✔ For her podcast *Geek Fu Action Grip,* Mur Lafferty showcases every week an essay of her own dry witticisms and irreverent look at the world. She spends an hour writing and rehearsing her material. If she incorporates material from other resources, she might need to tack on another half hour. That's pretty efficient preshow prep for a podcast of 15 to 25 minutes.

✔ On the opposite side of the production spectrum is *Area 51,* a fully scripted one-hour podcast that features comedic bits, polished banter between hosts Douglas Scott and Bobby Black, and extremely professional-sounding production quality. (See Figure 3-1.) *Area 51's* preshow prep begins with producer Marc Rose scripting comedy bits while recording host segments. "Because of the nature of this show, the Douglas and Bobby segments are improvised then cleaned up in editing." The average preshow prep time for the *Area 51* crew, according to Rose, ranges from two to three *days*.

Figure 3-1:
Area 51 takes its comedy seriously, and that means plenty of preshow prep!

A PureCastMedia.com podcast

These are two very different approaches: one for a 15-minute solo podcast and another for a one-hour production, complete with full cast and special effects. Both are popular podcasts that consistently run smoothly thanks to appropriate preshow prep. So how far should your prep go technically? That depends on what your podcast needs. Outlines and scripts can keep you on track with what you want to say, serving as roadmaps to keep you moving smoothly from Point A to Point B.

Both of these approaches to preshow prep work, but if you have never done any kind of planning like this, the secret to efficient preshow prep can be boiled down to three disciplines that podcasters follow:

✔ **Habit:** Many podcasters, especially podcasters emerging from corporate offices, prepare for podcasts in the same manner as business presentations. They jot down essential points on note cards to keep the podcast on track, but the points are the only material they write beforehand.

Organizational skills from the workplace can be easily applied to the podosphere. For example, Nicole Simon, in her day job as a consultant, gives presentations on various marketing strategies. Nicole's day-to-day job — addressing a roomful of people armed with only a single index card of key points — is easily applied to her preshow-prep practices for her podcast, *Useful Sounds*. With a collection of ideas and topics gathered between podcasts, she begins her one-take recording with a handful of points serving as a guideline.

✔ **Talent:** Some podcasters are truly the Evel Knievels of the podosphere, firing up their mics and recording in one take. These podcasters tend to have backgrounds in live entertainment, deciding in a moment's time when a change of delivery is required. This is a talent of quick thinking, and while it keeps material spontaneous and fresh, it is a talent that must be developed with time.

For example, Dan Klass is the demented mind behind the sharp and sarcastic podcast, *The Bitterest Pill*. His show is completely improvised. No prep time. Not a list of key points in sight. How can he do this? Dan's is a special breed of bravery: He's a professional stand-up comedian.

✔ **Passion:** This is a driving force with a majority of podcasters that keeps their podcasts spur-of-the-moment. With enough drive, inspiration, and confidence in their message, they keep their prep time to a minimum because it isn't a chore but a form of recreation.

For example, Jesse Obstbaum's podcast *The Mousepod* is all Disney, all the time. "My prep time is under an hour, assuming I'm not doing an interview for the show. I quickly jot down a bunch of ideas — probably twice as many as I need for the show — and then I have lots of books and articles about Disney," Jesse states about his preshow planning. He then lets his passion for Walt, Mickey, Goofy, Donald, and the gang drive him easily through 30 minutes (in some cases, an hour).

Choosing a Method for Recording Interviews

In your search to find the podcast that best reflects you, communicates the message you want to send out to the world, and makes the impression you want to make (among the thousands of podcasts being uploaded), you conclude that the best way to give your viewpoint credence is to bring in guests. Yes, along with Charlie Rose, Barbara Walters, and Tom Green, you're going to hold interviews.

Your podcast just got a bit more technically complicated.

Taping phone calls

Many times, interviews — particularly with authorities and luminaries in the field you're podcasting about — will be held over the phone. Do a Google search for the term "telephone recording devices," and you'll find a wide array of machines out there that will record, even in a digital format. What you choose depends on how much moola you're willing to spend:

- ✔ **Cassette recorders:** These economical recording devices utilize micro or standard tape cassettes, leaving it up to the podcaster to solve the problem in getting the conversation from analog device to computer. The simplest way of digitally capturing the interview is to simply play back the conversation and use an external microphone in front of the device's speaker to record the playback. That's a simple and cost-effective method, but it may not yield the highest sound quality.

- ✔ **Digital recorders:** On the opposite end of equipment cost and quality are digital recorders. You can attach them to a telephone (in the same manner as an answering machine), record over 20 hours of conversation, and then easily transfer the sound from device to computer via a USB port.

- ✔ **Analog-to-digital hybrid recorders:** Software applications such as CallCorder for the PC (for just under $40 from www.callcorder.com) or Phone Valet for the Mac (an investment of about $119 from www.parliant.com) turn your computer into the recorder. Using either a standard modem or another hook-up device (in the case of some software packages, it comes included), your telephone and your computer are connected. When the call comes in or when you make the call, you can then ask for permission to record the conversation (again, some software does this automatically) and then bring the phone call directly into your computer in the format of your choosing.

You can find these recorders and software packages at your local electronics store or online at a wide variety of prices.

Recording conversations with Skype

If you have never heard of Skype, do yourself a favor: Surf over to www.skype.com and familiarize yourself with the new application that turns telecommunications on its ear. Skype is "free Internet telephony," something akin to iChat's/AOL IM's Audio mode. It's more stable and, in some instances, provides clearer reception. What makes Skype more appealing to Internet users than iChat/AOL is the expandability of the application. You can record Skype conversations with various methods and use downloadable software to monitor levels and volume as you record (as detailed on www.raggedcastle.com/webcrumbs/archives/003724.html). Figure 3-2 shows an example setup that provides the ability to record Skype calls for editing into a podcast.

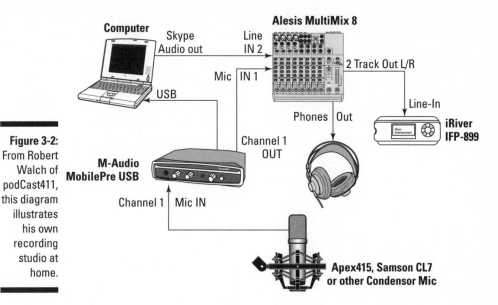

Figure 3-2:
From Robert
Walch of
podCast411,
this diagram
illustrates
his own
recording
studio at
home.

For Macintosh users, an easier solution for recording Skype calls is an application that is built specifically for the capturing and enhancement of audio: *Audio Hijack Pro* from Rogue Amoeba (www.rogueamoeba.com). Costing only $32.00, Audio Hijack Pro offers clear capturing of Skype conversations in the format and quality of your choosing, and the setup is easy.

Recording Skype calls using Audio Hijack Pro

With Audio Hijack Pro, Mac users can capture Skype conversations in an editable format by setting a few simple preferences. Your Skype recording settings are then saved for future use; you don't have to reset them each time.

You can give Audio Hijack a test run by downloading a fully working demo at www.rogueamoeba.com/audiohijackpro/ and recording a quick test chat. After upgrading to Pro, your settings remain in the application's preferences. Follow these steps to record:

1. **In the Recording Bin, click Default System Input (a microphone reading the current default audio input and output settings) to select it. In the lower-right corner of the window, make sure the Input tab is selected.**

2. **Confirm that the Input Device is Default System Input and that the Output Device is Default System Output.**

   This should match your Skype audio input/output settings.

3. **Click the Recording tab in the lower-right corner of the window and make changes as needed. These are your options (as shown in Figure 3-3):**

   - Change the format of your audio file (advisable if you want to edit the audio in your application of choice).

   - Designate a location for captured audio, filenaming conventions, and whether or not you wish to incorporate any script commands.

   - Incorporate ID3 tags (advisable if you are going straight to MP3/podcasting content).

   Note that when you change the Title in the Tags section of the Recording window, your Default System Input changes to whatever you have named it.

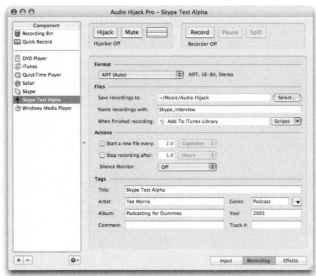

Figure 3-3:
The Recording window in Audio Hijack Pro gives you full control over the format and quality of your captured audio.

4. **Click the Effects tab in the bottom-right corner of the window.**

5. **Click inside the first Click Here to Insert Effect area and choose 4FX Effect⇨Application Mixer.**

   The Application Mixer opens, as shown in Figure 3-4. It gives you the ability to "hijack" or record incoming audio from the selected application.

6. **Click the Select button and choose Skype.**

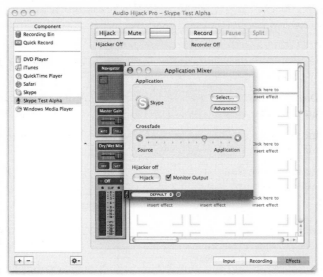

Figure 3-4:
With the
Application
Mixer, the
input signal
between
the Source
(micro-
phone) and
Application
(in this case,
Skype) is
controlled.

By default, the crossfade is set at 50%. The crossfade can be regarded as a *gain* or *input signal strength* ruler, giving more signal dominance to either the source recording signal or the application recording signal. If your voice is coming in loud and clear but your Skype caller is not, try adjusting the crossfade a few notches towards the application, giving Skype more dominance. Although you can adjust levels in post-production and easily re-record your questions and edit them in, it is more difficult to do when your interview has already been recorded. When recording Skype interviews, it is best to record with the Skype signal strong.

7. **In the Application Mixer, click the Hijack button and then close the window.**

   Skype automatically launches.

8. **In the Audio Hijack Pro main window, click the Hijack button and the Record button, and then place your Skype call (see Figure 3-5).**

   You're recording!

As stated next in this chapter, there are legal restrictions concerning the recording of telephone/Skype calls, and these restrictions vary from country to country, state to state, and region to region. Compliance with these laws is the responsibility of the podcaster. Always ask for permission (or better yet, get it in writing) before recording phone calls.

9. **When you're done, click to turn off the Hijack and Record buttons in the main window. Then go into the Application Mixer and turn off the Hijack feature there.**

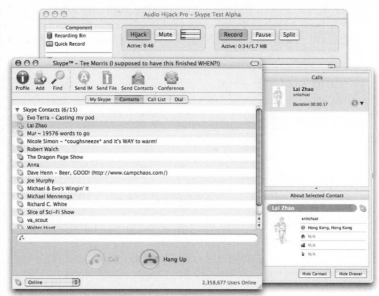

Figure 3-5:
After the Application Mixer and the Audio Hijack Pro main window are hijacking and recording, you're ready to place your Skype call and record your conversation.

When you're ready for your next interview, simply repeat Steps 7 through 9 and start recording!

The Audio Hijack free demo is a fully working version of Audio Hijack Pro with a failsafe built in to it in order to make it (and keep it) a demonstration application. After ten minutes of recording, the sound is slowly replaced by static. Upgrading to Audio Hijack Pro provides you with a fully working version of the software, granting you the ability to record hours of Skype calls in the format of your choice.

Recording Skype calls using SkypeOut

SkypeOut is a built-in feature that comes with Skype and gives you, the Skype user, the ability to dial a telephone number (either LAN or mobile) and use Skype to talk to that person at two cents a minute. Oh, and this charge is for all calls, anywhere in the world.

Follow these steps to start using SkypeOut:

1. **Go to My Account and login using your Skype username and login.**

   Links are provided on the My Skype tab in Skype's startup window or online at the Skype Store, located at `www.skype.com/go/store/`.

2. **Look for the message `SkypeOut is not active` (assuming you have not activated SkypeOut yet) and click the Buy SkypeOut Credit link.**

3. **Select the credit package you want (usually listed in euros in increments of ten, but each package lists the details of what you're buying) and then purchase it by using PayPal or any major credit card.**

   Your SkypeOut account is activated.

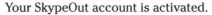

   When your credit is at $0, your SkypeOut goes inactive. Simply purchase another block of credit to reactivate it.

4. **Return to Skype and click the Dial tab.**

   Skype opens a numeric keypad emulating a telephone, as shown in Figure 3-6.

Figure 3-6: When SkypeOut is active, you can place phone calls to non-Skype users.

5. **Enter a phone number and click the green Call button.**

6. **Record the phone call by using either Audio Hijack Pro or Gizmo (both of which are described in this chapter).**

SkypeOut credits have a shelf life of 180 days after your last SkypeOut call. So if you go three months between calls, you might find that your credit is gone and your SkypeOut feature is inactive. If this happens or if you run out of credit, repeat Steps 1 through 3 to put credit back into your account and reactivate SkypeOut.

The Gizmo project: A new recording option

Affordable and hacker-safe solutions for podcasters seem harder to find for the PC and Linux podcasters out there. However, a new player is stepping into the area, offering a free alternative to Skype, and this new gizmo for your computer is simply called . . . Gizmo. Available for download at www.gizmoproject.com, Gizmo is an intuitive, multiplatform VoIP (Voice Over Internet Protocol) application (much like Skype) offering additional features that Skype lacks. One of these additional features is the ability to record conversations and save them in WAV format. Gizmo also informs both parties in the call that the phone conversation is being recorded and when recording stops.

If you are not podcasting with a Mac and are looking for an efficient and easy way to record interviews, take a good look at Gizmo, the latest option offered by the Internet to make over-the-phone interviews cost effective for start-up podcasts.

Ensuring trouble-free recordings

When it comes to recording telephone conversations, here are a few points to keep in mind before asking the first question:

> ✔ **Get permission to record telephone conversations, even if the interview is prearranged.** Laws (both federal and state) prohibit the recording of conversations without permission, and further restrictions limit broadcasting these conversations. If you plan to record and podcast a conversation, get the subject's consent beforehand, both verbally and in written communication (even e-mail) to make sure your legal issues are covered.

✔ **Test the equipment before the interview to make sure it works and have a backup plan in case something goes wrong.** If you have arranged a phone-in (or Skype-in) interview with someone for your podcast — say, a favorite indie musician or a local politician — prepare for the interview the day before (or a few days before): Skype (or phone) a friend to conduct a mock interview and make sure the recording setup not only works but also sounds good.

Bandwidth demands increase the more people you conference through your computer. Reception will be affected, so if you know more than one person will be conferenced into this interview, it's a good idea to test how many people you can effectively conference in one call.

And while this may sound a bit pessimistic, be ready for things to go wrong. Guests might not show up for interviews, and new high-tech toys, if not given a proper pre-interview shakedown, may not come through. Prepare to have plenty of topics to discuss on your own, and then your podcast can continue following a quick disclaimer. In podcasting, sticking to a regular schedule is reassuring to your listeners because they know you will offer new feeds consistently and punctually.

Prepping Your Green Room for Guests

A guest could be your dad, your mother-in-law, your best friend, or the man on the street. It could also be the friend of a friend who can get you on the phone with your favorite author, actor, or athlete, but now you have a second party to worry about. Regardless of who your guests are, even if they're the fastest of friends, working completely outline-free is *no longer* an option. Pull together a few questions, organize a direction and tempo for your podcast, and leave yourself some breathing room for impromptu or interesting off-topic tangents to emerge.

Welcoming in-studio guests

Removing the "technical difficulties" element usually means either taking the show to the guests or bringing the guests to the show. This kind of interview not only is the most fun to do, but also gives you direct contact with the subject so you can observe body language, facial expressions, and reactions to questions and answers.

When you have guests visit your facilities, which if you're a podcaster will probably be your house, make them feel at home. Offer them something to drink. Offer to take them on a tour of your humble abode. Introduce them to your family. The point is to be polite. You don't have to cook dinner for them, but offering a hint of hospitality, be it a glass of water (or a beer, if you've ever worked closely with The Dragon Page crew), is a nice touch.

If you're having in-studio interviews, it's also a good idea to get your home and yourself ready to receive guests. Sure, Tee has recorded quite a few podcasts in his pajamas, but because he's reading a book for his podcast, he's allowed. If fantasy and science fiction authors Terry Brooks and Catherine Asaro ever come over to his house for an interview, don't think he'd be greeting them in his Joe Boxer jammies with his Guinness slippers keeping his feet warm.

Okay, maybe he *would* greet them wearing the Guinness slippers, but he would be bathed and dressed and have his teeth brushed and hair combed. The key word here is *guest*. Treat them as such. Be cool, be pleasant, be nice. And if you're a guest on someone else's podcast, the same rules apply. Don't prop your feet up on the furniture, don't demand hospitality, and don't be a jerk during the interview.

The in-studio visit is an audition for both guest and host. If the guest is abrasive, abusive, and just plain rude, chances are the guest will never be invited back, no matter how well the previous interview goes. If a host asks unapproved questions, continues to pry into personal matters that have nothing to do with the interview, or seems determined to take over the interview spotlight as if trying to impress the guest, said guest may never return, even if extended an invitation. (Later in this chapter, we talk about the do's and don'ts of interviewing.)

Meeting guests on their own turf

Be cool, be pleasant, be nice. These same rules apply when you take your podcast on the road. You are now practicing — for the lack of a better term — guerilla journalism, ambushing unsuspecting people on the street with questions that may not strike you as hard and probing but could be to people who don't expect them.

A good approach in getting good interviews is to ask permission of your guests, be they passers-by or experts and authorities in the general vicinity, to interview them. Shoving a microphone in someone's face and blurting out a question is hardly a great way to introduce yourself and your podcast to the world. If the guest you wish to interview has a handler or liaison, it's good protocol to follow the suggestions and advice of the guest's staff.

When interviewing people on the street or in the moment, there are some easy ways to identify yourself. Michael Butler of the *Rock and Roll Geek Show* (rockandrollgeek.podshow.com/) uses a *mic cube* (the classic cube that usually has a logo identifying a network, a show, or an organization affiliated with the interviewer) around his microphone. There is also the simple greeting, "Hi, do I have your permission to record this for a podcast?" (Be prepared to explain what a podcast is, or you could always fudge it and say "broadcast." Keep the greeting simple!)

Just as with the phone and Skype interviews, first test and check your equipment. You are now out of the controlled environment of your home studio; you have to deal with surrounding ambient noise and how well your interview is recording in the midst of uncontrolled background variables. Set up your equipment; power up your laptop, mixing board, and mics; and record a few words. Then play back your tests and set your levels accordingly. When you have your setup running, you're ready to get your interviews.

Preparing for Interviews

There is an approach that all interviewers, be they Barbara Walters or Howard Stern, should take in talking to guests — a simple, basic plan in how to ask the questions that garner the best responses.

Surefire routes to happy, conversational guests

Chances are if you're new to podcasting, you have never held an interview quite like this — an interpersonal, casual chat that could get a bit thought-provoking or downright controversial, depending on your podcast's subject matter. The interview may be arranged by you, or it may be prearranged for you, but if you think what reporters do is easy, it isn't. There is a science to it, and here are just a few tips to take to heart so you can hold a good, engaging interview:

- ✔ **Know who you're talking to and what to talk about.** With interviewer Jana Oliver, host of two shows on Leisure Talk Radio (recently making the jump to the podosphere), the sheer number of guests she interviews can cause a problem: trying to find the time to read all her guests' books. So she does a different kind of homework on her guests. "If my guest wrote a book about Charlemagne, I will go online and do my own research into the topic. This has two effects: (1) I sound like I have a clue what I'm talking about and (2) It allows me to ask better questions."

It's also a good idea to visit guests' Web sites (provided they have 'em). You don't have to be an expert on their subject matter, but you should be familiar with it so you know in what direction to take the interview.

✔ **Have your questions follow a logical progression.** Say you're interviewing an independent filmmaker who is working on a horror movie. A good progression for your interview would be something like this:

- What made you want to shoot a horror movie?

- What makes a really good horror film?

- Who inspired you in this genre?

- In your opinion, what is the scariest film ever made?

You'll notice these questions are all based around filmmaking, beginning with the director's choice and ending with a director's choice. The progression of this interview starts specific on the current work and then broadens to a wider perspective. Most interviews should follow a progression like this, or can start on a very broad viewpoint and slowly become more specific to the guest's expertise.

✔ **Prepare twice as many questions than you'll need.** Some interviews you hear grind to a halt for no other reason than the interviewer believed that the guest would talk his head off on the first question. It is certain you are in for a bumpy ride when you ask a guest, "So has this been a pleasant experience for you?" and the guest replies, "Yes." (Yeah, this is going to get painful.)

Write down a series of questions that could fill up your podcast with brief, one-or-two-word answers. This way, if you find yourself struggling, you have a hidden stockpile of questions to call upon. If after a few yes and no answers, you can always fall back on the "would you expand a bit on that please?" question.

✔ **Never worry about asking a stupid question.** When asking questions that may sound obvious or frequently asked, remember: Chances are, your audience has never heard them *answered* before. Okay, maybe a writer has been asked time and again, "Where do your ideas come from?" or a politician has heard, "So, when did you first start in politics?" often. When you have a guest present for a podcast, there's no such thing as a stupid question; what's really dumb is not to ask a question that you think isn't worth the guest's time. He or she may be champing at the bit in hopes you *will* ask it.

So these are just a few things to keep in mind when putting together your questions for an interview. But before you start percolating and dream up a few questions based on the preceding tips, stop and think about the interviews you've listened to where things suddenly head south. Usually the interviewer ambushes the guest or tries to dig into something that is either out of the guest's scope or none of the interviewer's business. We've piled up the typical gaffes in a prime example of a *good* interview gone *bad*. Stay tuned.

Surefire routes to outraged, uncooperative guests

Every podcaster should know how to turn a pleasant conversation sour (uh, this *is* a satire and not a recipe, okay?); the following blunders should do it:

- **Ask inappropriate questions.** Keep in mind your podcast is not *60 Minutes, 20/20,* or even *Jerry Springer.* If you want to fire off "hard-hitting-tell-all-mudslinging" questions, think about who your audience is, who you are talking to, and if the question is within the ability of the guest to answer honestly and openly. If not, an awkward moment may be the least of your worries.

  Inappropriate can also mean irrelevant, wacky, off-the-wall, and far-too-personal questions. For instance, Hugo and World Fantasy Award-winning author Neil Gaiman, during a question-and-answer session with a ballroom full of people, was asked completely out of the blue: "Mr. Gaiman, what is your best score in bowling?"

  Gaiman looked at the con attendee, somewhat baffled, and then replied awkwardly, "Well, um, I can't really answer that question because I . . . don't . . . bowl. Never been bowling. Don't know how. So . . . ummm . . . sorry."

  Maybe silly, overly candid questions work for shock jocks, but when you have an opportunity to interview people you respect in your field of interest, do you really *want* to ask them something like, "Boxers, briefs, or none of the above?" Think about what you're going to ask before you actually do.

- **Continue to pursue answers to inappropriate questions.** If a question has been deemed inappropriate by a guest, don't continue to ask it. Move on to the next question and continue forward into the interview. Podcasts are by no means an arena for browbeating guests into submission till they break down in tears and cough up the ugly, sordid details of their lives. If this is the intent of your podcast, then you've picked up the wrong book; you need to get *Psychotherapy For Dummies.*

  Are there exceptions to this exception? We would say, yes, depending on the content of your podcast. Let's say after reading — and enjoying — *Podcasting For Dummies,* you decide you want to become the Tom Green of podcasting. Of course, if you're after irreverent material for your show and push that envelope as far as you can, your guests may or may not want to play along — especially if they don't get the joke. If that's the case, expect your guests to get up and walk away. Even in the most idyllic situations, guests can (and do) reserve the right to do that.

> ✔ **Turn the interview into the Me show.** Please remember that the spotlight belongs to your guest. Yes, it is your podcast, but when a guest is introduced into the mix, you are surrendering control of the show to him or her, and that is not necessarily a bad thing. Let guests enjoy the spotlight; your audience will appreciate them for being there, which adds a new dimension to your feed.

One final note on interviews: We have heard some guests say, "I'm doing these interviewers a favor by going on to their show." And we've been told by other show hosts, "We're doing you a great favor with this chance to showcase your work on our show."

Both of these opinions are not just arrogant, they are just flat-out wrong.

The reality is that host and guest are working together to create a synergy. The interviewer has a chance to earn a wider audience and display mastery of journalistic techniques. The guest has a chance to get into the public eye, stay in the public eye, and talk about the next big thing they have coming in sight of said public eye. Working together, guest and host create a seamless promotional machine for one another.

If you decide to take on the art of the interview, keep these rules in mind; you and your guests will have your best chance to work together to create something special.

Determining a Length for Your Show

If you've been using this chapter to develop your podcast, you've made serious progress by this point. Here's a quick checklist:

> ✔ You have a voice appropriate and fitting for your show's intent.
>
> ✔ You have considered how much preparation your individual feed needs — whether that's a detailed outline and intricate scripts, or a basic list of points to encourage improvisation and spontaneity.
>
> ✔ You have taken a closer look at interviews: the prep involved, how to approach guests — questions to ask and questions to avoid.

Now you're ready to podcast, right? The show is all set. The guest will be calling you later tonight. Your questions are set up in front of the microphone and organized, moving from broad questions about your guest's field to the specifics your guest is out promoting. Time to hit the Record button and start talking — yes?

Well, no. Have you thought about how long your show's episode is going to run?

The hidden value of the short podcast

There are many podcasts that run under ten minutes where hosts deliver their message and then sign off only moments after you thought they signed on. On average — and this is more like an understood average, not really a scientific, detailed study of all the podcasts out there — a podcast runs between 20 to 30 minutes per episode. So what about these ten-minute vignettes? Does size matter? Does time matter? (Woah. Deep.) Is there such a thing as too short a podcast?

Here are some advantages in offering a short podcast:

- ✔ **Shorter production time:** Production time is reduced from a week-long project to a single afternoon of planning, talking, editing, and mixing. With a quick and simplified production schedule, delivering a podcast on a regular basis — say, every two weeks, weekly, or twice a week — is easier.

- ✔ **Fast downloads:** You can be assured — no matter what specs you compress your audio file down to — that your podcast subscribers always have fast and efficient downloads.

- ✔ **Easy to stay on target:** If you limit yourself to a running time of less than ten minutes, you force yourself to stick to the intent (and the immediate message) of your podcast. There's no room for in-depth chat, spontaneous banter, or tangents to explore. You hit the red button and remain on target from beginning to end, keeping your podcast strictly focused on the facts. Shakespeare said, "Brevity is the soul of wit." Considering his words, ol' Bill would probably have podcast under 15 minutes if he were alive today.

Nothing wrong with keeping a podcast short and sweet. In fact, you might gain more subscribers who appreciate your efficiency.

A little length won't kill you

Now with that slick and fancy quote from the Bard about brevity, you might think, "Shakespeare said *that?!* Before or after *Hamlet?*" That's a good point because Shakespeare did, in fact, have a number of his characters say, "My lord, I will be brief . . ." and then launch into three-to-four-page monologues.

So what if Shakespeare decided to be brief in his podcast? Would he get any subscribers if his show ran longer than half an hour? What if he broke the 60-minute ceiling? Would the Podcast Police shut down his show?

Podcatchers (like iTunes, iPodder Lemon, and iPodderX) and subscribers, on reading your show notes and descriptions, should be able to figure out the average running time of your show. On a particular topic, some podcasts can easily fill two or even *three* hours. It's hard to believe even avid podcast audiences would want to sit and wait for such a mammoth download, but huge productions have some definite advantages:

- ✔ **If the show is an interview, you have anywhere from two to three hours with an authority.** It's something like having a one-on-one session stored on your computer or MP3 player. From marketing shows like *G'day World* or science shows like *Slacker Astronomy,* if a guest or authority is part of the podcast, you can rest assured your podcast will go a little longer than 30 minutes — and sometimes it should.

- ✔ **You're allowed verbal breathing room.** Discussion stretching past the 30-minute mark allows you and your co-hosts or guests to break off into loosely related banter, widening your podcast's focus and sparking discussion that can lead in other directions.

The cost of podcasts longer than 30 minutes is in bandwidth and file-storage — issues that smaller podcasts rarely, if ever, have to deal with. See Chapter 7 for a discussion of the bandwidth demands on your server.

Finding that happy medium

Is there such a thing as middle ground in the almost-completely undiscovered territory that is podcasting? How can you find a happy medium if podcasters can't agree on a standard running time?

The happy medium for your podcast should be a sense of *expectancy* or *consistency*. For example, in Tee's podcast of *MOREVI: The Chronicles of Rafe & Askana,* the running times for each chapter are across the board — the shortest is 20 minutes, 12 seconds, and the longest weighs in at a whopping 1 hour, 13 minutes, 24 seconds. The audience for *MOREVI,* however, understands this is a *podiobook,* an audiobook being podcast in a serialized format. Readers understand that chapters vary in size with a printed book, so it's no surprise when a podiobook follows suit. Some of the podcasts are short, sweet, and a quick bridge between one plotline and another. Other chapters reveal a new plot twist or introduce new characters, meaning that some length is in order.

Podcast *Galactica*

The SciFi channel has struck gold with an innovative approach on an old favorite from the '70s: *Battlestar Galactica*. With a new cast, a new look, and some gender-bending on the characters Boomer and Starbuck, the successful series rounds off a solid night of science fiction. *Galactica* in every episode takes delight in taking chances and challenging boundaries. In that spirit of taking chances (as well as being interested in reaching new audiences), Executive Producer Ronald D. Moore and SciFi.com decided to host a podcast: two hour-long episodes, similar to director commentaries on DVDs, providing an inside look at season one's finale "Kobal's Last Gleaming."

An hour inside Ron Moore's head? That's a sci-fi geek's dream come to life. But *two?!* Season one of *Battlestar Galactica* was so successful that its premiere, "33," won Science Fiction's highest honor — the Hugo — for Best Short Form Dramatic Presentation. The companion podcast of *Battlestar Galactica* was so successful that SciFi brought it back for repeat episodes and is currently running it with season two. Moore's casual chat lasts an hour (well beyond the average running time for a podcast ... not that anyone subscribing cares) and provides inside stories on how improvisational the actors can be on the set, delves into the decision process behind shooting schedules, and notes that Ron Moore doesn't have a problem referring to über-intense actor/director Edward James Olmos as "Eddie." Keeping the production values to the basics, *Galactica's* companion podcast adds a new dimension to the military SciFi epic by taking fans behind-the-scenes and into the imagination of its creator.

Podiobooks aren't the only place that variable length works. If your podcast deals in do-it-yourself home improvement, then explaining the construction of a bookshelf will be a far shorter show than one about adding an extension to your deck.

Give yourself some time to develop your show, your voice, and your direction. (You may just be finding out about the elements in this chapter. Developing them will take some time, trial, and error.) If you build some consistency and expectation for your audience, it's easier to introduce a little variation (even a happy medium) into your running time.

Right, then. Are your vocal cords warmed up? Is that glass of ice water within reach? Do you have a guest holding on Skype? After duly considering this map of what it takes to build a podcast that people will want to listen to, it's showtime: Take a deep breath, organize your notes one more time, and then exhale. (*Always* remember to exhale.) Time to click that intimidating red button and do your thing: It's time to record.

I Hear Music (And It Sounds like Police Sirens!)

In creating your own podcast, something that will give your show an extra punch or just a tiny zest is the right kind of music. Both of us are musicians (although Evo's the hipper one because he does the whole rock-and-roll thing. Tee is more into the classics: Wagner, Rimsky-Corsakov, Gershwin, and Ellington), and we both appreciate and understand the power of music and what it can bring to a podcast.

We also understand and appreciate the law. While you may think it is cool to "stick it to the man" and thumb your nose at Corporate America, the law is the law, and there are serious rules to follow when featuring that favorite song of yours as a theme to your podcast.

We want to make this clear as polished crystal — we are not lawyers. We're podcasters. We have looked up the law on certain matters so we know and understand what we're talking about, but we are *not* lawyers. We can tell you about the law, and we can give a few simple definitions of it, but we are *not* giving out legal advice. If you need a legal call on a matter concerning your podcast — whether it is concerning the First Amendment, copyright issues, or slander — please consult a lawyer.

The powers that be

The Internet, in the eyes of the government, is still regarded as a digital Wild West, an unknown territory that has avoided regulation for many years, granting those who use it a true, self-governed entity where ideas, cultures, and concepts can be expressed without any filtering or editing, unless it comes from the users themselves.

Does this mean we podcasters are free to do as we please? Well, no, not by a long shot. Although no specific laws are on the books (yet) — other than anti-spam regulations governing Internet usage — there are some rules and regulations that even podcasts must follow. There are also organizations that both broadcasters and podcasters *must* pay attention to.

The following organizations all have a say in the destiny of podcasting, and it is only going to benefit you as a podcaster to understand how their legislation, activities, and actions are going to affect you.

The Federal Communications Commission (FCC)

If you listen to Howard Stern, watch CBS News, or tuned in the infamous 2004 Super Bowl Halftime Show with Janet Jackson's "wardrobe malfunction," then you know about the FCC. This commission is the watchdog of anything and everything that gets out to the public via mass communications. The FCC keeps an eye on technology development, monopolies in the telecommunications industry, and regulating standards for telecommunications in the United States and its territories.

With all the good the FCC does in preventing monopolies, encouraging technological advancements, and upholding broadcasting standards, the FCC is most commonly known for enforcing decency laws, infuriating many artists and performers who describe it as a form of censorship. George Carlin even went so far as to write several routines based on the "seven dirty words" he could not say (he's way past two dozen now) to illustrate how the kibosh has expanded over the years to include words *and concepts*.

For podcasters, the FCC cannot regulate what is said (yet) because it does not consider the Internet a broadcasting medium. However, given recent legislation to reduce *spam* (junk e-mail) and the growing popularity of podcasting among mainstream broadcasters (such as Clear Channel and the SciFi channel), it may not be long before the law catches up with technology.

The Recording Industry Association of America (RIAA)

Sean Fanning. Does that name ring a bell? Sadly, it was Fanning who lost his battle against the RIAA when he contested that his file-sharing application, a tiny piece of software called Napster, in no way infringed on copyright laws and was not promoting music piracy. The RIAA led the charge in shutting down the original Napster Web site and continues to protect property rights of its members — as well as review new and pending laws, regulations, and policies at the state and federal level.

The RIAA will have a definite say as to why you cannot use a selected piece of music for your podcast. Simply put, it's not your music. Sure, you bought the CD and you own that CD, but the music you listen to is under the condition that you use it specifically for listening purposes only. (Didn't realize there were conditions involved, did you?) This means you cannot use it as your own personal introduction music that people will associate with you. This also means, no matter how appropriate your favorite song is, you cannot use it as *bed* (background) music for your advertising. Unless you are granted licenses and pay specific fees to the RIAA, you are in copyright violation when playing music without permission.

One way of getting music for themes, background beds, and segues is to look into what musicians and podcasters refer to as *podsafe music.* This is professionally produced music from independent artists who are offering their works for podcasting use. The demand for podsafe music has been so high that the Web site *Podsafe Music Network* (music.podshow.com) was launched, offering a wide array of genres, artists, and musical works. Find out more about this free service (shown in Figure 3-7), the conditions entailed in using podsafe music, and what it can do to benefit your podcast.

Figure 3-7: The *Podsafe Music Network* — professional music that is podcast friendly and waiting for your patronage.

The Electronic Frontier Foundation (EFF)

In addition to the big dogs who are passing the laws and legislation to restrain your podcasting capabilities, there is a group out there (with science fiction author and tech guru Cory Doctorow stepping forward as one of its more outspoken members) that looks out for you, the podcaster. The Electronic Frontier Foundation (EFF) is a donor-supported organization working to protect the digital rights of the individual, to educate the media, lawmakers, and the public on how technology affects their civil liberties, and uphold said civil liberties if they are threatened.

A good example of EFF's mission is its involvement in various legal cases concerning URL domain registration and *cybersquatters* (individuals who buy desired domains and then hold on to them, waiting for the highest bidder). The EFF stands up for the rights of legitimate Web-site owners who happen to own a domain that a larger corporation would desire to utilize.

The EFF, provided you have a strong case to contradict the findings of the RIAA and the FCC, will stand up for you and give your voice a bit of power when you're standing up to a corporate legal machine.

Creative Commons (CC)

Founded in 2001, Creative Commons is a non-profit corporation dedicated to helping the artist, the copyrighted material, and the individual who wishes to use copyrighted material in a constructive manner but may not have the resources to buy rights from groups like the RIAA.

Copyright protection is a double-edged sword for many in the artistic field. On the positive side of a copyright, your work is protected so that no one can steal your work for their own personal profit, or if someone makes the claim that you are simply ripping off their work, your copyright is proof that your egg came before their chicken. That is the whole point of the copyright: protection. The downside of this protection is that people now must go through channels for approval to feature your words or your work in an educational or referential manner; and while you are still given credit for the property featured, there is still a matter of approvals, fees for usage, and conditions that must be met. Also, there are many contributors of the Internet who simply want to share their work with others on no other terms but to contribute and share with the world. Copyrights complicate this.

This complication of the digital copyright, protections, and desire to exchange ideas, original creations, and concepts brought about the founding of the Creative Commons (`creativecommons.org`). This organization (shown in Figure 3-8) is dedicated to drafting and implementing licenses granting fair use of copyrighted material via the Internet.

Figure 3-8:
Creative
Commons
offers free
licenses for
use of
original
content in
podcasting.

In the case of the podcaster, you want to offer your audio content to everyone, not caring if listeners copy and distribute your MP3. As long as the listeners give you credit, that's all fine and good for you. CC can provide you with licenses that aid you in letting people know your podcast is up for grabs as long as others give credit where credit is due. CC provides these same licenses for artists and musicians who would not mind at all if you used their music for your podcast.

CC breaks down its licenses into four categories:

- **Attribution:** Grants permission for copying, distribution, display, and performance of the original work and derivative works inspired from it, provided credit to the artist(s) is given.

- **Noncommercial:** Grants permission for copying, distribution, display, and performance of the original work and derivative works inspired from it *for noncommercial purposes only.*

- **No Derivative Works:** Grants permission for copying, distribution, display, and performance of the original work only. No derivative works are covered in this license category.

- **Share Alike:** Grants permission to others for distribution of *derivative* works only. While the original work is not covered by this license, the terms of this permission are similar to the No Derivative Works license.

These four categories can be used as stand-alone licenses or can be mixed and matched to fit the needs of the podcaster or the artist offering content for the podcast.

The CC and its Web site give details, examples, and a FAQ page that answers questions concerning the granting of licenses for use of protected content. Just on the off-chance you do not find your answer on the Web site, it gives contact information for its representatives. CC is a good group to know and can open up opportunities for you to present new and innovative ideas and works in your podcast.

I can name that tune . . . I wrote it!

Using almost anyone else's music for your podcast can be an open invitation for the RIAA to shut it down. This is primarily to protect the artist's rights. Think about it — how would you feel if you were enjoying a popular podcast, receiving praise from all over the world, and while you're thinking about ways of taking the podcast to the next level, you turn on your radio and hear your podcast being broadcast on a top-rated radio station. Soon, your podcast is all the rage on the broadcasting airwaves — and you haven't made dollar one.

The same thing can be said for artists and their music. They work hard to produce their work, and now podcasters are using their music to brand their show, not bothering to compensate them for their efforts. Artists love to say that they "do what we do for the love of the craft" — and many do — but in the end, it's their *work* — and artists have to pay the bills too.

So how can you use a piece of music without suffering the wrath of the RIAA or FCC? Ask permission of the artist? Only if the artist owns the rights to the music and the recordings. Otherwise, you also need to get written permission from artists, musicians, record labels, producers. . . .

The best way to avoid the legal hassles is to avoid copyrighted material that is not your own.

If you want to use published pieces that are not royalty-free, then ask the artist directly (if you can) about getting permission to feature or use that music on a regular basis. Compensation to the artist may come in the form of a quick promotion at the beginning or end (or both) tags of the podcast. As long as you have written permission from the artists and the artists have the power to grant it (that is, haven't signed the power over to their label or publisher), then you should be able to use their work to brand your show or feature them on your podcast. (If you're not sure whether you have the appropriate permission, you may want to consult an attorney.) This is usually acceptable with independent artists because, in many cases, they also own the record label. Confirm this with artists. Otherwise, you run into the same legal issues if you were to use music recorded by Queen, Switchfoot, or U2.

Why not offer up your podcast as a venue for the musician to sell his or her work? Dave Slusher of *Evil Genius Chronicles* (`www.evilgeniuschronicles.org`) has written permission from the Gentle Readers to use its music as intro, exit, and background music for his podcast. In return, Dave eagerly promotes its CD *Hi, Honey*. This kind of promotion works well for the Gentle Readers as well as artist Michelle Mallone (`www.michellemalone.com`). After her music was featured on Dave's podcast, her sales spiked — both through her Web site and on iTunes!

I'll take the First: Free speech versus slander

Words can (potentially, at least) get you in just as much trouble as music. The legal definition of *slander* is *a verbal form of defamation, or spoken words that falsely and negatively reflect on one's reputation.*

So where does podcasting fit into all this? Well, the Internet is a kind of public space. Think about it — before you open your mouth and begin a slam-fest on someone you don't like in the media or go on the personal attack with someone you work alongside, remember that your little rant is reaching MP3 players around the world. Be sure — *before* you open your mouth to speak — that you are not misquoting an article or merely assuming that your word is gospel. It may sound like we're going back to our original rules for interviewing guests, but actually we're going even further with this cautionary word: When expressing jaded opinions, have real evidence to back up what you say — and put up or shut up!

It's worth repeating here: If you have an in-studio guest, never lose sight of that key word: *guest.* Be cool, be pleasant, be nice. Both of you — interviewer and guest — are working together to create something special for the podcast.

Chapter 4

So What Are You Waiting For? Record, Already!

• •

In This Chapter

▶ Setting your levels and parameters

▶ Focusing on volume and projection

▶ Capturing ambient sound

▶ Pacing and clock management

▶ Going off on tangents

• •

*N*ow comes the part of podcasting you've been waiting for — recording. This is it! You've got a high-performance or low-cost microphone pointing in the direction of your mouth, just waiting anxiously for you to begin podcasting.

So what's stopping you? Perhaps you have no clue how you sound to your recording equipment, or perhaps you're still trying to understand why your smooth and sultry voice sounds distorted when recorded. The problem could be in your audio application's sound settings. Too much pep in the voice, and you sound like Rob Zombie crooning a goth's delight. Too little amplification, and podcatchers would be better off if you just went out to your front porch and shouted out your podcast's content.

So before the podcast itself comes the process of *setting levels and parameters* — a fancy-schmancy way to say *fiddling with knobs and sliders* on your mixing board or your audio-editing software to ensure that the signal you're sending through the microphone is loud and clear.

Did Your Sound Check Clear the Bank?

If you show up early enough for a rock concert, you see those roadies setting up microphones, playfully waving to the crowd as they speak quickly into a microphone "Check one, check two, check-check-check!" It's a staple for rock-and-rollers to do such a mic check because the fans expect it. Okay, maybe the mic levels were set earlier that day, but it adds to the atmosphere to do that "last-minute check" before the band hits the stage.

With podcasting, your own mic check should be more involved. In Chapter 3, we recommended you perform a mic check just to assure yourself (and, if applicable, your guests) that the equipment is working. The idea is not only to confirm that your mic is picking up sound, but also to check the volume of the voices — yours, and the voices of anyone else involved in this podcast.

Understanding dB levels

Setting levels is quite easy, provided you know where your *decibel (dB) input levels* are displayed on your software. The *decibel* unit is used to express the intensity of sound, beginning at zero for the least perceptible sound to approximately 130 for an intensely loud sound level. Your VU (Volume Unit) readout measures how "hot" you are (that's the power of your voice, not how good you look) on the microphone. Audio *signal strength* (measured in decibels) is the amount of power that goes into the signal — which affects how clearly it can be heard and how hard it hits the ears. "Loud and clear" is good; too much signal strength causes distortion, and that's a pain to listen to.

In vintage radio and audio equipment, this dB display was the VU meter — the little needle that bounced in response to your voice. Later, the needle was replaced by lights that reacted when you spoke into a microphone, going from green to yellow to orange to red. What they said was pretty easy to translate:

- **Green:** Well, I can hear you, but wow, are you quiet!
- **Yellow:** I can hear you better, but you're still kind of soft.
- **Orange:** Hey now, that's a mighty fine voice you've got there.
- **Red:** Wow — that's a *powerful* voice you've got there!
- **Red with double bars:** Why are you shouting?

With each application, VU meters will appear different (as you see with Audacity in Figure 4-1), but they all serve the same purpose: to make sure your content is heard clearly. Your aim, as you speak and watch the indicators speak back, is to keep your dB levels bouncing in the high level (low red) without lighting up those double bars. When you attain that average, your voice is rising and falling within a balanced dynamic range of around 0 dB. In this case, a big fat zero is a good thing. It means your audio equipment and your voice are in balance so you can produce a strong signal without distortion.

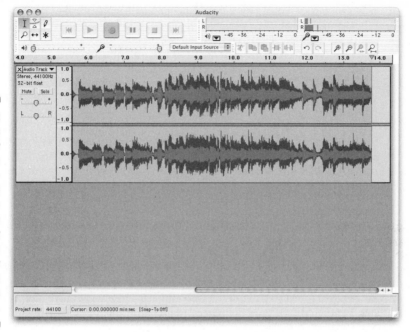

Figure 4-1:
VU displays
for Audacity
(shown in
the upper-
right corner)
respond to
your voice
and allow
you to
monitor how
loud you are
when
recording.

Because microphones, audio-capture cards, and mixing boards all work at different sensitivity levels, it's best to test your voice before you record. If your levels are in the green, it means you're loud enough to be heard by your equipment, but still may be *undermodulated,* or so soft that people will have to crank up the volume on their computers or portable MP3 players, consequently blowing out their eardrums on their next podcast or CD. Undermodulated voices tend to register into the negative dB numbers.

Calling in the crew

It'd be great to set your levels so "0 dB" is always where your lights remain, but recording is a real-world activity. Sometimes your meter may never reach yellow, and other times it might hit the double red bars. If your goal is to maintain perfect levels from the beginning to the end of a recording session, an audio crew can work with you in rehearsal and performance, adjusting levels when you go loud and when you go soft.

The downside of hiring a crew does mean an added expense to producing your podcast. Even if the crew is a collection of audio geek friends, it can still cost you in sending out for a *lot* of pizza every time you record.

Overmodulated voices also tend to cause problems for listeners. They will have their MP3 players set for a pleasant, comfortable volume . . . and suddenly your show begins with guns blazing and pipes blaring. As your levels reach deep into the red, listeners fumble for their players and try to turn down the sound so the program can be understandable through its own distortion. Sadly, the modulation is such a problem that your voice crackles and growls as it tramples the volume limits of your recording equipment, even at the lower volume.

In achieving a balance in your audio, you could spend the day setting and resetting those levels in quest of dB nirvana. (That's time spent, but not *well* spent.) It makes more sense to practice till you get a pretty good sense of what your best working level is and get comfortable speaking into a mic at that level. Time to go mano-a-mano with setting the levels.

Setting your levels

Your mission, should you decide to accept it, is to keep your levels in the neighborhood of 0 dB, dipping and spiking when necessary. For podcasting, consistency is key. Setting levels consists of only a few steps:

1. **Begin talking into the mic about your podcast topic or plans.**

   This can be a scripted test read or just you talking off the top of your head, speaking in the manner and mood of your podcast.

2. **While you're talking (or if you're monitoring by playing back your test takes), keep an eye on your dB levels.**

   If they're spiking into the double-red/red area or remaining in the green, then check your input volume settings on your mixing board or audio-editing software.

3. **Re-record your voice at the new settings.**

   Try to speak in the same manner and inflection as you did on the first recording.

4. **As you review the second take, watch the dB input levels and adjust accordingly.**

After you set your levels, make a note of the settings somewhere other than your computer (using, say, a PDA or its retro ancestor — a legal pad and pen), in case your preferences are lost or fiddled out of whack by somebody's child or best friend playing spaceship in your studio. (Yes, even adults enjoy playing spaceship with really super-cool looking equipment!) That way, even if something awful happens to your application's preferences or your mixing board, you always have your last known settings to reference.

Fire Sign Podcasting: Volume and Projection

Even if you never much felt like portraying Hamlet, podcasting is like acting: You're trying to captivate an audience. So here's a time-honored actor's technique, normally used for doing an aside or "focusing on the horizon" during dialogue with other actors: *Fire Sign Acting.* It's called that because the best focal point to pick was the always-visible fire-exit sign (or vicinity) at the back of the theater. Actors were trained to *project* their voices so the back row could hear the dialogue as clearly as the front row, without anyone having to screech or bellow.

If you're wondering why you'd have to project your voice when a perfectly good mic is sitting in front of you, remember that technology isn't the be all and end all solution. While Chapter 2 describes several models of microphones, this chapter touts the art of setting levels, and a quality microphone (plus some care with levels) helps a podcast immensely.

So will Fire Sign Podcasting.

Suppose, for example, you're podcasting without the benefit of that MXL 990 Cardioid Condenser Mic with Shockmount you've been saving up for, and you're currently working with that modest Griffin Technologies iTalk (retail cost about $39.99) handy — and you're including several people besides yourself in this podcast. Then the volume and projection of each voice is as important as it would be in a mic-less theater.

Microphones such as the iTalk are inexpensive and easy to use (especially if you're recording podcasts on the move), but they have a very limited range. If you don't hold that mic close enough to your mouth, it may pick up more of the surroundings and less of you. Also, mics like these don't give you much nuance to play with if you have to wrestle with the levels in *post-production* (which can include tweaking less-than-perfect recordings to "sweeten" their quality by using filters and output settings). Trying to balance levels in post-production is similar to working with a bad scan in Photoshop: You can make some improvements, but a bad scan is still a bad scan. The same thing can be said for audio files. Moral: Know what your microphone can do, and use it to provide the best original audio possible by (for example) having everyone in the podcast speak directly into the mic within its range. Unless you're all in a football huddle, that means voice projection — Fire Sign Podcasting.

To improve your chances of creating files that need less tinkering in post-production, you need to know how voice projection works. The techniques may sound a little weird — okay, *really* weird — because normally most of us don't pay much attention to *how* we talk. But professional actors and voice talent use these techniques (in varying styles and approaches), and they work. They can make recording sessions, both in studio and on location, a breeze. Here's the drill:

1. **Take a nice, deep breath allowing your stomach to push out a bit.**

   The action in pushing out your stomach gives your *diaphragm* (the curved muscle separating the abdomen from the lung area) enough tension that you can support your lungs' current air supply and control exhaling. It also gives your voice a little extra kick.

2. **Hold the microphone you're using (iTalk, eMic, whatever) a short distance away from your mouth and *direct your voice* to the microphone.**

   The difference between talking *into* the microphone and directing your voice *to* it is focus:

   - Talking *into* the microphone means you have your mouth closer to the mic and are talking in a more conversational tone (while still supporting your voice).

   - Directing your voice *to* a microphone means the microphone isn't as close to you — instead of a conversational tone, you now have to make your voice heard across an expanse.

   So, instead of speaking into thin air in the vague direction of the mic (or the person next to you), speak in the exact direction of the mic, pointing your voice directly at the recording device (as shown in Figure 4-2). Even if the mic isn't omnidirectional, it can pick up your voice better this way.

3. **Begin talking, using either scripted or improvised material, and remember to talk a bit louder than usual because you're competing with background noise.**

   When talking, open your mouth a bit wider and slightly over-enunciate. The distance between your mouth and the mic can play havoc with your consonants; make sure they sound clear.

4. **Play back your final file and tinker with it using your audio-editing software package. (See Chapter 5 for the lowdown on editing.)**

   When you have a pretty clear idea of what will make this file sound good, write down these settings on that same legal pad where you jot down your studio levels, and make a note that your post-production should *start* at these levels. Because every recording situation is different, don't expect your post-production process to use the same settings as your field recordings.

Figure 4-2:
Set your micro-
phone at a
comfortable
distance,
close
enough to
overpower
ambient
noise, but
avoid
microphone
contact.

In an ideal world, you could test this type of recording in the setting where you'll be podcasting, practicing voice projection and volume so traffic, crowd noise, or boomy echoes don't drown you out. If you have a chance to test-record yourself in the setting you'll be in (be it a hotel room, outdoors, or on location), do it. In practice, most podcasts-on-the-go never know where they'll wind up, but a dry run can help. You'll be better prepared for post-production if you take your portable equipment outside and try recording in the midst of kids playing, weed-whackers whacking, and blustery days when the wind is particularly strong.

And speaking of the background noise filtering in . . .

Noises Off: Capturing Ambient Noise

Part of the charm that is podcasting is just how varied the content is, as well as how spontaneous the shows tend to be when the record button is hit. Some podcasters believe that a "true" podcast (whatever *that* is!) must record everything in one take and deliver its content to listeners completely unedited. This supposed mark-of-authenticity includes any background noise (also called *ambient* noise) you happen to capture while recording — you know, rustling trees, birdcalls, pounding car stereos, jackhammers, the usual.

Identifying ambient noise you want to edit out

As we discuss in Chapter 5, how much you edit depends on what kind of content you're presenting. For example, if you're doing an off-the-cuff, off-the-wall podcast about your life and a typical day in it, you may just grab the iTalk, plug it into your iPod, and head out the door, recording every step along the way. This kind of podcast can be (note we said *can be*) easiest to record. You're podcasting a slice of Americana . . . or Britanniana, if you're in the United Kingdom . . . or Australiana if you're podcasting from Down Under. Especially if your goal is to capture the look and feel of your culture, ambient noise is not only welcomed, but desired. Up to a point.

Some podcasts cringe at the mere mention of ambient noise — podcasts like . . . well, like Tee's. Since January 20, 2005, he's been podcasting *MOREVI: The Chronicles of Rafe & Askana,* a swashbuckling epic fantasy adventure featuring martial arts, nail-biting cliffhangers, dark sorcery, swordplay, and a hint of romance to make things interesting. So imagine: He's worked to create a magical setting with voice, story, music, special effects . . . a world completely shattered by real-world blunders like school buses, kids at recess, UPS trucks, the Virginia Commuter Rail system, and air traffic from two nearby airports. (Oh, and he became a dad in summer 2004. Even if you love the *source* of the ambient noise, sometimes it just doesn't fit what the podcast is trying to do.)

For this sort of podcast, when you schedule recording sessions is the start of your production. The rest is soundproofing and editing. On average, if you record 30 minutes' worth of material, you can usually expect to edit out 10 to 15 minutes on account of ambient noise (especially if you're recording during the day). If you live in a noisy neighborhood, figure out which times are quietest and use those to record the imaginary bits that would suffer from unwanted ambient noise. To continue reducing the intrusion of the outside world and still maintain a budget, some creativity is in order, as we describe in the next section.

Minimizing ambient noise

Truth be told, there really isn't an easy solution to podcasting in a noisy world. One not-so-cost-effective answer is to rent a studio and record your podcast there. Unless you have a sponsor who will bankroll your costs, your "hobby" could easily max out credit cards and cast a hungry eye upon your nest egg. (Let's not even go there.)

A somewhat-less-expensive option is to soundproof your home-based recording room. That may sound simple, but it can involve a lot of home improvement before you have one room in which you can be sure the only sound is yours.

And that's seriously frowned upon if you're renting an apartment. So, let's keep this affordable:

- ✔ Stuff towels under the door. It decreases the amount of sound from inside your house filtering into your recording area.

- ✔ Keep the microphone as far away from your computer as possible; then its fan (if audible) simply becomes part of the natural ambiance (also known as *white noise*) for the podcasting room.

- ✔ Turn off any ceiling fans, floor heaters, additional air conditioners, or room ionizers. The fewer appliances that are running, the less chance exists of additional ambient sound being created.

- ✔ If you do encounter ambient noise that you don't want in your podcast, simply give it a few moments. Wait until the noise subsides, pause, and then pick up your podcast a few lines *before* the interruption. That's for the sake of post-production: With a substantial gap in your podcast activity, you can easily narrow down where your edits are needed.

When noise interferes with your podcast, leaving gaps of silence so you know where to edit isn't exactly a foolproof method. Always set aside enough time to listen to your podcast — and *really* listen, not just play it back while you clean the office or call a friend. Make sure levels are even, no segments are repeated, and the final product is ready for uploading and posting.

Many podcasts rely on ambient noise to set a mood, but sometimes reality just doesn't cut it. If you want to put more craft into the setting for your podcast, the ideas in this section should help you keep the background down to a dull roar.

When holding podcasts-on-location, make sure the ambiance — be it a particularly busy crosswalk at a street corner, a frequented bar, or backstage at a concert — does not overwhelm your voice. Background noise belongs in (well, yeah) the background. Its intent is to set a tone for the aim of the podcast, not to become the podcast itself. It would also be a good idea, if possible, to do a few test recordings in the space to see how much volume you'll need and how close to the mic you have to be in order to be heard.

Now Take Your Time and Hurry Up: Pacing and Clock Management

Podcasts, whether short and sweet or epic and ambitious, all share something in common: the need for *pacing*. As a rule, you don't want to blurt out the aim or intent of your podcast in the opening five minutes and then pad the remaining ten or 15 with fluff. Nor do you want to drone on and on (and on . . .) till suddenly you have to rush frantically into why you're podcasting on this particular day about this particular topic. Give yourself ample time to set the mood comfortably and competently, and make it to the intent without dawdling. Why rush your moment in the spotlight? Enjoy your podcast, but make certain you don't overstay your welcome. The trick in pacing a podcast is really understanding how much time you have to get your message across.

So the big question is how to really grasp how much time you really have. Where to start?

You can start with the here and now: Find a clock, watch, or stopwatch and for one minute (and *only* one minute) sit quietly and do nothing, say nothing, and remain perfectly still. That one minute will feel like a short eternity. Now imagine that one minute times 15. (No, no, no — do *not* repeat this exercise for 15 minutes. There's a fine line between an exercise and a complete waste of time. . . .)

You have a good amount of time on your hands, so you should make certain that in your podcast you take your time getting to the message. The journey you take your listeners on doesn't necessarily have to occupy all of 15 or 20 minutes, but you have time to play. That is the most important thing to remember as you set your best podcasting pace.

Take the potato out of your mouth and enunciate

This following section is dedicated to Evo's co-host of The Dragon Page, Michael R. Mennenga. We love the guy, but, man, does he need to take a breath, give himself a moment, and think before speaking. It's rough enough when your co-host is constantly riding you like a Triple Crown winner, but when Bruce Campbell (Ash from the *Evil Dead* films, and Elvis from *Bubba Ho-tep*) puts you in your place, an intervention is in order.

And sometimes, all you need to sharpen your speech and your vocabulary is to take a breath.

It is not out of the ordinary to fire up the mic and launch into your podcast with enough energy and vitality to power a small shire in England. Nothing wrong with that — until you go back and listen to yourself. Your words, phrases, and thoughts are running together and forming one turbulent, muddy stream of thought. Yes, that is your voice, but even you're having a tough time keeping up and understanding what the podcast is about and what the podcaster is saying . . . and you're the podcaster!

One way of getting a grip on pacing yourself through a podcast is *enunciation* — pronouncing your words distinctly, explaining your topic clearly — and there is no better way to do that than to slow your speech slightly and listen carefully to certain consonants (for example, the *t, s,* and *d* sounds). In fact, it isn't a bad idea to *over*-enunciate. In the excitement of recording, over-enunciation actually forces you to slow down, clean up your pronunciation, and make your voice easily understandable.

Speaking a few tongue-twisters before going on mic helps your enunciation, as well as warms up your voice and prepares it for the podcast you're about to record. Here are some easy ones that emphasize the problem consonants lost when speaking too quickly:

- ✔ Toot the tin trumpet, Tommy, in time.
- ✔ Pop prickly pickles past the peck of parsley.
- ✔ See sand slip silently through the sunlit seals.
- ✔ Will Wendy remember wrecking the white rocker?

If you perform a search online for tongue twisters, you can find a wide variety of classic and original warm-ups for the voice. You can also take the twisters you find and compose your own. Proper enunciation may help you set a comfortable pace and keep you from rushing through your presentation.

And now let's take a break for station identification

Ever notice that certain podcasts suddenly break in with a show ID or take some other marked break, and then (if they are lucky enough to have sponsors) play their sponsors' spots? They're trying to emulate — maybe make themselves easily syndicated by — conventional radio. You know — the broadcasting industry. *Clock management* is the careful, standardized interruption of a typical radio broadcast — usually every 15 minutes in a one-hour slot — for such necessities as station identification, show identification, public-service announcements, and (of course) commercials.

This opens up the great debate as to whether or not podcasting should become a commercial venue, but tailoring a podcast for the broadcast airwaves, or even scheduling in quarterly breaks in the hour, can actually work in your favor.

Clock management usually works in this fashion during an hour:

- ✔ :00 — programming break, station identification, show ID, PSAs, advertisements
- ✔ :15 — programming break, PSAs, advertisements

✔ :30 — programming break, station identification, show ID, PSAs, advertisements

✔ :45 — programming break, PSAs, advertisements

These breaks vary in length, but can last anywhere from two minutes to five minutes. While we list "show ID" (something like "You're listening to Dragon Page's *Cover to Cover* with Michael and Evo . . .") being at the top of the hour and on the half-hour, you can really drop in a show ID anytime you feel like it. Coming back from a break, you can ID yourself, just to remind people what they're listening to.

No surprise that this is where hardcore podcasters get a bit restless. They find clock management and show ID redundant, if not frivolous. Why bother to break or even drop in a show bumper? People have downloaded your feed specifically. They know what they're listening to, so what purpose does clock management serve?

It all comes back to what you see for your podcast's future. If you intend to remain in the *podosphere* (as the aforementioned hardcore podcasters refer to the community of podcasters and loyal listeners), then it really comes down to your format, your way. No constraints from the FCC or RIAA. It's just you, the microphone, your listeners, and caution to the wind. However, if you set your sights for the broadcast airwaves — be it AM, FM, or satellite radio — then you have to format your show to fit the standards. This may not sound like a challenge, but when Michael and Evo took their Dragon Page show from a pre-recorded venue to a live call-in show, a jump that appeared no larger than a hop actually became a leap, particularly in the dynamics between the two of them and the pace of the show.

Writing with experience

Tee's coming to *Podcasting For Dummies* with experiences from podcasting his debut novel and contributing to other podcasts, but it's the co-writer of this book, Evo Terra, who continues to apply many of the techniques discussed in this chapter in the three shows *Cover to Cover, Wingin' It,* and *Slice of Scifi*. Along with Michael R. Mennenga, these three shows not only continue to raise bars and set standards in podcasting, but are enjoying successful jumps from podcasting to broadcast radio.

Michael and Evo's *Cover to Cover* already adhered to the broadcasting standards of clock management because it initially started as a syndicated radio show. With the habit already in place, their spinoff shows *Wingin' It* and *Slice of Scifi* were easy to work the same way. The advantage to sticking with this format is their shows are ready for the jump to standard broadcast radio. At present, radio may seem like a far jump from podcast, but the jump is possible as *Cover to Cover* now runs on XM Satellite Radio.

Think about the possibilities of your podcast, and where you see yourself with it several months (or years) down the road. Maybe a bit of management and organization will aid your podcast in jumping to the airwaves.

Concerning Tangents, and Their Val — Oh, Look, a Butterfly!

It is hardly surprising that broadcasters who have no experience in broadcasting will stray from their topic once the microphone goes hot, and then lose themselves in the thickets and thorns of tangents. Defensive podcasters claim that's part of the charm of podcasting, but that charm fades as the topic gets more serious. If (for example) you launch a podcast intent on addressing the growing concern of television violence and wander into *American Idol* trivia, don't be surprised if your audience wanders away.

It's worth repeating: Stay focused on the intent of your podcast. Remaining true to your podcast's intent is not just a matter of staying within your running time; it also makes clear to your listeners that yes, you have a message and you *will* deliver it. You haven't promised something substantial only to let your mind and commentary wander aimlessly. When people listen, you want them to feel assured that what they will hear is exactly what you've offered.

"Say, that reminds me of something . . ."

Of course, tangents can also be creative opportunities. You don't necessarily treat tangents as strictly *verboten* in podcasting. Say your commentary begins with "Anyone notice how cell phones are no longer just cell phones but tiny PDAs that can be easily monitored and hacked into?" and then suddenly break off on a tangent about cell phone etiquette and the lack of manners it brings out of people. This is a tangent that will *keep your listeners engaged* — and that can count as much as staying on topic.

What if your podcast isn't so structured, though? There's nothing wrong with hitting Record and forging ahead into the great unknown of the next 15 or 20 minutes, so long as you have an idea of where you want to go. If, say, your podcast is about movies but your review of *The Fantastic Four* suddenly goes into the decline of the comic book industry (regardless of the onslaught of comic-books-to-film productions), then you still have a sense of focus. However, if your review of *The Fantastic Four* wanders off into how your cat is throwing up hairballs every time you podcast or that your car's sunroof chose to stop working, blah, blah, what the heck is going on here? Your audience may grow frustrated enough to stop listening. Tangents are terrific in moderation, but put some reins on 'em and keep them at least (well, yeah) tangentially related to the subject matter of your podcast.

"But getting back to what I was saying earlier . . ."

When you're podcasting for 15 or 20 minutes (or longer . . .), it's okay to take the scenic route with your podcast, but make sure that you return to the point you wanted to make in this particular (weekly, bi-weekly, or monthly) installment. The listener's delight in podcasts is often the revelation that individuals who (in many cases) have never set foot in a recording studio can produce entertaining, and even informative, shows. Sometimes meandering back to the point is part of that delight.

For instance, a podcast might begin with something read in the headlines — say, a new marketing strategy launched by Team Mobile to reach a wider client base. This can lead to a variety of topics in the discussion, such as the following:

- ✔ Multipurpose cell phones that play MP3s, video clips, text messages, or (why not? maybe soon) podcasts
- ✔ Costs for services from various carriers
- ✔ Ways that carriers could bring down the costs of services
- ✔ Continued shortcomings and disappointments from the cell-phone industry

But in the last five to ten minutes, a simple segue like "So, to recap our thoughts on this bold marketing strategy from Deutch Telecomm and Team Mobile . . ." can successfully steer you, or you and your co-hosts, back to the aim and intent of your podcast. If you return deliberately from a tangent, your listening audience arrives back at the point and knows the destination as well as the scenery they went through to get there.

Get your listeners there and back again. Not only will they appreciate it, but they will tell others about your podcast, and your subscribers will grow in numbers.

Chapter 5

Cleanup, Podcast Aisle 7!

Although a high-tech activity like podcasting doesn't exactly qualify as quaint, "the charm of podcasting" is (as Steve Jobs describes it) a *Wayne's World* approach to broadcasting. In *Wayne's World*, two Illinois teenagers, Wayne and Garth, shoot a television show in Wayne's basement. They rock and roll their afternoons away for their local cable-access station, all on the budget that their allowance (and perhaps the odd sponsor or two) can swing.

Podcasts, much like *Wayne's World,* are usually done on a shoestring budget and shot in one take, with no editing. All the trip-ups and tangents are captured for posterity and sent out to MP3 players everywhere. This is part of the homespun appeal that podcasting not only is known for, but prides itself in nurturing as new and innovative podcasters enter the podosphere.

While podcasting purists may harbor animosity toward the editing process, sometimes it makes all the difference between a listenable podcast and an incoherent mess of senseless rambling. For example, you might want to eliminate the sound of a train going by, or silence a cough that would otherwise distract your listeners from a brilliant riposte. This chapter shows you how to use editing to shape your podcast while retaining its natural atmosphere, adding depth to that atmosphere with music, and then give the final touch to your podcast's format with an introduction and exit.

A Few Reasons to Consider Editing

Take a serious look at the script and the mood you want to convey with your podcast. From there, you will be able to judge how intense your editing workload will be. The following list explains some instances where editing is needed — and (trust us) your podcast will benefit from it:

- **Ambient noise:** As explained in Chapter 4, *ambient noise* is the natural and spontaneously occurring noise you may pick up when recording your podcast. In some productions, such as *podiobooks* (books podcast one chapter at a time, in a serialized format), moods and atmospheres must be maintained. In others — say, a sketch comedy like *Area 51* (area51show.com) — continuity and clarity are established, requiring a certain amount of editing simply to control ambient noise. If you are conducting an in-studio interview and suddenly a passing siren or the rumble of a garbage truck makes it into your recording, the noise can disrupt the momentum of the interview and distract the audience.

- **Running times:** Another good reason to edit your podcasts: running times. You just wrapped your latest podcast with a great interview, and you're confident that you have plenty of material for your 30-minute podcast. And then you check again and realize that you have recorded over *90* minutes' worth of interview. And you love all of it! Now here's where editing works in your favor. Your listeners expect 30 minutes, give or take a segment or two, from your podcast. You could run the whole thing, unedited, but that might test the patience of your audience (not to mention their bandwidth and file storage). Or you could divide it into two 45-minute interviews, breaking up the airplay of the interviews with two smaller podcasts in-between the segments. In this approach to editing, everyone wins.

  Editing can easily increase your productivity with podcasts. True, some podcasters define "editing" as cutting and deleting material, but there's more to it. Editing can actually help you rescue discussions and content that would otherwise be hard to shoehorn into one podcast.

- **Scripted material:** Some podcasters argue that the true podcast is done in one take, but as podcasting matures as a medium, audiences grow more and more demanding. Expectations for a podcast change when your podcast includes scripted material. Editing is a necessity in these situations. With dramatic readings and productions, moments of "ah" and "um" should be edited out to maintain the clarity of the story, as well as maintain the mood or atmosphere established in your reading.

  With the rising popularity of audio literature in the podosphere, professionalism and performance are the keys to a good product — and usually that means (yep) editing. If you feel that editing would mar the spontaneity of your podcast — but still want to present literature or other scripted material — ask yourself how good you think *Lord of the Rings* would had been if Ian McKellen or Viggo Mortensen did everything in one take. Imagine their dialogue sounding like this:

  Gandalf: Frodo . . . he, uuummm, grows closer to, you know, the end. I wonder if, um, he's, ahh . . . alive.

> *Aragorn:* Ummm . . . what *sneezes suddenly — sniffle sniffle* . . . what does your heart *ahem* tell you?
>
> Not what we would call riveting drama. With scripted material, editing is a must.

The Art of Editing

Editing out breaks, stammers, and trip-ups may sound easy, but there's a science to it. If you cut off too much from a clip, one word comes right on top of another, and you sound unnatural. There is also the problem of having pauses that seem to last too long between thoughts. When you're editing voice, the key is to review, review, review.

There are lots of audio applications out there, each with its own way to edit out stumbles and bumbles (and moments of silence to honor a lost thought). The same principles apply to all of those applications:

1. Find the unwanted content.

2. Give your clip a second or two of silence as leader or "play area" between edits.

3. Review the edit, making sure it sounds smooth and natural; an effective edit doesn't sound like an edit.

But instead of talking about it, how about you do it? In this section, we go into basic editing using GarageBand (`www.apple.com/ilife/garageband/`) and Audacity (`audacity.sourceforge.net`) as examples. These are two very common audio-editing software packages in podcasting, and both serve as our benchmarks in how to create podcasts. If you're using some other audio-editing software package, the steps are similar enough for you to apply to your own project.

Editing voice with GarageBand

You can use GarageBand to edit out awkward gaps of silence or eliminate coughs and stammers from your podcast. To prepare for such edits, split your audio into smaller segments in order to isolate the audio that you want to remove. You do that by following these steps:

1. **Determine where in the track you want to make the edit by clicking and dragging the playhead to the beginning point of your edit.**

   Use the Time Display readout to see exactly how long the gap of silence runs. The playhead tool is the triangle connected to a vertical red line. When creating segments, you want to place this line at the beginning and ending points of your edit. (See Figure 5-1 for details.)

2. **Isolate the area that you want to delete: Move the playhead to where you want the edit to begin, and then choose Edit⇨Split to make the first cut.**

   Figure 5-1 shows the first cut.

3. **Now move your playhead to the location where you want the edit to end. Then choose Edit⇨Split to make your next cut.**

   As you edit, give yourself a second or two of silent "play area" at the beginning and end of your edits. It makes the editing of two segments sound like one continuous segment, and they'll be a little easier to mix together.

4. **Single-click the segment between your two cuts and then press the Delete key.**

   If you're working with GarageBand for the first time, note that the first track of audio is selected by default. To deselect the segment you're editing, single-click anywhere in the gray area underneath the track(s) you're working on.

Playhead

Figure 5-1:
Click and drag the playhead to the beginning point of your edit. The Time Display gives you an idea of where you are in the project's duration.

Time Display

5. **To join the two remaining segments, click and drag the right-hand segment over the left-hand audio segment, overlapping the two (as shown in Figure 5-2).**

   The selected segment overlaps and takes priority over the unselected segment, effectively erasing any content there.

Figure 5-2: To shorten the silence, move one edit over another.

6. **Click and drag the playhead to any point before the edit and hit the Play button to review.**

7. **If the edit doesn't sound natural, undo the changes (by choosing Edit⇨Undo Change of Position Region) and try again.**

   Because you're allowed multiple undos in both versions of GarageBand, you can step back in your project to begin at the first Split command.

If you want to find out more about GarageBand, I recommend Dr. Mac's *GarageBand For Dummies.* Bob Levitus gives you the grand tour and keeps you in the know on how to work this terrific application.

Editing voice with Audacity

Audacity users can follow these steps to make a basic edit:

1. **Find the segment that you want to edit.**

    To view the entire timeline of your project, click the Fit Project in Window tool, shown here in the margin.

You can easily navigate between the segments of your timelines and the project timeline as a whole with the Fit Project in Window and Fit Selection in Window tools, located in the top-right section of the project window.

2. Click the Selection tool and then click and drag across the unwanted segment.

The unwanted segment is highlighted, as shown in Figure 5-3.

Right about here would be a good opportunity to use the Fit Selection in Window tool to make certain the selection border does not go into the recorded content you want to keep.

3. Single-click the segment between your two cuts and then press the Delete key (Mac) or the Backspace key (Windows).

You can also use Edit➪Cut or ⌘+X (Mac)/Ctrl+X (Windows) to remove the unwanted segment.

Do not use the Trim command (HERE'S THE COMMAND NOT TO USE: Edit➪Trim or ⌘+T for Mac/Ctrl+T for Windows). While you may think you are trimming away unwanted content, this command works differently from the ⌘+T command in GarageBand: As when you crop an image, it trims off *unselected* material — leaving you with only the content you wanted to edit out. Ack!

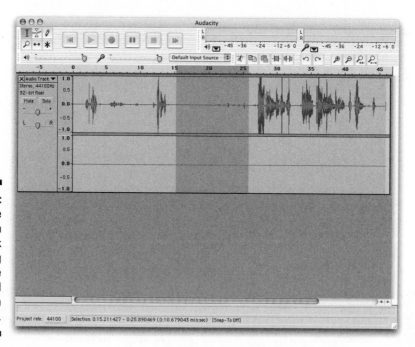

Figure 5-3:
With the Selection tool, click and drag across the unwanted content in the timeline.

Hate editing? Get real . . .

Are there exceptions to the rule? Absolutely! Yes, a performance is at its best when your actors are stammer-free, but back in 1938 there was a radio drama that was chock-full of trip-ups, stutters, and "fluffs" as Paul Jenkins of *RevUp Review* (www.revupreview.co.uk) calls them. With all this going against its production, the Mercury Theatre terrified a nation with its adaptation of H.G. Wells' *War of the Worlds*, arguably the first "reality-based" entertainment (well, a realistic *simulation* of reality, anyway) unleashed on America — the fluffs intensified the illusion of reality. If your podcast is primarily entertainment anchored in reality, then you can probably avoid the arduous editing process. Again, it depends on the content you're podcasting.

4. **Review the clip. If the edit does not sound natural to you, undo the changes via the menus (Edit⇨Undo Change of Position Region) or ⌘+Z (Mac) or Ctrl+Z (Windows), and try again.**

   You are allowed multiple undos in Audacity, giving you the ability to go back to the beginning point of your editing just in case you are not happy with the sound of the edit.

Making Your Musical Bed (And Lying in It): Background Music

On listening to podcasts of people in interview situations or in round table discussions, there can be a strange sense of isolation, especially if the conversation hits a pocket of *dead air* (when conversation or the signal stops), and only silence is recorded or broadcast.

A few podcasters like to add a little bit of atmosphere in their individual podcast with *bed music* — a background soundtrack that's usually two to three minutes long, and looped so it can play again and again throughout the podcast, if desired. Sometimes the bed music will last only a minute or two into the podcast when the hosts return from the break, and some hosts prefer to keep it going from beginning to end, fading it out if they are bringing in any other sources of audio (voice mail, other podcast promos, ads, and so on).

 Regardless of how long the loop is, you must obtain permission from the artists to use their music and give them audible credit — either at the beginning or end of your podcast. These are conditions of Web sites such as PodSafe Music Network (music.podshow.com/). Other options include using music loops found in GarageBand, Audition, or Soundtrack.

As you add music as a background bed, incorporate sound effects, and bring in pre-recorded audio from other sources (such as an iRiver or a Skype call), the sound of your podcast gets more complex. Balance becomes not only harder, but also more essential. (Note, for example, the various volume levels of the multiple tracks in Figure 5-4.)

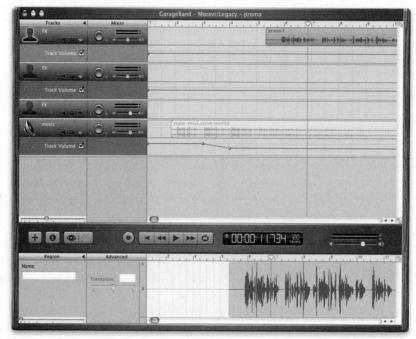

Figure 5-4:
Adding multiple tracks is easy. Balancing them can be challenging.

Finding the right balance

Bed music should add atmosphere to your podcast. That means finding a proper balance between the talking of the hosts and the soundtrack. The following sections explain why you want to avoid music that's too soft or too loud.

What is that noise?

If your music is too soft, your looped music could be mistaken for unwanted ambient noise of someone listening to music in the next room. Or it could be regarded as some kind of technical difficulty such as a stray *signal bleeding* (another wireless audio signal accidentally being picked up by the same frequency as your own wireless audio device) into the podcaster's wireless microphone. Music too indistinct to hear can be a distraction, particularly in quiet moments or pauses in the conversation. Your audience might end up hammering out e-mail after e-mail (asking what's making that annoying noise) or trying to figure out what that faint music in the background is.

Could you speak up? I can't hear you for the music . . .

When bed music is too loud, your voice is lost in the melody. Music, especially classical music and selections that rise and fall in intensity (like any good Queen album), can be really tricky to mix into a conversation.

You do want to allow your audience to hear the music in the background, but the music, if it is being used as background music, probably isn't the point of the podcast. It shouldn't be so loud that you have to pump up your own voice track to be heard.

Never sacrifice audio clarity so bed music can be heard and identified clearly. If you want to showcase music, then showcase music properly. Otherwise, your bed music should remain in the background as a setting, not in the forefront of your podcast.

Applying bed music the right way

When you're setting audio levels, you want to find the best blend of music and voice, ensuring one doesn't overpower the other. Both tracks should work together and not struggle for dominance. Always listen to your podcast before uploading it to the Internet — review, review, review, and find that balance.

To avoid music that is either too soft or too loud, keep the following points in mind as you apply the bed music:

- Experiment with levels for the music *before* you record voice. Watch your VU meter and set your music between –11 to 16dB, depending on the music or sound effects you are using.

- When you're comfortable with the bed's level, lay down a voice track and see how your project's overall levels look (as well as sound) on your VU meter. Remember, your aim is to keep your voice in the "0" or red area without overmodulating. With the music bed now behind your voice, it's much easier to hit the red without effort.

- Avoid "uneven" music, or music that suddenly dips low and then has moments of sudden intensity. The best music-bed-friendly loops have an even sound (whether driving and dramatic or laid-back and relaxed) and an even level.

- Experiment with putting your music at the beginning and at the ending of your podcast instead of throughout. In these cases, music beds announce upcoming breaks and pauses in your podcast.

Setting a Gentle mood for his listeners

Dave Slusher of the *Evil Genius Chronicles* (www.evilgeniuschronicles.org) showcases independent singers and songwriters such as Michelle Malone, Arts & Sciences, and The Gentle Readers, always asking permission before featuring their works. His bed music, playing from the beginning to the end of his podcasts, comes from The Gentle Readers' CD *Hi Honey.* To show his appreciation for the permission, Dave offers a special *Evil Genius* package that includes a T-shirt promoting his show, bundled with the *Hi Honey* CD. With this arrangement, Dave and The Gentle Readers can *both* successfully promote their works.

Setting volume levels for bed music

Each audio application has its own way to change volume dynamically — but the basic process is the same. In the sections that follow, you find out how to use GarageBand and Audacity to bring music into your podcast at full volume, and then balance it to be just audible enough in the background.

Setting volume levels with GarageBand

Follow these steps to set volume levels with GarageBand:

1. **Click to select the track icon (usually represented by a silhouette of a person) that *your voice* resides on.**

   This selects all segments in this track only.

2. **Click and drag your playhead to anywhere between five and ten seconds into the project.**

   If you look at the Time Display in GarageBand and see a musical note in the left corner, single-click it. Doing so switches the display out of Beats and Measures mode and into Time mode.

3. **Click and drag the beginning of your vocal track (your voice) to the playhead.**

   You now have ten seconds of lead time between the beginning of the timeline and your podcast.

4. **In the Finder (or Explorer), open a window and find the music file you want to use as your bed music. Click and drag the file into GarageBand, just underneath your podcast track, as shown in Figure 5-5.**

Figure 5-5:
A simple
drag-and-
drop from
an open
window
to your
GarageBand
window not
only imports
music but
also adds a
track to your
podcast.

GarageBand allows you to import a variety of audio formats into its tracks via the drag-and-drop method — but it won't let you import or incorporate MP3 files into a project. This is not necessarily a bad thing; an MP3 file is a *compressed* file, similar to a JPEG file in digital photography. Compressed files (film, photo, audio, whatever) are usually far from ideal for editing. When using sound effects or bed music, use AIFF or WAV files. Compressed audio files can be exported into AIFF or WAV files easily via QuickTime Pro (available for both Windows and Mac).

5. **Expand the new track of audio you just imported into the project by single-clicking on the Expand Track (the upside-down triangle) tool located in the collection of tools grouped with the music track.**

   You should see a thin blue line against a simple grid. This is your *track volume control*. If your playhead is not at the ten-second mark, be sure to put it there.

6. **Click at the point where the playhead line and the volume control line intersect.**

   You have now created a *control point* — a place you can click and drag to change volume levels at various times. (See Figure 5-6.)

Expand track tool   Control points

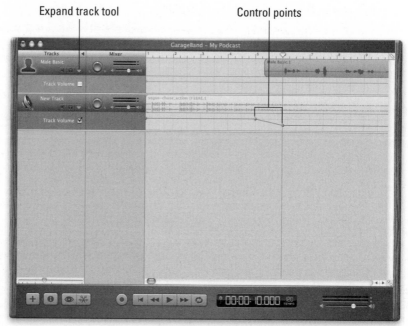

Figure 5-6:
Creating a
volume
curve for a
fade-down
requires two
control
points and
gives you
dynamic
control over
the track's
output.

7. **Move your playhead back two seconds to the eight-second mark. Also at the eight-second mark, click the volume control to create another control point.**

8. **Return to the first control point you created (in Step 6). Click, hold, and drag the control point halfway between the bottom of the track-volume partition and its current level.**

   You have just created a *volume curve.* Now the sound dips lower, allowing for a voiceover to be heard with music softly playing in the background.

9. **Move your playhead back to the ten-second mark, as shown in Figure 5-6.**

   Doing so completes your *fade-down* (the automatic fading of the music to a subdued volume behind the voiceover).

10. **Select the podcast track and click and drag your podcast segments to where the content begins at the ten-second mark.**

    You now have a bed of music behind your podcast.

11. **Bring the playhead back to the beginning and review your podcast. Change the levels as needed to set the music at a level you think works best.**

Setting volume levels with Audacity

If you're using Audacity, you can set volume levels by following these steps:

1. **Activate the Selection tool and then click at the ten-second mark of your timeline, placing an edit line there.**

2. **Click the Time Shift Tool button on the toolbar, shown in the margin.**

   The Time Shift tool takes an entire track of content and places it elsewhere along the project's timeline.

3. **Single-click your audio and drag it to the edit line you created in Step 1.**

4. **Choose Project⇨Import Audio and browse for the music file that you want to use as bed music. Then select the file and click Open to begin the import process.**

   Unlike GarageBand, Audacity does allow for importing or incorporating MP3 files into a project. Just remember the earlier technical note that an MP3 file is a *compressed* file, similar to a JPEG file in digital photography. When you're editing — be it film, photo, or audio — you should not be working with compressed files (it's just too easy to lose a bit too much quality along the way). You can use them in Audacity, but do so at your own risk.

5. **Click the Envelope Tool button on the toolbar.**

   The Envelope Tool allows you to dynamically control the audio levels over a timeline. Clicking at the beginning of the audio track establishes the first volume setting, and the second click (at the ten-second mark) establishes the new volume level.

6. **Select the track of recently imported music by single-clicking its name on the left-hand side of the project window.**

7. **Click at the beginning of the music and then click at the point where your podcast begins (the ten-second mark).**

   Two sets of points appear in your track of music.

8. **Click and drag the second set of points to the 0.5dB mark.**

   You now have a fade-down of the music that maintains its subdued volume behind the voiceover.

9. **Activate the Selection tool, click at the beginning of the timeline, and then click Play to review your podcast.**

   Now you can change the levels as needed to set the music at a level you think works best.

Making an Entrance: Intros

Now that your podcast has a solid lead-in and a cue to fade out — or you have a loop throughout your podcast that sets a tone — your podcast is beginning to solidify. It's establishing an identity for itself; be proud of the way this podcast of yours is maturing.

But when the microphone comes on, do you always know what those first words are going to be? For some listeners, you are about to make a first impression. What do you want that first impression to be? Are you looking for something spontaneous every time, or do you want to create a familiar greeting for you and your podcast that makes listeners feel like old friends?

It's up to you, but think about how strong a first impression a cool intro can make. Consider the ten simple words that became the signature introductions for George Lucas' *Star Wars* saga:

> *A long time ago in a galaxy far, far away . . .*

This intro leaves an unforgettable first impression. But even if you're not vying to be the next George Lucas, the first impression is always important. No matter who you are, this is a moment that can either establish you as a personality (and a podcast) that people will enjoy and anxiously await from episode to episode, or make winning over audiences a little harder. You want the first impression to be fascinating, lasting . . . and positive.

Consistent, iconic intros can serve as a polished touch of preparation or a subtle flair of professionalism. You are announcing to your audience that the show is on the launchpad, you're ready, and the journey is about to begin.

Theme music

How about a catchy theme? Just as television and motion picture themes establish a thumbprint for themselves in pop culture, an opening theme — be it a favorite song (used *with permission!*) or an original composition — can be just the right intro for your podcast. Radio Daddy (radiodaddy.com) provides quick and quirky theme songs (both opening and closing riffs) customized for your show. Earlier-mentioned software applications such as GarageBand, Cakewalk, Soundtrack, and Audition all offer royalty-free loops that can be easily edited into your own podcast intro.

Intro greeting

Some podcasters use quick, snappy intro greetings for their podcasts. For example, Adam Christianson opens every show with a heavy rock riff and the salutation "Hey, Mac Geeks, it's time for the MacCast, the show for Mac Geeks by Mac Geeks . . ." that kicks off his podcast, *The MacCast* (www.maccast. com). Others create an imaginative setting; for Michael and Evo's *Slice of Scifi* (sliceofscifi.com), the sultry voice of *Deep Space Nine's* Chase Masterson announces (in the style of a flight attendant), "Thank you for flying Trek United. Please return your tray and seats into your upright positions. . . ." Whether elaborately produced or just a simple welcome, a consistent greeting serves to bring listeners into your corner of the podosphere.

The elements you're looking for in a spoken introduction are

- ✔ The show's name.
- ✔ The name(s) of the host(s).
- ✔ The location of the podcast.
- ✔ A tagline that identifies your show. (Here's a good example from *Slacker Astronomy:* "A podcast for astronomy and anything else that floats above our heads.")

Sit down and brainstorm a few ideas on how to introduce your particular podcast. For example, try these approaches on for size:

- ✔ "Good morning, Planet Earth! You are listening to *My Corner: A Slice of Cyberspace*, and I'm your host, Tee Morris . . ."
- ✔ "From Washington, D.C., welcome to *My Corner: A Slice of Cyberspace*."
- ✔ "With a perspective on politics, technology, and life in general, it's Tee Morris with the *My Corner* podcast."

As you see in these examples, you can mix and match the elements to drop into an intro. Come up with what feels right for you and your podcast, and stick with it. Once you've put together your greeting, you can either keep it pre-recorded and use it as a *drop-in* (an isolated audio clip that you can use repeatedly, either from podcast to podcast, or within a podcast) at the introduction of your podcast, or you can script it and record it with each session. Whatever method you choose, a greeting is another way of bringing your audience into your 20 to 30 minutes (or five minutes to an hour and a half) of time on someone's MP3 player.

Exit, Stage Left

Now that you have reached the end of your message or the time limit you have set for a podcast, what do you do now? Do you just say "Thanks, everyone, see you next time . . ." or just a basic "'Bye," and then it's over? Or do you want to go out with a bit of fanfare? Whatever you decide, an *outro* is much like an intro — as simple or elaborate as you want to make it. Your outro is your final word, closing statement, and grand finale. (At least for this podcast.)

In practical terms, putting together an outro is no different from putting together an intro — it's the same approach, only you're doing it at the end. So review the earlier suggestions for intros and consider what seems a likely direction for an outro.

Some podcasters figure there's little more to think about for an outro than what to say and how to present it. Sure, you could keep it simple — say "'Bye" and switch off, no fuss, no script, just do it, done, and then upload. But other podcasters see the outro as more like an art form. Before taking a shortcut to the end, check out the following sections for some ways to spiff up your outro.

Leave the audience wanting more

Continuing your podcast to its final moments is a gutsy, confident, and exciting outro, carrying your audience all the way to the final second. This is one of the toughest ways to end a podcast, but if it's done right, it can only make your podcast better.

For example, all the *Area 51* shows conclude with a quick-and-overly-peppy commercial for the "Pink and Chewy Candy-Coated Bubble Gum Network" (offering entertainment that sounds frighteningly close to what's on the major networks), the question "So, like, uh, how was that?" and the reply of one guy applauding slowly, fading out to silence. With this exit, the crew at *Area 51* keeps the jokes flying right up to the last audible second. No plugs. No endorsements. The show keeps going, and just when you think the show is catching a second wind, it ends. The content continues right up to the end.

Catch phrase sign off

Your outro can be the final word from the host, and it should be your bow during the curtain call. A signature farewell is a classy way of saying "This podcast is a wrap. Thanks for listening."

For example, throughout the years that journalist Walter Cronkite reported the news to America, he always ended with the words, "And that's the way it is . . ." followed by the date. Evo has taken a similar approach with his intro for The Dragon Page's *Cover to Cover:* "Our work is done here." On *Slacker Astronomy,* one of the hosts signs off with, "For you, for fun, for the voices in our heads."

If you can't think of anything overly clever, a consistent exit such as "This has been my podcast. Thanks for listening . . ." works too.

Credits roll

Another possibility for your outro could be a scripted list of credits: Web sites where past shows can be downloaded, resources can be endorsed, and special thanks can be given to various supporters of your podcast.

When listing credits, take care that your list of thank-yous and acknowledgments doesn't ramble on for too long after every podcast. Some podcasters reserve a full list of end credits for special podcasts, such as an "end-of-the-season" or even "final" episode. By and large, a minute can serve as a good length for ending credits — plenty of time to mention relevant Web sites, tuck in the obligatory "Tune in next week . . ." statement, and ask for a vote of support on your favorite podcast directory.

Coming soon to an MP3 player near you

Just as television shows drops teasers of what will be coming up next week, podcasters can also give quick hints as to what is planned for future podcasts. Mark Jeffrey's *The Pocket and The Pendant* (pocketandpendant.com) and Scott Sigler's *EarthCore* (scottsigler.net) had already been pre-recorded for the intent of podcasting. This gave both authors a terrific advantage to edit together montages of audio clips and even record a quick synopsis of what was to come in the next episode.

Previews for future podcasts tend to be difficult to plan — mainly because of the spontaneous nature of podcasting that the medium prides itself on. Many podcasters have no idea what will be on the agenda for their next show until the day or even a few hours before recording, and other podcasters prefer to start up the audio equipment and speak with no prep time for their latest installment. For those podcasts that can provide glimpses of things to come, this kind of outro serves as a commitment to their audience that there will be more content coming through the RSS feed, and that programming is being planned for future installments.

As mentioned with intros, your outro can use one of these approaches or combine them. Find what best fits your podcast and stick with it. The more consistent your podcast is, the more professional it will sound — spontaneous but focused, right?

Part III

So You've Got This Great Recording of Your Voice. Now What?

The 5th Wave   By Rich Tennant

INSTEAD OF AN RSS AGGREGATOR, GLEN SUBSCRIBES TO AN RSS AGGRAVATER SERVICE.

©RICHTENNANT

Okay, that was "Swarming Mosquito". For the next half hour we'll be listening to "Whining Dental Drill".

In this part . . .

For every would-be podcaster who salivates at the thought of creating a recording, ten more faint at the thought of the technical hurdles involved in getting their work online. This part shows you how easy the technology really is and how to make it work for you, and guides you through the (elementary) process of launching your show into the *podosphere*.

Chapter 6

Shrink That Puppy and Slap a Label on It

In This Chapter

▶ Downsizing audio files with MP3 compression (getting 25 pounds of sugar into a 5-pound bag)

▶ Dissecting ID3 tags: They're not just for music anymore

You've finished your final edit (and for those who think we're skirting blasphemy whenever we use the "E" word, trust us — creativity sometimes demands a sacrifice). At last you're ready to compress your mondo-supersized AIFF or WAV file down to the format that inspires terror and indigestion to RIAA representatives everywhere: *MP3.*

The MP3 format was designed to reduce the amount of data (via 10:1 compression) required for digitized audio, while still retaining the quality of the original recording. This type of audio is used for quick-and-easy file sharing much to the chagrin of the music industry, and it is this "outlaw format" that podcasting utilizes to get content efficiently from podcaster to podcatching client. The MP3 format is the best way to keep the file small enough in size to make it a quick and easy download. Although creating MP3s is a very quick and easy process, you do need to make some tradeoffs between quality and compression.

A Kilobit of Me, and a Whole Lot of You: Understanding Kbps

The compression process begins with proper *Kbps (kilobits per second)* settings. Kbps is a method of measuring data transmission from one point to the next. The higher the Kbps value, the more data being transferred between two points. The more data being transferred per second, the better the quality of information. With each rate of data transfer (or, because you're dealing with sound, the *audio bit rate*) offered by recording applications, you can digitally reproduce the various qualities of audio:

- ✔ 8 Kbps (matching the vocal quality of a telephone conversation)

- ✔ 32 Kbps (yielding audio quality similar to AM radio)

- ✔ 96 Kbps (yielding audio quality similar to FM radio)

- ✔ 128 Kbps (matching audio CD quality, and the most common Kbps used for MP3 compression of music)

- ✔ 1411 Kbps (maximum quality for CD audio, with stereo playback, 16-bit audio quality, and modulation at 44.1 kHz)

You are not married to this listing of Kbps by any stretch of imagination. Figure 6-1 shows what Audacity offers in its Preferences — plenty of variations from five common settings. Tweak till you find the Kbps best suited for your podcast.

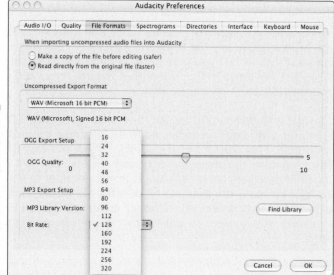

Figure 6-1:
You find a wide variety of bit rates for compressing your podcast to MP3 with Audacity.

It's a tradeoff: The higher the bit rate, the larger your file size is — but the smaller your bit rate, the lower your audio quality is. A good idea is to experiment: Compress your podcast using one bit rate, save it that way, and then change your bit rate to something higher (or lower), do the same, and play back each clip to compare how they load and how they sound. Note any changes in sound quality and file size. When you find that happy medium between quality and compression, stick with that number for your current and future podcasts.

In this section, we're changing bit rates using Audacity and iTunes. If you're using applications like Audition or Soundtrack, you can check your documentation or online help to find out where you make these changes.

Changing bit rates in Audacity

Changing bit rates in Audacity is an easy and painless process. The only hassle is that you have to know where to look in your Preferences and where to look under which option. To deal with it, follow these steps:

1. **Choose Audacity⇨Preferences (Mac) or choose File⇨Preferences (Windows).**

   The Preferences window opens.

2. **Choose the File Formats tab.**

3. **Select your desired bit rate from the Bit Rate drop-down list in the MP3 Export Setup area (refer to Figure 6-1).**

If the Bit Rate drop-down list is grayed out and you can't make a selection, you need to install the LAME Library first, as described next.

Here's a funny thing about Audacity. It's a great tool for creating MP3 files — especially considering its price! — but *Audacity can't make MP3 files all by itself.* It recruits a little help from an *exporting library* file, a separate download from Audacity itself. The LAME Library is not a huge download, but it's a bit of a hassle if you have been recording or are nearing the end, and now you have to make *another* download.

The good news about this extra step is that once you locate the LAME Library, you don't have to repeat this process again unless you move the library to another location.

Here are the steps you need to follow to download and install LAME:

1. **Download the LAME Library from** `audacity.sourceforge.net`.

2. **After you've downloaded the LAME Library, look for the LameLib file (Mac) or** `lame_enc.dll` **file (Windows) and save it in your Audacity program folder.**

3. **Repeat Steps 1 through 2 in the preceding step list.**

4. **Click the Find Library button.**

   The Export MP3 message window appears, as shown in Figure 6-2.

5. **Click Yes in the message window.**

   If you click No, you return to Audacity's main interface without installing LAME.

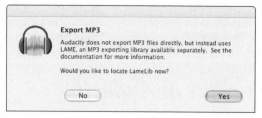

Figure 6-2:
Audacity's
way of
saying,
"I can't do
this alone."

6. **Locate the LameLib file (Mac) or** `lame_enc.dll` **file (Windows) on your hard drive.**

   If you saved the file in your Audacity program folder, choose Applications⇨ Audacity folder (depending on what version you download) in the Finder window (Mac) or My Computer⇨(Main Drive)⇨Programs⇨Audacity (Windows).

7. **Select the file and click Open.**

Changing bit rates in iTunes

If you're having way too much fun editing your podcast in GarageBand, you will notice that you have no options for exporting to MP3. In fact, you can't even import an MP3 into GarageBand for editing. That's because GarageBand prefers to work with full-sized AIFF or WAV files.

Notice, though, that GarageBand encourages a direct export to iTunes. Apple's plan is that you work your magic in GarageBand, and then perform any final touches (such as compression and tagging) in iTunes. It's a seamless relationship, and these two applications really play well together.

The release of podcast-friendly iTunes made compression and bit-rate changes easy (though it required one more step than Audacity). Follow these steps:

1. **Choose iTunes⇨Preferences (Mac) or choose Edit⇨Preferences (Windows).**

   The Preferences window opens.

2. **In the Preferences window, choose Advanced⇨Importing.**

3. **Choose Custom from the Settings drop-down menu.**

   The MP3 Encoder dialog box opens, as shown in Figure 6-3.

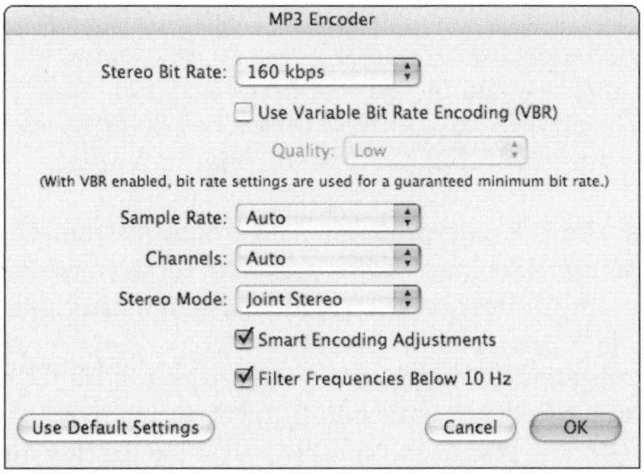

Figure 6-3:
The iTunes
options for
sampling
rates.

4. **Select your desired bit rate from the Stereo Bit Rate drop-down menu.**

   You can also choose to make your channels mono or stereo, and what your sampling rate is. (See the upcoming section for more about sampling rates.)

5. **Click OK.**

   You return to the Importing tab. The default settings for your MP3 compressions are now in the Details area.

Care for a Sample, Sir? (Audio Sample Rates)

After you have a grasp of bit rates, you're ready to move on to *sample rates*. This may strike you as a tad redundant, particularly when you see the list of common audio-sample rates. A strange *déjà vu* makes you wonder whether you're in the real world or exist merely as part of the Matrix. No biggie — sometimes technology *is* redundant.

As we discuss in the previous section, the bit rate is a measurement of how much audio data is transferred between two points, such as the computer and your headset. The *sampling rate* is a measurement of audio samples taken from a *continuous signal* (a signal of varying quantity, defined over a period of time) in order to create a *discrete signal* (a signal made up of samples from a continuous signal).

Think of a sampling rate like this. When you talk with a friend about how good *The Fantastic Four* was and how cool it was to hear actor Michael Chiklis say "It's Clobberin' Time!" — that is your *continuous* signal. Your words are coming out effortlessly, and do so until you take a break either for a breath or to give your friend time to compare *Fantastic Four* to *X-Men*.

Your friend then says, "You should podcast your opinions of movies." So you buy *Podcasting For Dummies* by Tee Morris and Evo Terra (a good book, we hear!), put together your studio, and then start recording thoughts on your favorite movies. The microphone sends your voice as a signal to the computer's audio software and samples that particular segment until you hit the Stop button. Whenever you hit Record, your computer samples your voice each time it receives the signal — and then compiles all the separate samples to create a continuous track of speech. The higher the sampling rate, the truer-to-life the digital reproduction of your voice sounds.

The most common audio sampling rates found in MP3 encoders are

- ✔ 8,000 Hz / 8 kHz (telephone-quality recording or lo-fi)
- ✔ 22,050 Hz / 22 kHz (equal to AM radio transmission)
- ✔ 32,000 Hz / 32 kHz (equal to FM radio transmission, minimum sound quality on miniDV digital video camcorder)
- ✔ 44,100 Hz / 44 kHz (audio-CD quality)
- ✔ 48,000 Hz / 48 kHz (digital TV, DVD, films, maximum sound quality on miniDV digital video camcorder, and professional-grade audio recording)

As with your audio recording applications, you have a range of bit rates available — and you can type in your own custom sampling rates.

Lower sampling rates mean smaller amounts of memory to store for your MP3 files — but your overall quality takes a loss. As with bit rates, experiment with several and find out which rate works best for you.

Changing sample rates in Audacity

Sample rates are located in the Preferences window and are extremely simple to either change or customize to your podcast's personal needs. Follow these steps to customize sample rates in Audacity:

1. **Choose Audacity➪Preferences (Mac). Choose File➪Preferences (Windows).**

   The Preferences window appears.

2. **Click the Quality tab.**

3. **Select your desired bit rate from the Default Sample Rate drop-down menu (as shown in Figure 6-4), or enter your own custom sampling rate by selecting the Other option and entering a number.**

   If you're entering a custom sampling rate, make sure you enter the rate in *hertz* (Hz) and not *kilohertz* (kHz). For example, if you decide your sampling rate is 22.05 kHz, you have to enter **22050**, not 22.

4. **Click OK.**

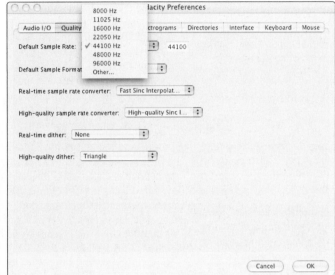

Figure 6-4:
Changing
your audio
sampling
rate in
Audacity.

Changing sample rates in iTunes

iTunes makes the process of changing the sample rate easy — what else would you expect from Apple? Follow these steps to change the sample rate in iTunes:

1. **Choose iTunes⇨Preferences (Mac). Choose Edit⇨Preferences (Windows).**

   The Preferences window appears.

2. **Choose Advanced⇨Importing.**

3. **Select the Custom option from the Settings drop-down menu.**

   The iTunes MP3 Encoder dialog box opens (refer to Figure 6-3).

4. **Select your desired sampling rate from the Sample Rate menu.**

Setting the standard for a new kind of book, a new kind of podcast

When Podiobooks.com was launched, we knew setting an audio standard for current and future podcasters would be important. But what setting could podcasters easily follow, and that listeners would find comfortable? In the end, we looked to The Dragon Page and its podcast (that is also syndicated on XM Satellite Radio and AM/FM radio stations) as a benchmark. Now, Podiobooks.com asks for the following parameters:

✓ 64 Kbps

✓ 22.050 kHz / 22,050 Hz

✓ Stereo

We haven't yet discussed mono or stereo output in this chapter, for one reason: It all depends on the method you use for recording — and on how you are listening:

✓ **Mono:** Mono is appropriate if you don't have stereo speakers or if your audio files were recorded with one audio channel (that is, one audio track). When it comes to file size, mono files take up half the memory of stereo files, therefore the download will be faster.

✓ **Stereo:** If you're listening to your podcasts with a portable MP3 player or stereo speakers connected to a computer, then export to Stereo. For iTunes users, an option is offered in the MP3 Encoder's Stereo Mode called *Joint Stereo*. With this option, one channel carries identical audio data present on both channels, and the other channel carries unique audio data. At bit rates below 128 Kbps, this approach may improve the sound quality of converted audio.

When setting standards for Podiobooks.com, The Dragon Page folks turned to its own, as this new service is a spin-off of its initial podcasts, *Cover to Cover* and *Wingin' It.* Therefore, it stands to reason that consistency between shows and special presentations is paramount. This is something to consider when setting standards for yourself.

Apple loves to make things easy for its users, and we love that. However, Apple sometimes takes out the *"I did it MY WAY!"* alternative and does not allow for custom settings. Here, iTunes keeps this sampling to the common settings, so you are given no leeway.

Note that Apple iTunes offers up your sampling rates at *kilohertz* (kHz), a more common, recognizable presentation of a sampling rate. Again, this is Apple looking out for you, keeping it to the basics.

5. **Click OK.**

You return to the Importing tab. The default settings for your MP3 compressions are now visible in the Details area.

You can take a look at the podcasts your aggregator is pulling down and check the settings. Check the MP3 Summaries in iTunes by pressing ⌘+I (Mac) or Ctrl+I (Windows). Settings may vary from file to file. As you work out the final technical details of your podcast, make sure that one of them is the setting that best suits your needs and (of course) your ear.

ID3 Tags: They're Not Just for Music Anymore

Is it soup yet? Not quite yet. Adding ID3 tags is the final step before you can upload the podcast to your Web site. This is the final detail (okay, batch of details) that not only tells other podcasters who you are, but also tells listeners what your podcast is all about, and which episode they're listening to.

Because this is a final detail, we find that some podcasters either skip it or just don't care how they tag their podcasts. And there goes any hope for effectively organizing their particular podcasts in your computer's MP3 player. Maybe some podcasters are unaware of where or how to identify their podcasts — or want to get their content out to the fans ASAP without taking the time to implement these tags.

Whatever the case, we entreat you: Stop the madness, stop the insanity, and stop the monkeys. Proclaim your true self for the sake of MP3 players everywhere — and implement your ID3 tags!

Tell me about yourself: All about ID3 tags

First created in 1996, *ID3 tags* were designed to be added to audio files in order to have the artist, album, and track title displayed in a computer's MP3 player when the file is played back. ID3 tags, in the early days, liked to crash MP3 players. The MP3 tags are more stable than their earlier versions, and now include composer, bit rate, and even genre.

Of course, another question that comes to mind is *why* would a podcaster want to even bother with ID3 tags?

Take a look at a podcast you're listening to, regardless of whether it's on your portable MP3 player or the player on your desktop. Your podcatching client probably organizes your various feeds by the date downloaded, either with the most recent show at the bottom or at the top of your playlist, depending on the player's preferences. Each individual podcast has a title, artist, and podcast title. If your MP3 player is particularly sophisticated, it also displays artwork associated with your show.

Now hop from podcast to podcast in your MP3 player, and you can tell which people care — or don't — about identifying their shows. Some podcasts simply use obscure numbers that could be a date, but when you hear two episodes of the podcast back-to-back, you find out the number and the date read at the intro of the show (provided there is one) don't match up (confusing). With ID3 tags in place, you can now look at your portable MP3 player or your desktop player to get an idea of what you are listening to.

ID3 tags can include the following:

- ✔ Name
- ✔ Artist
- ✔ Album
- ✔ Track Number
- ✔ Year
- ✔ BPM
- ✔ Composer
- ✔ Genre
- ✔ Comments

With these ID3 tags, you can now set apart individual podcasts from one another, making each one unique but keeping it grouped with your podcast show.

1Dentity crisis: Making 1D3 tags work for podcasting

By now you have noticed that some of these ID3 tags really don't work for podcasting. Album? Track number? Composer? You're podcasting, not producing music. Your responsibility (as a podcaster) is to redefine the following tags we have found useful for the podcasting medium:

- ✔ **Name:** This should be the name or number of your podcasting episode. Examples are `Area 51: Show #15 - Heir Check` and `Cover-to-Cover: Show #160, Chapters 32-34 - Phalanx`.

- ✔ **Artist:** This one is pretty self-explanatory. You're the artist behind this podcast, so let people know who you and your group are. Put in your name (or at least the pseudonym you're using as a podcaster) or the name of your podcasting team. For example, `Area 51`, `Michael & Evo`, `Scott Sigler`.

- ✔ **Album:** This tag may trip you up. It can be either the name of your show or your show's Web site. Good examples are `Area51show.com`, `The Dragon Page`, `EarthCore`.

- ✔ **Track Number:** Purely optional, this ID3 tag allows you to make sure your podcasts remain in some kind of sequential order. For Scott Sigler's *EarthCore* and the *MOREVI* podcast, the track numbers coincide with the chapter numbers.

- ✔ **Year:** The year of your podcast.

- ✔ **Composer:** This one can be tricky if offered by your MP3 creator. You can enter in your engineer's name, or the originators of the material. For example, *MOREVI's* artist is listed as `Tee Morris`, but the composers are `Tee Morris & Lisa Lee` because the original work was co-written.

- ✔ **Genre:** Recently, the Podcast genre was not offered in drop-down menus of MP3 creators, but with the growing popularity of the medium, it is becoming more and more of a common genre, now recognized by iTunes. You can always list your podcast as *Spoken Word* or *Comedy* but don't be surprised if *Podcast* is not an offered option.

- ✔ **Comments:** Similar to comments you leave in XML, you can give a quick two or three lines of show notes for your podcasts. It's also a great place to put in any copyright notices and special mentions.

Reminiscent of John Cleese's aside in a *Monty Python* robbery sketch ("Adapt, and improve. That's the motto of the Round Table"), we podcasters must adapt these ID3 tags to our podcasts to improve how they appear in our players. On playback, the ID3 tags appear on the listeners' interfaces, offering a quick glance at the content of the podcast (as shown in Figure 6-5).

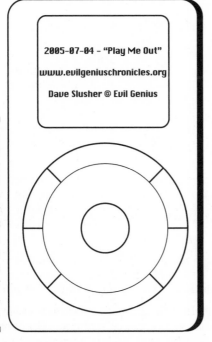

Figure 6-5: How properly tagged podcasts appear in an MP3 player's interface (in this particular example, an iPod).

2005-07-04 – "Play Me Out"

www.evilgeniuschronicles.org

Dave Slusher @ Evil Genius

Creating and editing ID3 tags in Audacity

When you're ready to create an ID3 tag, open Audacity and follow these steps:

1. **Choose Project⇨Edit ID3 Tags.**

   The Edit ID3 Tags (for MP3 Exporting) window opens (shown in Figure 6-6). The ID3v2 option, by default, is already selected.

2. **Fill in these fields:**

   - **Title:** The episode name or number
   - **Artist:** The podcaster or name of the podcasting crew
   - **Album:** The show's name or Web site
   - **Track Number:** The field is optional, unless numerical order is a priority in your podcast
   - **Year:** The podcast publication's year

Figure 6-6:
The Edit ID3
Tags (for
MP3
Exporting)
window in
Audacity.

> Edit ID3 Tags (for MP3 exporting)
>
> Format:
> ○ ID3v1 (more compatible)
> ● ID3v2 (more flexible)
>
> Title: Podcast #01
>
> Artist: Tee Morris
>
> Album: Podcasting for Dummies
>
> Track Number: 01   Year: 2005
>
> Genre: Indie
>
> Comments: loser look at details of my podcast.
>
> Cancel   OK

3. **From the menu of numerous genres, select the option best suited to your podcast.**

   Audacity doesn't offer a Podcast option, but you can always select Speech to indicate this is a non-musical podcast.

4. **Give a quick, brief description of your podcast in the Comments field.**

   Do not make your "Comments" a long, detailed description of your podcast's content. Keep it simple and brief. For example, if *The Dragon Page* were to write in comments for Show #174, it would not say "On this show we interview Brandon Sanderson about his debut novel *Elantris*

and then turn our attention to Steve Alten's latest novel, *The Loch*," but boil down this description to "Show 174 — Interviews with Brandon Sanderson and Steve Alten."

5. Click OK.

And that's it — you're done! The Audacity-generated MP3 is now tagged and ready for uploading.

Creating and editing ID3 tags in iTunes

You can add a few more ID3 tags into iTunes than you can with Audacity, and iTunes also gives you a bit more flexibility in customizing genres and even incorporating artwork.

iTunes also makes adding and editing ID3 tags extremely easy. Follow these steps:

1. Choose File⇨Get Info or press ⌘+I (Mac) or Ctrl+I (Windows).

The Info window appears, which gives you a summary of your MP3 file.

2. Fill in the following fields (shown in Figure 6-7):

- **Name:** The episode name or number.

- **Artist:** The name of the podcaster or podcasting crew.

- **Year:** The podcast publication's year.

- **Album:** The show's name or Web site.

- **Track Number:** This is optional, unless numerical order is a priority in your podcast.

- **Composer:** Fill in this field if you have a separate sound engineer, a tech guru handling the editing, or if you're doing the work yourself.

- **Comments:** A quick, brief version of show notes.

- **Genre:** Select one of the offered genres from the drop-down menu, or you can select the genre in the field and type **Podcast** (or whatever genre you want to use to classify your work).

  One of the cool bonuses of iTunes is how you can create custom genres. Choose File⇨Get Info⇨Info and enter your own genre there. Or go to the MP3 in your iTunes Library and single-click in the Genre column and edit the genre name. When you return to the Info window later, you can see your custom genre offered as an option on the Genre drop-down menu.

3. Take a last look at your ID3 tags to make sure everything is spelled properly and listed the way you want it, and then click the Artwork tab.

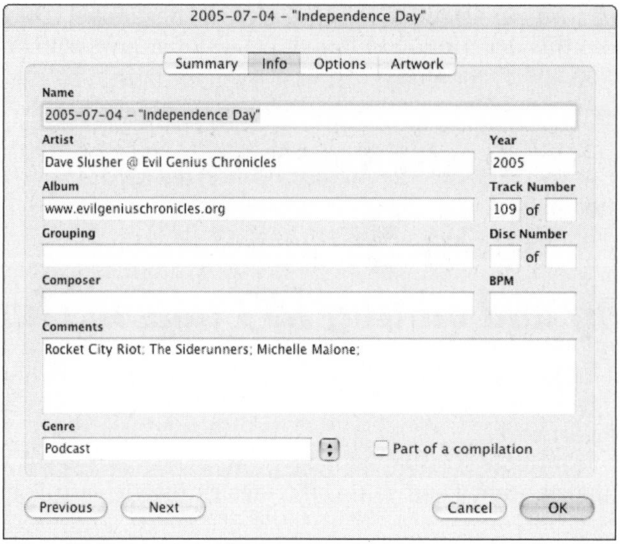

Figure 6-7:
So many options are available in the Info window of iTunes.

4. **Drag and drop a desired piece of artwork into the Artwork field. Or click the Add button and find the artwork you want to have associated with your podcast.**

   If your logo is in a format that iTunes recognizes, it appears in the Artwork field.

5. **Click OK.**

Art for art's sake

Album artwork, commonly seen in many desktop MP3 players and now in iPods that display photos, is a nice option for podcasters who want to brand a podcast with a logo. Mur Lafferty's *GeekFu Action Grip* logo is an edgy, anime-style caricature of our host. Then you have *Slice of Scifi*'s Andorian within reach of a classic radio microphone. These are icons associated with their shows, and this kind of branding is becoming more and more common in podcasting, especially with the iTunes Music Store becoming podcast friendly.

But what is the best way to make sure iTunes (and for that matter, the iTunes Music Store's Podcast Catalog) will recognize your artwork? Just make sure that your logo fits the following parameters:

- 300 x 300 pixels, both in width and height
- 8-bit channel, RGB mode
- JPEG (.jpg) format

Keep in mind that when you compress your artwork, overcompression can distort and deteriorate its visual quality. Some JPEG settings work in numbers 1–10 or 0–100. As a rule, if you compress your logos no more than 5/50, your artwork should retain visual quality.

Chapter 7

Move It on Up (To Your Web Server)

*Y*ou've managed to figure out what it is you wanted to say (or play), went through the trials and tribulations of the editing process (or not), and faithfully employed correct ID3 tagging (nonnegotiable). That's great, but no one is going to hear your contribution to the podcasting world until you put your files up on the World Wide Web.

In Chapter 1, we cover the hosting provider selection process. In this chapter, we take an extensive look at the mechanics of the process, including how to appropriately name and organize your files. And if you expect a high number of listeners, we walk you through some advanced hosting options that can help keep your hosting fees at a manageable level.

Podcasters have a variety of options when it comes to moving files. Specialized software is employed by many, and some podcast-specific hosting companies make moving your files to the Web as simple as point and click. And for the "old school" folks out there, text-based applications baked right in to the operating system might be the preferred method.

While they each do things differently, all of them help you accomplish the same job — moving files from your personal computer to their new home on the World Wide Web.

Uploading Your Files with FTP

FTP (File Transfer Protocol) is the method by which you can transfer files from one destination to another over the Internet. You likely transfer files every day, from your desktop to your documents folder, from an e-mail to your desktop, or even MP3 files from your podcatching client to your MP3 player.

Transferring files to and from the Internet isn't much different, at least on the surface and even at any depth necessary for podcasters to ply their trade. Lucky for us, specialty software exists to make this process even more simple. In reality, FTPing files around has become as simple as drag and drop.

Some podcast hosting services, such as Liberated Syndication (`libsyn.com`), make this simple process even simpler by providing a Web form to handle the uploading of podcast files, as described later in the chapter in the "Uploading to a Podcast-Specific Host" section. Browser-based systems certainly remove the complexity for many, but it doesn't hurt to understand the processes outlined in this chapter. Many experienced podcasters need more flexibility than the limited functionality a browser-based FTP process allows.

Understanding the parts that make FTP work

Regardless of what software, forms, or other assistance you use to move files around, the concept of FTP is the same. In this section, we identify each part of the FTP process and show how they work together to get files from your computer to your Web server.

FTP has been around for quite a while now. As such, archaic and seemingly nonintuitive names abound from the start — such as the two computer systems involved:

- ✔ **Local host:** The local host is the computer you are sitting in front of and are initiating the file transfer from. If you're using a laptop to connect to your Web server, your laptop is the local host. If you're at work, and are logging in from a workstation, your office computer is the local host.

  The *local directory* or *local path* is the folder on your local host that contains the files you want to transfer. You can change local directories at will, but most FTP programs have a default starting place. Feel free to move around after that.

- ✔ **Remote host:** The remote host is the computer or Web server to which you've connected. It's likely the spot where you're trying to get your MP3 files to go so you can start podcasting.

Not surprisingly, the remote host has its own *remote directory* (the folder on the remote system where you drop your files). Again, you can change or navigate through remote directories just as you can change the file folders on your computer.

Making your connection

You need three pieces of information to initiate an FTP connection:

✔ The IP address or hostname of your Web server

✔ Login name

✔ Password

Your hosting company should have provided this information to you. If you don't have it handy, find it. You're not going any farther without it.

All FTP programs do the same job in the same way, but have slightly different methods of going about it. After you grasp the concept, using just about any FTP client is a simple process. Here are the general steps you follow to set up a connection in any FTP client:

1. **Launch your FTP client and create a new connection.**

   Because this step is what FTP clients are designed to do, they usually make this process very simple.

2. **Enter the hostname of your Web server, username (login), and password.**

   This step identifies the remote system and shows you have access to the files and folders it contains.

3. **Connect.**

   Depending on the speed of your connection, the connection is established in a matter of seconds.

For purposes of illustration, the following sections show you how to use Cyberduck (cyberduck.ch/), a free and handy FTP program for the Macintosh system, and SmartFTP (www.smartftp.com), a similar program for the PC. You can find many FTP programs as freeware, shareware, and shrink-wrapped software, for every brand of modern day operating system. We picked these two for their ease-of-use and streamlined approach to getting the job done, but you are encouraged to use the FTP program of your choice.

Step by step with Cyberduck

Mac users can follow these steps to set up an FTP connection in Cyberduck:

1. **Click New Connection in the upper-left-hand corner.**

   The Connect dialog box appears, as shown in Figure 7-1.

2. **In the Server text box, enter the name of your server.**

   Depending on the requirements of your ISP, this name can be in the format of ftp.mydomainname.com or perhaps simply my_domain_name. com. And of course, you need to be sure and use the name of your Web server. Chances are you don't really own the domain my_domain_name. com, right?

3. **Leave the Path text box blank.**

   Every Web server is configured differently, and most ISPs have things configured to put you in the appropriate place. Later, you may wish to add something to this line so you don't have to move around file folders each time you connect.

4. **Enter your username and password.**

   The hosting company should have provided this information. If your hosting company is the same company that is supplying your connection to the Internet, it might be the same information you use to check your mail. But if you toss some additional money each week at a hosting provider, it's likely something completely different.

   Select the Add to Keychain option to store your username and password for the next time you connect.

5. **Click the Connect button in the lower-right corner.**

   If you entered things properly, you now see the file folders on your remote Web server. If you didn't, you get an error message or a login failed dialog box. Correct what's wrong, and try it again.

And when your connection is established, choose Bookmarks⇨New Bookmark. Give your newly created connection a catchy name, and simply double-click the given name the next time you need to connect.

Step by step with SmartFTP

SmartFTP suffers a bit from toolbar overkill, but it certainly cuts down on the number of steps for setting up an FTP connection:

1. **On the Login toolbar (shown in Figure 7-2), enter your server name, login name, and password.**

   Leave the port at 21 and leave the Anonymous check box deselected.

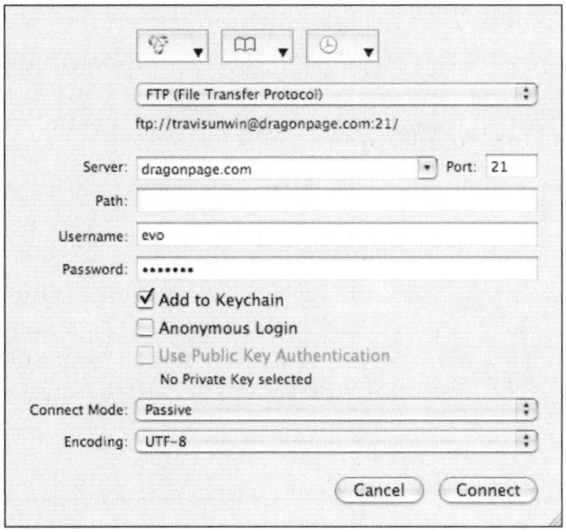

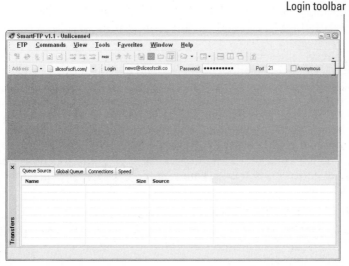

Figure 7-1:
A properly configured Cyberduck FTP connection.

2. Press the Enter key.

A new window appears, and if you did things right, you're now connected to your Web server. If you entered something wrong, you get an error message at the bottom of the new window. Correct your mistakes, and try it again.

Login toolbar

Figure 7-2:
A properly configured SmartFTP connection.

From here, you can now navigate through the folders on your Web server much as you do on your computer's hard drive. You can move up or down the file system, finding the spot where you want to drop your podcast files.

Unmetered and unlimited explained

Okay, I guess we can't throw out technical terms without saying something about them:

✔ **Unmetered bandwidth** refers to the policies of certain hosting companies, like Liberated Syndication and Podlot (podlot.com), that do not base their monthly charges on the amount of files transferred (podcasts downloaded) each month.

✔ **Unlimited server space** is an even more elusive option, and theoretically means you can host one or 1,000 different podcast media files on the Web server and be charged the same flat fee. We don't know of any hosting company offering unlimited server space currently, so you can stop salivating now.

A place on your Web server for your stuff

Logging in to your Web server for the first time can be an intimidating process. In this section, we show you how to place your files in a location so you can easily create links to your podcast files.

Don't be intimidated by the odd directory names on your Web server. The only one you really need to know is Public_html. Other hosts may call it www or simply html. If you don't have one of those three, poke around until you find one that has a bunch of files in it that end in .html.

Look, but don't touch. Going into folders doesn't hurt anything, but doing silly things such as deleting, renaming, and moving files you know nothing about is a bad idea. All those strangely named folders do something, and they're likely necessary to make your Web site work right. Remember the proverb "'Tis best to leave functioning Web servers lie . . ."

After you find your home (or *root*) directory, take a look around. You may see lots of different files and a few folders. We show you how to add even more files to this system, so now is a good time to think about organizing and housekeeping.

Start by creating a special place to keep your podcast files. Making a new folder exclusively for your podcast media files not only separates your podcasts from your other critical Web server files, but also allows you to quickly see what is currently live and what needs to be cleaned up.

Unless you have unmetered bandwidth and unlimited server space (see the sidebar for more details), you only want to keep a few of your more recent podcast media files online. Evo only keeps the last four episodes of one of his show online. It gets expensive to keep more than that available. Of course, your audience may love you so much they want to go back and listen to every episode. As a podcaster, you have to balance what is good for your fans and what is good for your pocketbook.

In your root directory, create a new folder called media. With Cyberduck, you need to simply choose File⇨New Folder, followed by entering the name in the resulting dialog box. On SmartFTP, choose Commands⇨New⇨Folder and enter the name.

After you create the new media folder, click (double-click for Cyberduck) the name of the folder to open it. You're now inside your totally empty media folder, and ready to load it with your podcast media files.

Adopting an effective filenaming convention

In Chapter 6, we talk about the importance of "the little things," such as ID3 tags. Equally important is how you decide to name your podcast media files. In this section, we illustrate the importance, not only to you as a podcaster, but also to your listening audience. While no hard and fast rules exist for naming files, following some common conventions allows everyone to easily find your podcasts.

A good naming convention of a podcast accomplishes the following:

- ✔ **Easy sequential ordering:** Files should not appear at random in your directory. They should line up — first, second, third, and so on.

- ✔ **"At a glance" recognition for your listeners:** Calling a podcast media file *my media file* doesn't help very much. Calling it `Bob's Fencing Podcast` certainly does.

Here's an example of a well-named podcast media file, if we do say so ourselves:

```
DPWI_012_052505.mp3
```

While the structure may not be obvious, this filename adheres to both rules and even adds one more:

- ✔ **DPWI:** This abbreviation stands for (The) Dragon Page *Wingin' It!*, one of the many podcasts Evo produces each week. Starting off the filename with these four letters organizes the files together in the media folder. For listeners who can only see the filename on their MP3 player, they can quickly recognize that files starting with these four letters belong to his show.

✔ **012:** This is Episode 12 of his show. Referring to each show with a sequential number is a good idea, giving you and your fans a common reference point that is easier than "remember when you did that one show with that one guy who said that funny thing? Man that was great!" Having the episode number right after the name also ensures that the files "stack up" right in the media folder, as well as in your listener's MP3 players.

✔ **052505:** The date Evo posted the live file. He uses 05 instead of 5 so that dates from October (10), November (11) and December (12) don't intermingle with January (if he used 1 instead of 01).

Between each element, he adds an underscore (_) simply to provide a clear distinction of each part for his eye, or anyone else's eye who might look at the filename.

Do not use any spaces or special characters in the naming of your files. Stick with A-Z, 0-9, dashes, and underscores. Slashes (/, \), octothorps (#), ampersands (&), and others can and likely do cause problems when creating RSS 2.0 files or when clients are handling the files. If you want to space things out, use underscores (for example, use My_Podcast.mp3 instead of My Podcast.mp3).

The following examples are from well-respected podcasters who all follow the guidelines we set forth earlier:

✔ BP2005_05_27.mp3

✔ Area51show-2005-05-26.mp3

✔ cnMay27.mp3

✔ DSC-2005-05-26.mp3

Note how they identify the name of the podcast and provide a sequential way of ordering the files. The year of the podcast ahead of month and day also ensures that 2005 files are always grouped together. If they had used the month first, as we traditionally think of dates in the United States, files would be mixed based on the month they were released, regardless of the year.

If thinking that way seems a little too strange for you, do what Evo does. Stick a sequential number in front of your date, and don't worry about it.

Some podcasters (including Evo) have experienced intermit resetting of ID3 tags when renaming MP3 files. Be sure and re-check your ID3 tags if you rename your file. After you establish a naming convention, this problem rarely happens.

Uploading your files

After you set up a folder for your podcast media files and decide on a file-naming convention, you're ready to move your freshly named files to the Web server.

Both Cyberduck and SmartFTP support *drag-and-drop* file transfers. If you're new to FTP, the FTP program interface may be easier for you to use.

For Cyberduck, follow these steps:

1. **Choose File⇨Upload.**

2. **Browse your system to find the podcast media file you want to upload.**

3. **Click the Upload button.**

For SmartFTP, follow these steps:

1. **Choose Commands⇨Upload⇨Direct⇨Select Files.**

2. **Browse your system to find the podcast media file you want to upload.**

3. **Click the Open button.**

Depending on the size of your file and the speed of your Internet connection, the file may transfer in a matter of seconds or a matter of minutes. When completed, the file appears in your FTP client and is ready to be linked in your show notes and RSS 2.0 feed, as we discuss in Chapters 8 and 9.

Uploading to a Podcast-Specific Host

Podcast-specific hosting companies significantly simplify the uploading process; many include Web-based forms that take the place of additional computer programs to handle the uploading process. They also take care of archiving, RSS 2.0 creation, and even ID3 tagging.

While this Web-based uploading process is simple, we prefer the flexibility of using an FTP client. Or maybe we're old school . . .

For the purposes of illustration, we use an account with Liberated Syndication (libsyn.com) for the examples. If you haven't already, you need to sign up with Libsyn and create your own account. Then follow these steps:

1. **Log in to your account.**

   Enter your username and password and press the Login button.

2. **Click the Settings tab to access your blog and podcast settings.**

3. **Enter the information for your blog and/or podcast. When you finish, click the Save Changes button.**

   The blog settings are very simple — things like the name of your blog, the e-mail address of the author, and what category you want it placed in. Nothing here is mission critical, so fill it out however you want to see it listed. You can always come back and change it later.

4. **Click the Media Files tab.**

   If you've never uploaded any media files, no media files are listed.

5. **Click the Upload Media button on the left navigation bar.**

   You're taken to the upload page, as shown in Figure 7-3.

6. **Click the Browse button, which is to the right of the HTTP Upload box.**

   The File Upload dialog box opens.

   Note: HTTP upload is another name for form-based transfers.

7. **Find the podcast media file you want to upload and either double-click the file or click Open.**

8. **Click the Load File button.**

   Depending on the size of your file and the speed of your Internet connection, the page may refresh in a matter of seconds or a few minutes. After completion, the screen refreshes, and your podcast media file displays. Note also that the text box under Advanced Users contains a string of RSS 2.0 code. Remember this spot, as we revisit it in Chapters 8 and 9.

Figure 7-3:
Adding
media files
to a Libsyn
account
doesn't
require an
FTP client.

For those of you who like to try it before you buy it, Libsyn lets you log in to a demo account, move files around, and generally get a feel for how it works before you sign up. Not that the very inexpensive monthly fees will break most of you or anything. But it's nice to know how your future home might work.

Using Your Blogging Software to Upload

Many popular blogging tools, such as Movable Type and Word Press, allow bloggers (and podcasters) to upload files without the need for special FTP software, much like the HTTP process outlined in the previous section.

However, podcast media files often exceed the file size requirements for these services. For this reason, we recommend not using your conventional blogging software to handle your podcast media file uploads.

Consider that blogs are primarily used to communicate texts. While you can easily extend the functionality of a blog to support and indeed power a podcast, the site management tools are designed for text and images.

Movable Type, for example, has a file size limitation of 5MB. Unless you're posting two- or three-minute podcasts, you'll likely exceed this limitation on every file.

WordPress does allow file uploads, but not without editing the configuration files, and setting the maximum file size and allowable file extensions. You can upload, but it does take a significant amount of work that exceeds the scope of this book.

Uploading with Command-Line FTP (Speaking of Old School . . .)

We've talked about FTP clients and Web-based forms to handle the uploading process for your podcast media files. Each option requires you to either download some specialty software or make a selection of a hosting company that offers HTTP transfers. There is another way . . .

Every PC and Mac user has a built-in FTP program. Neither is elegant nor pretty, and is the antithesis of simplicity at first glance. But these built-in tools are handy to know about, especially if you can't install new programs (library or shared-student computers may have this restriction) and/or your hosting provider does not provide a Web-based HTTP transfer option.

We talk about command-line FTP in this section, and it comes with none of the conveniences and assurances as the other options we covered earlier in this chapter. But it is a sure-fire way to get your files up no matter where you are. (Almost.)

Setting up a folder for your podcast media file

Before we get into the program itself, you need to move the podcast media file to a staging area on your desktop. Follow these steps:

1. **Create a new folder on your desktop.**

   We recommend naming your folder something like *media* or *media staging.*

2. **Move your podcast media files to this folder.**

   Drag and drop the files from a new Finder window, My Documents, or wherever you may have them stored.

Accessing Terminal on a Mac

If you're a Mac user, follow these steps to use Terminal to access the podcast files you want to upload:

1. **From Applications, open the Utilities folder and activate Terminal.**

   A small window appears, reminiscent of old-time computers where unstyled black text appeared on a white background, or vice versa. Your graphical interface is gone, and you might as well move the mouse out of your way for a bit; you won't be using it.

2. **Type `cd Desktop/media` at the flashing cursor prompt.**

   Your local directory changes to the media file staging area that contains the podcast files you're about to upload.

   Be sure to substitute the name of your folder if you've named it something else beside *media.*

Jump ahead to the section "Uploading your files" to find out how to finish the uploading process.

Accessing the command prompt on a PC

PC users can follow these steps to use the command prompt to access their podcast files:

1. **From the Start menu, choose All Programs➪Accessories➪Command Prompt.**

   A small window appears, reminiscent of old-time computers where unstyled white text appeared on a black background, or vice versa. Your graphical interface is gone, and you might as well get your hand off the mouse for a bit; you won't be using it.

2. **Type** `cd Desktop\media` **at the flashing cursor prompt.**

   Your local directory changes to the media file staging area that contains the podcast files you're about to upload.

   Be sure to substitute the name of your folder if you've named it something else beside *media*.

   The backwards slash (\) is different than what you normally use when typing Web addresses or URLs and is normally located above the large Enter key on most keyboards. Using a forward slash (/) doesn't work on a PC.

Now you're ready to upload your files as described in the following section.

Uploading your files

After you access the podcast files you want to load (see the two preceding sections), the uploading process is the same on a Mac or a PC. (Bet you never thought you'd see that happen, huh?)

Follow these steps to upload your files:

1. **Type** `ftp my_domain_name` **and press the Enter key.**

   For example, we typed `ftp dragonpage.com`, and then pressed Enter.

   A variety of text appears in this window, followed by a prompt to enter your name.

2. **Type your username and press Enter.**

   If your username is accepted, you get some positively reaffirming text, followed by another prompt.

3. **Type your password and press Enter.**

If you've typed your password correctly, several more lines of text describing the server appear, followed by a new prompt. You're now connected to (and controlling) the remote server.

4. **Type** `cd www` **and press Enter.**

That step takes you to the root directory where your files are accessible to Web browsers and podcatching clients. Depending on your server configuration, it may be `public html` or simply `html`. You may need to check with your ISP if neither of these works for your situation.

5. **Create a media folder for your podcast media files.**

Type **mkdir media** at the prompt and press Enter, followed by **cd media** and press Enter to move to that folder. You've just created a connection between your local media folder and your remote media folder.

6. **Type** `put my_podcast_file.mp3` **at the prompt.**

Change the name of the file to reference the file in your local directory. Type the name exactly as it appears, with proper capitalization, because case is important.

That's it! If you've done things properly, you've now placed your podcast media files on the server and are ready to create your show notes and/or create your RSS 2.0 file. You can exit the command line by typing **quit, exit,** or **close**, depending on the application.

Advanced Hosting Options

Many podcasters dream of being famous. As we indicate in the beginning of the book, popularity is a double-edged sword in the world of podcasting. Every time new subscribers add your feed to their podcatching clients, and every time a new listener downloads your latest media file from your Web site, your precious bandwidth begins to disappear.

Some forward-thinking podcast-specific hosting companies such as Liberated Syndication provide unmetered bandwidth to podcasters, keeping the costs down even when popularity finds its way to a podcaster's front door.

But for others, switching hosting providers may not be a simple matter. Companies, organizations, and educational institutions may have a complete IT infrastructure, and the politics of not using in-house systems can come with a cost that far exceeds the few dollars Libsyn charges.

Organizations such as these may have a large base of customers, contributors, and alumnae or students to draw their audience from and can expect to have impressive numbers of listeners as soon as their podcasts are released. A savvy IT professional understands the heavy load this new venue can place on the existing servers and network architecture.

The following sections give an overview of two advanced hosting options that are designed to lower the bandwidth load created by a successful podcast. Because this book is designed with the beginning podcaster in mind, we give you a general overview of these services.

BitTorrent

BitTorrent has come under fire recently as the MPAA and RIAA are stepping up their efforts to reign in illegal file sharing of copyrighted material. Regardless of the controversy surrounding the contents of the files being shared, this technology presents a sound solution to the problem of intensive bandwidth. But like all solutions, it's not for everyone.

BitTorrent is the latest incarnation of peer-to-peer file sharing, where individuals share files with one another, rather than downloading them from individual Web sites. These files can be music, programs, videos — anything you can think of.

For an in-depth discussion of the technologies that make BitTorrent work, visit www.bittorrent.com. The technically savvy can find a plethora of information on the various aspects of BitTorrent, from creating a tracker to the protocol specification for encoding files. The rest of us can stare blankly at the pages, unsure of how we got here — and why we came.

BitTorrent solves the bandwidth issue by replacing the traditional "big file stored on one computer" model with a "big file sliced up into bite-sized pieces shared among friends" paradigm. Allow us to explain.

If you want to get Dave Winer's latest Morning Coffee Notes (morningcoffee notes.com) podcast, your podcatcher pulls the file down from his server. If your mother comes along next and also wants to download the file, she gets it in the same way. And if your Uncle Charlie wants the file as well, he also downloads it directly from Dave's server. The burden is on Dave's Web server to push all that traffic down to every user.

If Dave used BitTorrent, things would be different:

1. Dave creates a small piece of code, called a .torrent file.

    This file acts as the treasure map keeping all the pieces and parts (which we're about to get into) nice and organized for all the people who are trying to get Dave's latest show.

2. Dave posts this `.torrent` file to his Web site and includes it in his RSS 2.0 feed.

3. When you (and each member of your extended family) access this file with your podcatching client, the `.torrent` file connects your computer to a *tracker,* which keeps track of everyone trying to download this particular file.

4. Here's where it gets interesting. By the time your uncle comes on board, he's actually pulling parts of Dave's file from you and your mom, at the same time you and your mom are actively downloading other parts of the file from Dave's server.

5. When Evo tries to download Dave's file, the `.torrent` file and the tracker work together to start sending him files from the three of you, as well as Dave's system.

The net result is that Dave spends less on bandwidth, and Evo gets a whole bunch of simultaneous downloads of individual pieces of the file, which show up on his computer faster than if he tried to download directly from Dave!

Complicated? You bet! But as you can see, BitTorrent is beneficial for everyone. Well, that all depends.

You see, BitTorrent only works well when a lot of people are *seeding* the file to others. If there are no seeds, files are downloaded at a standard rate, and the whole thing is moot. So while it can be great to help distribute the load for recently released podcasts that have a large subscriber base, it's not as helpful for archives of past shows, or podcasts that have a small subscriber base.

As of this writing, only a handful of podcasters are using BitTorrent technology to distribute their feeds. Creating the `.torrent` file and registering with a tracker is non-trivial, to say the least. Currently, developers are working on solutions to lower the technical barriers that could allow more podcasters to use this very beneficial technology.

CoralCDN

Coral is a relatively new player in the content distribution network (CDN) scene. Sponsored by the National Science Foundation, Coral reduces the bandwidth load on podcasters by distributing and sharing podcast media files throughout a network of *caching* servers around the world. Once a podcast media file has been cached, it's replicated throughout the network as more downloaders request the file, theoretically causing the file to be accessed from the origin Web server a single time.

This can be a great boon to podcasters who are on the receiving end of the *Slashdot* effect. When a popular Web site — such as Slashdot (`slashdot.org`) as the name indicates — points a link at your podcast, your bandwidth can suffer a serious blow. If you're using Coral to distribute your media files, you can lessen that load by orders of magnitude, because the caching servers on the Coral network, not your Web server, handle the distribution of the podcast media files.

The Coral network has some innovative methods of internal load balancing and intelligent redirect mechanisms to ensure a highly available network. Podcasters are assured files are transmitted faithfully, and podcatchers receive the subscribed episodes — even under heavy loads.

Any podcaster can start using Coral immediately. It requires no sign up, no software to buy, and no server configurations to make.

You can modify server settings to automatically use Coral with your podcasts. Editing the configuration files in Apache server is a bit outside the scope of this book, however. For more information, visit `coralcdn.org`.

Using Coral to distribute your podcast feeds is as simple as adding the following to your media file URL:

```
.nyud.net:8090
```

Evo recently experimented with using Coral to distribute his *Slice of Scifi* podcasts. A generous donor was hosting this Web site, but increased awareness in the podcasting community was causing it to be hit hard in the bandwidth department. Prior to using Coral, his podcast files had links that looked like:

```
http://www.sliceofscifi.com/slicePod/Slice_009_052605.mp3
```

To have Coral cache the file and distribute it throughout its network, he simply altered the filename:

```
http://www.sliceofscifi.com.nyud.net:8090/slicePod/Slice_009_
        052605.mp3
```

So what happened when he did that? From the end listener's point of view, absolutely nothing. Both URLs access the file just fine. Only one came directly from my Web server, and the other comes from a caching server on the Coral network.

But podcasters can notice a big change. Evo's Web stats program showed a significant drop in the number of downloads for the show, as his Web server is only sending the file to the Coral network and not to individual listeners.

For the next 12 hours, any requests for his media file were handled by one of the many Coral caching servers instead of his Web server. If a request came in after the initial 12 hours, the network re-examined his file to see if it had changed and restarted the process all over again.

Coral is designed for static content. After you alter the URL to your podcast media file, this file is served for the next 12 hours. If you suddenly realize you forgot to put an ending tag on your file, had your levels set too low, or linked your last confessional by mistake, the whole world (or at least your subscribers) are going to know about it for the next 12 hours, and you can do nothing to stop it. You can put your eyes back in your head now . . .

Many of your listeners who use their at-work connections to enjoy your show may likely have problems accessing your episodes if you use Coral. Because of some overly complicated Web server port configurations that you don't need to know about, many corporations inadvertently block access to the connection path (ports) Coral uses to distribute content. Remember how we said Evo had recently experimented with Coral? He's switched back. Too many e-mails from listeners who could no longer listen. For Evo, Coral wasn't worth the bandwidth savings, and he decided to go with the unmetered plan of Libsyn instead. If you are not expecting a huge at-work listener base, then Coral may be worth the minimal loss of your listener base to save on your hosting fees.

Archiving Aging Media Files

Podcast media files are big. Earlier we suggested you keep only the most recent shows online and in your RSS 2.0 feed. But your listeners likely won't care about server space and bandwidth issues. If they find a connection with your podcast, some of them are going to want your older podcast media files as well.

As a podcaster, you're in a difficult position. On the one hand, you want to keep your listeners happy and share your previous shows, music, art, voice, and ideas with them. But unless you're getting paid by the listener, happy listeners don't pay your server costs. If listeners want your old files, they'll likely be sensitive to your constraints and happy to go through a few reasonable hoops as long as they get what they need. Here are a few novel suggestions on how to deal with this good-to-have problem:

✔ Set up a rotating archive feed.

✔ Use the Internet archive.

✔ Rent a new server and charge for access.

The follow sections explain these points in more detail.

Set up a rotating archive feed

An archive feed takes a bit of dedication on your part. Unless you're completely maxed out on your server space, you likely have room for one more podcast media file. This method takes that unutilized space and puts it to good use satisfying your hungry audience.

Every day or two, upload one of your previous files (because no podcasters ever delete any of their own podcasts from their personal computer) to your Web server and create a custom RSS 2.0 feed just for this file. We discuss how to create RSS 2.0 feeds in Chapter 9. Meanwhile, on your regular podcast, mention that you have a new feed created for archived shows and tell all interested listeners to subscribe to that new feed as well. Repeat this process every few days. You may wish to start from your first show so you don't forget where you're at!

Use the Internet Archive

The Internet Archive (www.archive.org) is a 501(c)(3) organization dedicated to the preservation of digital content. It provides the service free of charge, but it has some catches:

- ✔ The archives are a community center. If your podcast is protected by exclusive copyright, it can't be contained in the archive. Creative Commons licenses are allowed, however, and even recommended.

- ✔ Joining the Internet Archive is free, and there is no charge to *hold* your content. Notice we said *hold* and not *host*. Think of the Internet Archive as a library. Content is added to a library for the benefit of everybody. Hosting companies are at your beck and call. Librarians are not.

- ✔ As a free service, it offers no guarantees of uptime and reliability. This is a non-profit organization; so we suggest you don't store your critical podcast media files here. But storing previous editions is another matter all together.

Rent a new server and charge for access

If your content has a good following, your listening audience may be willing to pay for access to previous content. Several syndicated radio programs and magazines take this approach now, providing the most recent episodes as a free download but charging visitors and listeners to access older editions of the content.

While this idea may smack in the face of the free nature of podcasts to date, nothing is stopping you from making a "for fee" podcast feed where you can house all your old episodes. The major podcatching clients iPodderX and iPodder Lemon both support secure connections.

Chapter 13 covers more ways you can derive income from your podcast, including paid subscriptions.

Chapter 8

Posting Show Notes

In This Chapter

▶ Understanding good show note etiquette

▶ Planning your show notes

▶ Deciding on your level of detail

▶ Using images effectively

▶ Posting with searchers in mind

*I*n the world of traditional broadcasting, programs and episodes are usually self-sufficient. In other words, what you see (or hear) is what you get, and accompanying documentation usually isn't made available.

Not true in the podcasting world.

A good podcaster does more than simply talk about an article, band, recipe, or upcoming event — he encourages listeners to get more information on the subject. You can accomplish this via show notes, and they're an effective tool traditional broadcasters can only dream of.

Show notes are brief summaries of each podcast episode. They can take the form of an outline, a bulleted list, or just a few sentences of text. In this chapter, we show you how to effectively use show notes to enhance the listener experience of your show and bring in additional traffic to your podcast through search engines.

Getting additional traffic means additional bandwidth consumption, which can cause issues. Flip to Chapter 7 for tips on ways to reduce the load on your servers, or optional hosting plans that don't charge for additional bandwidth.

Show Note Etiquette

Several schools of thought exist on how to approach show notes. Some say you should be very brief, only using notes to hold URLs and other pieces of important offline data that your listeners may not have had time to write down as the show was playing.

Others suggest show notes should be filled with information on each and every concept touched upon in the show. We prefer a more moderate approach, and your personal tastes and style go a long way in determining what is right for you.

Regardless of the length of your prose and the level of detail you wish to explain, all podcasters should follow some basic rules of etiquette:

- ✔ **Use intriguing and informative titles.** Your title is your pitch; you're a huckster competing for the attention of listeners. Some listeners may know all about you; others could be seeing something from you for the first time. Include key words in your title that accurately and specifically represent the contents of this episode, as well as generate some excitement and make the episode sound interesting and intriguing to potential listeners.

- ✔ **Include links to all the locations mentioned in the podcast.** If you're talking about a trip to the local museum, provide a link to the museum's Web site in your show notes. If you mention another podcast, link to it. Good linking brings good karma, and it may provide some interesting and potentially helpful "Hey you linked to me!" comments (and backlinks) from others.

- ✔ **Be concise.** Remember, these are show *notes* and not show *transcripts*. Leave the colorful anecdotes for the podcast media file and keep your notes short and to the point.

Figure 8-1 displays how Robynn of the *Projekt Podkast* (projektpodkast.com) uses show notes. The notes include plenty of backlinks and a brief sentence about the conversation she had with the band members. A thing of beauty, to be sure.

When we think of show note etiquette, we're reminded of a commercial that aired years ago for a small car company. The premise was "if everyone drove one of our tiny cars, traffic congestion would vanish, the demand for fossil fuels would drop, and the world would be a generally nicer place."

We're convinced that if every podcaster followed these three simple show note guidelines, the podcasting world would be a better place. The impact on traffic jams and oil consumption remains questionable, but one can dream . . .

Figure 8-1:
Robynn
from *Projekt
Podkast*
properly
implements
show notes.

Planning the Post

The amount of time you spend planning your show notes is inversely proportional to the amount of time you spend during your show prep (see Chapter 3). For those of you who forgot everything from your Algebra II class, allow us to paraphrase: The more you prepare for your show, the less time you spend working on the show notes.

Examine the notes you used when you recorded your podcast. Did you talk about any Web sites? Find the URLs and make sure you spell them right. We highly recommend the copy-and-paste technique for URLs, rather than relying on your typing skills, especially for lengthy URLs.

If you recorded and/or edited your show hours or days before you started the notation process, replaying the media file with pen and paper at the ready is a good idea. Look for need-to-know moments and jot them down as the show plays. After it finishes, use a search engine to find additional URLs you may wish to provide to your listeners on topics included in your show.

It's all in the details

Now is a good time to figure out what level of detail you're going to employ in your show notes. Several factors can influence your decision, and audience expectation and personal choice are among the more important.

Here's a good rule: The deeper you dive in to a single topic, the less detailed your notes need to be. That may sound counterintuitive, and please keep in mind this is only a general rule and not cannon law. For example, if your podcast episode features a 20-minute interview with Sir Arthur C. Clarke about the symbolic differences between _2001: A Space Odyssey_ the novel and the movie, you likely won't have much more than a link to buy the book and/or rent the movie.

Show note details serve two primary purposes:

- ✔ To act as a table of contents for the episode
- ✔ To allow listeners to skip ahead if they so chose

As the podcaster, you can decide how much or how little you embrace these purposes. Here are some approaches that other podcasters have adopted:

- ✔ **Add a time stamp.** Some podcasters, such as Dawn and Drew (`dawnanddrew.com`), put the exact time stamp of when they change topics, which is quite frequently. Time stamps can be quite helpful to your listeners if you cover a wide range of topics in a given episode, and want to assist possible listeners in jumping around.

- ✔ **Write your show notes in complete sentences and paragraphs.** Taking cues from the world of blogging, many podcasters follow a similar approach to Kris Smith of _The Croncast_ (`croncast.com`). Kris writes his show notes in prose, using complete sentences and paragraphs in place of bullet points and time stamps. This approach feels better to potential readers, giving them a flavor of the show without having to listen. However, we've also heard listeners complain that key elements are difficult to find in this format.

- ✔ **Create more than a one-line summary.** Still other podcasters, such as Dave Winer (`morningcoffeenotes.com`) take the opposite approach, and post a simple one-liner that isn't much more than a title. We suggest new podcasters not follow his lead, as it doesn't do much for helping attract new listeners. Dave is a seminal figure in the world of podcasting and gets most of his listeners because he's Dave Winer, not because he posts great show notes.

A picture is worth a thousand words

Some podcasters include a representative image or two in their show notes. While random graphics only serve to increase your bandwidth consumption and clutter your page, well-selected images can add flavor and dimension to your show notes.

Before you add an image to your post, keep in mind these three considerations:

- ✔ **Is the image protected by copyright?** Posting someone else's creative work without first securing permission (which may include royalties and fees) is stealing, pure and simple, and can land even the most well-meaning podcaster in a heap of legal trouble.

- ✔ **Can you link directly to the image, or do you need to copy it to your server?** Some sites, such as Amazon.com, allow you do link directly to images as they sit on the Web site. These sites have a huge technology infrastructure and can handle remote hosting images that appear on other sites. But many smaller and personal sites can't handle the load a popular podcast or blog can put on their systems if they allowed direct linking to their stored images. In these cases, copy the image to your own server before adding it to your page. If you're going to do this, it's good karma to provide an "image courtesy of . . ." link to the original site. Again, this assumes you've received the appropriate permissions to copy the file. When in doubt, don't.

- ✔ **Does the image fit on your page?** Images too small or too large aren't doing your listeners any favors. Make sure the image you select is the right size. You can add `width=x height=x` declarations to your image tags to control the size, but keep in mind that this distorts the image. Previewing your post with resized images is a must. If your HTML is a little rusty, check out *HTML 4 For Dummies,* by Ed Tittel and Mary Burmeister (Wiley), for additional help.

We can't stress enough how important it is that you not take, post, modify, or use any image without the express permission of the copyright owners. The act of someone posting an image to a Web site does not give you carte blanche to use it as you see fit. When in doubt, leave it out.

Posting Your Show Notes

If you've planned and prepared, posting your podcast is easy. And if you've decided for the minimalist approach or don't really care to utilize show notes, this process can go quickly as well.

In this section, we show you how to enter your show notes by using Movable Type and Libsyn as examples. If you use another tool to make your posts, or if you create your notes by hand, you still get value out of these examples as we show you things to consider along the way.

Posting in Movable Type

Follow these steps to post show notes in Movable Type (`www.movabletype.org`):

1. **Create a new entry.**

   Click New Entry from the navigation bar or choose Main Menu⇨Create Entry.

2. **In the Title text box, enter the title of your podcast.**

   We cover some titling tips in a moment. For now, simply enter a basic description of what this episode is about. "Fishing trip to Alaska" for example.

3. **Chose the appropriate category for the podcast from the Primary Category drop-down list.**

   Evo uses the highly descriptive Shows category to segregate podcast entries from regular text entries for his blog. You may have a different setup, so choose accordingly.

4. **In the Entry Body text box, type your detailed show notes.**

   Follow a chronological order and list the various topics covered in your show, one on each line. Be sure and add URLs to any Web sites you mention. Movable Type makes this easy with the HTML editing buttons at the top of the Entry Body box (see Figure 8-2).

   These buttons may not display for you if you're on a Mac and you use Safari. Chances are, other browsers may not be able to display these buttons. If that happens to you, try Firefox (`www.mozilla.org/products/firefox`).

   Many podcasters use a hybrid approach to show notes, including general notes in the Entry Body section, with more detailed notes, complete with time stamps and links, in the Extended Entry section. This cuts down on clutter for the resulting posts, while enabling those who wish to access the more detailed nuts and bolts of a particular episode. Others make extensive use of the Excerpt and Keywords sections. If you want to, go ahead!

5. **Add the link to your podcast media file.**

   In Chapter 7, we show you how to move your podcast media files to a server on the Web. Now we put that to good use.

   a. On a new line, type a text description for your link.

      This can be your choice, but to keep this simple we recommend `Download this show`.

   b. Highlight the portion of the text you want to link.

Click to add a hyperlink

Figure 8-2:
Movable
Type makes
adding
HTML to
your posts
as easy as a
click of a
button.

For illustration purposes, use your cursor to highlight *this show* on the line of text you just created.

c. Create the link by clicking the hyperlink button, shown in Figure 8-2.

The Enter URL window appears, as shown in Figure 8-3.

Figure 8-3:
Enter a URL
to create a
hyperlink to
a podcast
media file.

d. Enter the URL of the podcast media file. Then click OK.

Don't remove the `http://`. Type the full path to the file, such as `http://www.mysite.com/media/MS001_103105.mp3`.

Your notes now contain a properly hyperlinked reference to your podcast media files. Figure 8-4 shows a fully filled out New Entry window, utilizing the Extended Entry field as well.

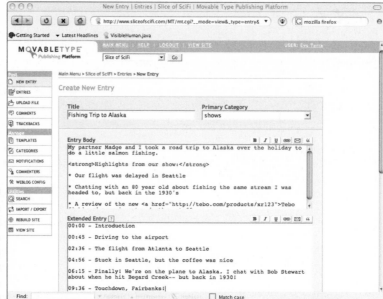

Figure 8-4:
Completed
Movable
Type screen
with show
notes.

In the next chapter, you find out about creating the RSS 2.0 feed so that people can subscribe to your podcast. Assuming you've installed the MT-Enclosures plug-in, Movable Type makes RSS feeds easy. Don't worry about it for now because we cover it in detail in Chapter 9.

6. Click the Preview button to see a sample of how the post will look when it's published.

Make sure you typed your URLs right and check your spelling and spacing. If you see anything that needs fixing, click the Re-edit This Entry link and make your corrections.

7. Click Save This Entry to publish the post.

The post is published to your site, and the process of creating your properly constructed RSS 2.0 file is started (which we cover in depth in Chapter 9).

8. Check your site.

Visiting your Web page is a good idea to make sure everything looks as you expected it to. If it doesn't, simply edit the post and resave your changes.

Posting on Libsyn

Because Libsyn (`www.libsyn.com`) is a dedicated podcast hosting provider, the steps are quite intuitive and a bit different than those used by bloggers.

1. **To create a new post, click the** `podcast/blog` **tab or the link of the same name from the main page.**

2. **Select the Podcast radio button.**

   Libsyn also allows text-only posts to the site. Great for times when you want to post some text without a media file, such as to say "I'm on vacation for the next two weeks . . ."

3. **Choose a category for your podcast from the Category drop-down list.**

   Categories on Libsyn work like they do with most blogging applications. To keep this simple, choose Podcast from the list.

4. **Enter a title for this episode.**

   We cover some titling tips later in this section. For now, simply enter a basic description of what this episode is about — "Fishing trip to Alaska" for example.

5. **Skip the Post Image drop-down list for now.**

   Yes, you can put something in there if you must. But it's not required. See our earlier comments on using images in this chapter if you decide you can't live without one. (But you probably could . . .)

6. **Enter the detailed show notes in the Post Body text box.**

   This is the appropriate place for your detailed show notes. Follow a chronological order and list the various topics covered in your show, one on each line. Be sure and add URLs to any Web sites you mention.

   Simply typing the URL in this section isn't quite as effective as providing a true hyperlink. Making a hyperlink isn't difficult, though it may look that way to those not familiar with the mysteries of HTML.

   Hyperlinks follow this convention:

   ```
   <a href="link/to/website/or/web/page">Name of link</a>
   ```

   Basically, you fill out what's between the quotes, replace the name of the link, and you're done. Here are a few real-world examples:

   ```
   <a href="http://dragonpage.com">The Dragon Page</a>
   <a href="http://teemorris.com/podcast">Morevi podcast</a>
   <a href="http://marsrovers.nasa.gov/gallery/images.html">Pictures from
           Mars</a>
   ```

7. Chose your podcast media file from the drop-down list.

If you haven't uploaded the show yet, Libsyn makes it easy. Simply click the Browse button and navigate to the appropriate file in your media folder (which we show how to set up in Chapter 7).

8. Select the Auto Ping check box.

This helps spread the word about your podcast, telling audio.weblogs. com that a new episode of your show is ready. We talk more about pings in Chapter 10.

Because Libsyn doesn't allow you to preview your post first, we highly recommend checking your spelling and double-checking your links before you proceed. An ounce of prevention and all that. Figure 8-5 shows how your post looks on Libsyn before it is posted.

9. Click the Post button.

Libsyn makes it hard to screw up, requiring you to fill out the appropriate fields before allowing you to continue. If you're successful, you see a nice green check box next to your brand new post.

10. Check your page.

Click the link to your show name and see how it looks in the real world. Check your links, spelling, and layout. If it's not the way you want it, close the window and click the name of your post to edit it further.

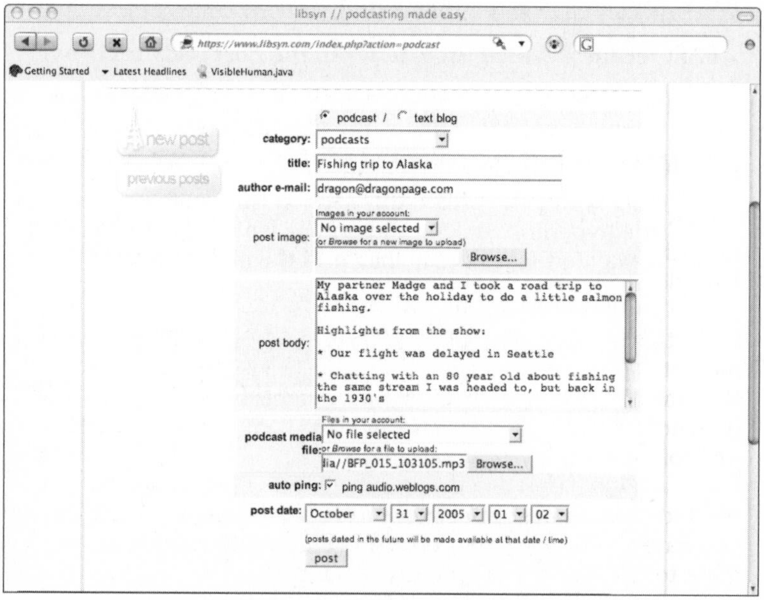

Figure 8-5:
Filling out
show notes
on Libsyn.

Boosting Search Engine Rankings with Good Show Notes

One of the more tangible benefits of quality show notes is the impact they can have on your listings within search engines. With the exception of brand-new search engines such as Podscope (`podscope.com`), traditional search engines cannot (yet) scan and index the contents of your podcast media files. As such, you need to provide text for the search engine spiders and bots to examine and evaluate for index inclusion.

We go into more detail about spiders and bots in Chapter 11. For now, you just need to know that they are simply tools that search engines use to find and present interesting information when people search for a particular topic.

Podcasters can learn a lot of tips and tricks from bloggers and other Web site owners on how to boost search engine rankings. Many include page-level changes to positioning of elements, correct usage of headings, meta and image tags, and backlinking techniques. All of that conversation is far beyond the scope of this book. Grab a copy of *Search Engine Optimization For Dummies* by Peter Kent (published by Wiley) and break out your code editor if you want to make a bigger splash.

In this section, we show you some best practices to implement right away that can make your notes (and podcast) more accessible to search engines — and ultimately search engine users.

Loading up your titles

Search engines (and searchers) pay close attention to titles. You should consider the title of your individual podcast episodes every bit as important as the title of a given Web page.

Important as they are, most podcasters struggle with effective titles. The biggest problem comes from confusing titles with descriptions. If your title starts with "In this episode . . . ," stop right there. You're writing the description, not the title. A title is a string of well-chosen and crafted words that has no room for superfluous baggage.

We find that the best titles come from a re-examination of your show notes. If you haven't made your notes yet, you may find coming up with a solid title quite tough. Here's the process we suggest:

1. **Read your show notes and pull out the key elements, thoughts, or themes covered on the show.**

2. **When you have your list of elements, try to boil each of them down to a single word or phrase, if possible.**

   Think about the types of people who might be interested in the contents of your show, and pick common words they are likely to search on.

Using the Alaskan fishing trip from earlier in this chapter, we've come up with the following completely made-up topics and themes from an imaginary show:

- ✔ Sleeping in the Seattle airport while the flight was delayed

- ✔ Interesting discussion with 80 year-old angler during the flight

- ✔ Great success with a Tebo XR-123 Kevlar pole

- ✔ Seeing bears fishing in the same stream

- ✔ Discovering a great new recipe for salmon gumbo

- ✔ Mountain biking the last day

Okay, not the most interesting show on the planet (at least from our point of view), but you see what you can do with that.

The first step is to figure out what's important. Not just to you, but to your listeners and potential listeners. If you're a comedian, the airport delay and the old man on the plane might be good places to start. If this is a more serious fishing show, the experience with the new pole and the aged angler are the key points.

But if your show is a relatively serious outdoorsman show, and you're trying to entertain and attract like-minded anglers. Getting rid of the fluff is a good idea. You can select the key points and boil them down to the following:

   Ancient anglers, space-age fishing gear, and salmon gumbo from Alaska.

That's a solid title, giving searchers a good tease of what they can expect. Notice how it doesn't cover everything and it shouldn't try. That's the job of the description where you can go into even greater detail on those three elements, plus the many other things you talk about on the show.

The title also carries good keywords likely to be of interest to fishermen or wanna-be-fisherman considering a trip to Alaska, looking for new equipment (we have it on good authority fishermen call their equipment *gear*), and maybe even those interested in wild game cooking.

Chances are, you know your audience much better than we do. Think about how people are likely to search, and write your titles for that. Keep them short, don't try to cover everything, and employ more detailed descriptions to carry the rest of your story.

Soliciting backlinks

Backlinks are the Holy Grail of search engine optimization. A *backlink* is simply a link from one Web site to another Web site. Sites that have a lot of backlinks pointing to them are considered "more important" to the computers that control how and where your site shows up on a search engine. In order to get backlinks from others, you have to create links to their Web sites in your show notes.

In the highly suspect Alaskan fishing trip we've used throughout this chapter, you could link to several things, and a few that you really should link to. For example, you could provide a link to the airline that messed up the flight, but what's the point? On the other hand, you most certainly want to create a link to a place to buy or read more about the new gear, and likely would want to link to the outfitter.

After you make the links and post the show, you need to start soliciting backlinks:

- ✔ Write to the Tebo corporation to tell them you're posting a review of one of its products. Getting big companies to link to you doesn't always happen, but sometimes it does. And getting backlinks from big popular sites is very beneficial to your rankings.

- ✔ Send an e-mail to the outfitter you booked the trip with and maybe even the hotel.

- ✔ Notify various fishing bloggers and podcasters about the new episode. It only takes a few moments of your time and is information they would or should welcome.

A fine line exists between asking for backlinks and spamming someone. Make each e-mail personal, provide the exact link you want them to use, and tell them why you think it's important for them to link it. If you can't think of a good reason why that site should link to you, then you shouldn't ask for it.

A Word on OPML Show Notes

Hang out in the podosphere long enough, and you'll hear the cryptic acronym OPML thrown around. OPML stands for *Outline Processor Markup Language*, and it's a big part of what makes up the infrastructure used in podcasting.

It's the *O* in the acronym that matters most to viewers: outline. The output of an OPML file (when used properly) looks like an outline, but with collapsible sub-points under each main point. Programmers get all giddy at the last three letters because you can pass it lots of information along with the hierarchical arrangement of text.

OPML is both cool and powerful, but it's also esoteric in shape (by definition) and somewhat beyond the scope of this book. Still, it's good to know what it is and how the podcasting world uses it, even if you never implement it with your podcast.

Most of the directories either import their data from or export their data to OPML. When you look at a particular node in the iPodder.org directory, you're looking at information that is controlled by an OPML file. When you view the list of podcasts in the iPodderX Top Picks directory, you're viewing information that came from an OPML file.

OPML has been breaking out from being a behind-the-scenes player for nearly as long as podcasting has been around. It's been slow going, probably because most podcasters don't really see how creating OPML files can help their podcasts.

In all likelihood, most podcasters never find themselves in a situation where they're creating OPML files for their shows. They'll likely use it everyday, as OMPL creation could be built in to various applications, but only a few folks need to sit down and say "Well, it's time to create my OPML file."

OPML is a bit too technical for detailed discussion in this book, but it is worth mentioning in this chapter because it makes up such a large part of the podcasting landscape, even if podcasters and podcast listeners never notice it.

For more information on OPML, we recommend going straight to the master himself, Dave Winer. He's created a site just for OPML at www.opml.org. It's not for the neophyte or faint of heart. But if you have development in your bones, you just might find some interesting applications for it.

Chapter 9

Geeking Out on XML and RSS

*Y*ou've entered the dark and murky waters of XML and RSS generation — a region of the podcasting sea that strikes fear into the hearts of the uninitiated, causes mild-mannered podcasting preachers to break out into curse words that would make a sailor blush, and has soured more than one would-be independent media producer on the whole prospect of podcasting.

Relax. For the most part, the trials and tribulations you might have heard others had to go through are mostly overblown. If it were as hard as some have made it out to be, there wouldn't be as many podcasts as there are available today. The XML-and-RSS step wasn't designed to be complicated, it's just quirky in that direction, and it's been tainted by the experiences of a few who jumped in a little too fast, without a trusty guide to show them the path.

This chapter shines a big bright spotlight on XML and RSS elements, showing you that they aren't as mean and scary as they've been made out to be. After reading this chapter, you'll have a solid strategy for generating your podcast's RSS 2.0 file, some options for dealing with multiple media files, and the confidence to tweak your RSS file as you see fit.

You're probably asking yourself: "Do I need to know all that"? Well, yes and no. Granted, you'll likely be using blogging software or some podcast-hosting company that takes care of the RSS 2.0 feed for you. It's still a good idea to know what goes on under the hood, in our opinion.

Getting a handle on TLAs (three-letter acronyms)

XML stands for e*X*tensible *M*arkup *L*anguage. "Markup" is a lot like what your teacher used to do to your homework, only more useful: "marking up" a text file with some special tags that control how the text is used by various applications, like a podcatching client. This is good news for those of you without advanced degrees in computer science: It's text (in this case, English or something a lot like it) that tells other text how to present itself.

"Extensible" means developers can add additional tags beyond the original "set" that was designed for XML. In other words, a developer can add to the *code base* of XML, adapting it to individual needs. Okay, feel free to forget that if you want — you won't have to worry about creating new tags, thanks to RSS 2.0.

RSS is a '"flavor" (modified version) of XML, and it stands for *Really Simple Syndication.* (*Syndication* is the process of getting the goods — whether Web site update, news bulletin, or podcast — to the intended audience.) Luckily for us podcasters, XML was extended to RSS, which was further extended to create RSS 2.0. And inside RSS 2.0 is where you find the appropriate tags and elements that make podcasts work.

You'll hear podcasters use the terms *XML* and *RSS* interchangeably. Sometimes they say the version number (2.0) out loud and in print, other times it's simply implied. There is at least one other version of XML that works with podcasting: Atom. No, it's not a TLA, because it has four letters and it doesn't stand for anything, but it is a version of XML. The good news is that most podcatching clients read either Atom or RSS 2.0 files; the differences between Atom and RSS 2.0 files are, for the purposes of this book, minimal. In fact, advanced RSS 2.0 feeds often incorporate Atom elements, further blurring the differences between the two formats. To minimize headaches, this chapter focuses on RSS 2.0 as the preferred method of syndicating your podcast to podcatching clients. And yes, iTunes fans, we do cover the extra tags your podcatcher of choice has made us all deal with.

If you want an even deeper dive into the world of RSS syndication — because you can do some *really* cool stuff with it — we highly recommend Ellen Finkelstein's *Syndicating Web Sites with RSS Feeds For Dummies* (Wiley Publishing, Inc.).

Elements That Make the RSS Go 'Round

The main function of your RSS 2.0 file is to distribute your media files to people who have subscribed to your podcast. RSS is nothing more than "marked up" text with special tags. (For more about the technical aspects of RSS, check out the nearby sidebar.) Here's a sample RSS 2.0 feed:

```
<?xml version="1.0"?>
<rss version="2.0" xmlns:content="http://purl.org/rss/1.0/modules/content/"
          xmlns:itunes="http://www.itunes.com/DTDs/Podcast-1.0.dtd">
<channel>
  <title>The Great Outdoors Podcast</title>
```

```
<link>http://www.mypodcast.com/</link>
<description>The best podcast on the planet. Period. With your host,
          me!</description>
<webMaster>evo@mypodcast.com</webMaster>
<managingEditor>evo@mypodcast.com (Evo Terra)</managingEditor>
<pubDate>Mon, 31 Oct 2005 12:02:28 -0800</pubDate>
<category>Outdoors</category>
  <image>
    <url>http://mypodcast.com/images/logos/tDPWi100x86.jpg</url>
    <width>100</width>
    <height>86</height>
    <title>The Great Outdoors Podcast</title>
    <link>http://mypodcast.com</link>
  </image>
  <copyright>Creative Commons Attribution 2.5 License</copyright>
<language>en-us</language>
<docs>http://blogs.law.harvard.edu/tech/rss</docs>

<!-- iTunes specific namespace channel elements -->
<itunes:subtitle>The best podcast on the planet. Period. With your host,
          Me!</itunes:subtitle>
<itunes:summary>This podcast blows the doors off all other podcasts that have
          ever come before or who will try afterwards. I'm not kidding. It's
          that informative and earth shattering. You'll
          see...</itunes:summary>
<itunes:owner>
  <itunes:email>evo@mypodcast.com</itunes:email>
  <itunes:name>Evo Terra</itunes:name>
</itunes:owner>
<itunes:author>Evo Terra</itunes:author>
<itunes:category text="International">
    <itunes:category text="Canadian" />
</itunes:category>
<itunes:category text="Sports" />
<itunes:link rel="image" type="video/jpeg"
          href="http://mypodcast.com/images/logos/tDPWI300x300.jpg">The
          Great Outdoors Podcast</itunes:link>
<itunes:explicit>no</itunes:explicit>

  <item>
  <title>TGOP 013 - Ancient anglers, space age fishing gear and salmon gumbo
          from Alaska.</title>
  <link>http://www.mypodcast.com/tgop013.html</link>
  <comments>http://www.mypodcast.com/tgop13.html#comments</comments>
  <description>Show Notes Cabin Fever Outfitters is the company that booked
          this trip. Can't recommend them highly enough! I had a great time
          catching fish and exploring the great Alaskan wilderness on a
          mountain bike. And you won't want to miss my review of the Tebo
          XR-123 Kevlar pole that I used to land the big one! Download The
          Great Outdoors Podcast Episode #13</description>
  <guid isPermaLink="false">1808@http://www.mypodcast.com/</guid>
  <pubDate>Mon, 31 Oct 2005 12:02:28 -0800</pubDate>
<category>Outdoors</category>
```

```
<author>editor@muypodcast.com</author>
<enclosure url="http://mypodcast.com/media/TGOP013_10312005.mp3"
           length="24849394" type="audio/mpeg" />

<!-- RDF 1.0 specific namespace item attribute -->
<content:encoded><![CDATA[<p><strong>Show Notes</strong></p>

<p><a href="http://www.cabinfever.com/">Cabin Fever Outfitters</a> is the
           company that booked this trip. Can't recommend them highly enough!

<p>I had a great time catching fish and exploring the great Alaskan
           wilderness on a mountain bike. And you won't want to miss my
           review of the <a
           href="http://tebofhishing.com/products/XR123.html">Tebo XR-123
           Kevlar pole</a> that I used to land the big one!</p>

<p>Download <a href="http://mypodcast.com/media/TGOP013_10312005.mp3">The
           Great Outdoors Podcast Episode #13</a></p>]]></content:encoded>

<!-- iTunes specific namespace item attributes -->
<itunes:author>Evo Terra</itunes:author>
<itunes:subtitle>My recent trip to Alaska, plus my
           adventures.</itunes:subtitle>
<itunes:summary> Show Notes Cabin Fever Outfitters is the company that
           booked this trip. Can't recommend them highly enough! I had a
           great time catching fish and exploring the great Alaskan
           wilderness on a mountain bike. And you won't want to miss my
           review of the Tebo XR-123 Kevlar pole that I used to land the big
           one! Download The Great Outdoors Podcast Episode
           #13</itunes:summary>
   <itunes:category text="International">
       <itunes:category text="Canadian" />
   </itunes:category>
   <itunes:category text="Sports" />
   <itunes:duration>00:45:00</itunes:duration>
   <itunes:explicit>no</itunes:explicit>
   <itunes:keywords>outdoors fishing Tebo salmon mountain
           biking</itunes:keywords>
   </item>
   </channel>
 </rss>
```

Okay, that's a lot to digest in a single sitting. The next sections of the book break it down into individual parts to show you how un-scary it really is.

If you're currently using (or planning to use) software to generate your RSS 2.0 feed, it'll take care of just about all this brouhaha for you. It's still a good idea, however, to have solid grasp of this section in the event you want to make some modifications to your RSS 2.0 feed in the future. (Most podcasters do, sooner or later.)

Well, your "feed generator" may not be of much help with the iTunes-specific stuff. iTunes burst on to the podcasting scene without much advanced notice (read: ANY). And when it did, it came up with unique tags instead of reusing what RSS 2.0 already provided. Take a good hard look at the tool you are using to generate your RSS feed and see if it has any iTunes-specific tags. If not, you may have to break out the manual and see how you can add them yourself. It's scarier than it sounds, trust us.

Do you have anything to declare?

All RSS 2.0 documents should start with a *declaration statement.* Think of this declaration as working with a "Hello, my name is . . ." badge. This statement identifies the contents of the file, allowing podcatching clients and other XML parsers or readers to know what to expect and how to handle the contents. Some declarations wear their hearts on their sleeves, some are terse, but all RSS 2.0 documents do the initial honors with these first two lines of text:

```
<?xml version="1.0"?>
<rss version="2.0" xmlns:content="http://purl.org/rss/1.0/modules/content/"
          xmlns:itunes="http://www.itunes.com/DTDs/Podcast-1.0.dtd">
```

With those two lines of text, you've declared that the document is written in XML version 1.0 and is of the special flavor RSS 2.0. Additionally, it calls out two specialized *namespaces,* which we get into in a bit. You might want to write those two lines on your forehead backward (metaphorically speaking, of course) so you'll always see 'em in the mirror as a reminder: They are what you use to start every RSS 2.0 file you create as a podcaster.

A *namespace* is denoted by the `xmlns:` statement, followed by the URL of the "home" of the namespace. In the preceding instance, we call the namespaces for the *encoded content* module as well as iTunes tags. Purists will argue that *encoded* content isn't necessary and that even the iTunes tags are optional. But they both go a long way toward getting your podcast listened to by the most people.

What's on this <channel>?

An RSS 2.0 document contains a single `<channel>` statement, complete with lots of other information to help describe the channel. A channel can contain multiple `<item>` statements, and each `<item>` can have lots of other information to describe the individual item.

Okay, here's a real-world example to clarify the issue: NBC is a "channel" on your television. Depending on the day of the week and the time of the day, various different "items" are made available for viewing. It's not an accident that podcasting works the same way.

In the following sections, we examine the contents of the `<channel>` declaration from the example at the beginning of the chapter. (We cover `<item>` tags in the later section "Loading up on `<items>`s.")

<title> tag

You use the `<title>` tag to hold the title of your channel or the title of your overall podcast. Here's the title from the example just given:

```
<title>The Great Outdoors Podcast</title>
```

This line of text says, "Here's what's inside me." It never changes, unless you decide to change the name of your podcast. Don't abbreviate or shorten the name unless you have a very good reason for doing that.

Almost every markup language uses this format of beginning and ending tags encapsulated in angle brackets, or greater-than and less-than signs. The ending tag uses the same name, but it's preceded by a / character to tell the software that the tag is now closed. In the example just given, you can think of the code as talking to the podcatching client, along these lines: "(The next thing you'll read is the title.) `The Great Outdoors Podcast` (That was the end of the title.)"

<link> entry

Here's a good place to put a link that leads back to your Web site or blog. The beauty of RSS and podcasting is that the listeners don't have to be looking at your Web page to listen to your show. This link allows them (through their podcatching clients) an easy way to find your Web site if they so desire:

```
<link>http://www.mypodcast.com/</link>
```

<description> entry

Your description, much like your title, will rarely (if ever) change. Find a good description for what your shows are about. The following example is pretty poor (just kidding, okay?), so try to put in some words that truly identify what your podcast is about:

```
<description>The best podcast on the planet. Period. With your host,
          me!</description>
```

<webMaster> and <managingEditor> entries

The Webmaster is the person responsible for the technical accuracy of the information contained in the feed. The managing editor is the person responsible for the messaging and content contained within the tags. For most podcasters, these both reflect the same e-mail address. Note that the `<managingEditor>` tag requires a name in parentheses to follow the e-mail address.

Okay, maybe the words `webMaster` and `managingEditor` aren't a perfect fit with podcasting, but including an e-mail address for the person responsible for this feed as well as the content is an excellent idea. We've e-mailed the keepers of various feeds to report problems we've encountered with their feeds — and each one has been very appreciative. Although having that information can help improve the podcasting experience for everyone, many feeds don't provide contact information. If you make it easy for people to help you, you're ahead of the game. Include a valid e-mail address in your feed.

```
<webMaster>evo@mypodcast.com</webMaster>
<managingEditor>evo@mypodcast.com (Evo Terra)</managingEditor>
```

<pubDate> entry

At the `<channel>` level, this tag indicates the last time the feed was updated. It is very important that you follow the correct convention when adding this element — you can't just put any old date in here.

Getting the `<pubDate>` (publication date) correct is terribly important, but it's often overlooked by podcasters in a hurry. Don't fall into this trap. Include a publication date and make sure you do it right:

```
<pubDate>Mon, 31 Oct 2005 12:02:28 -0800</pubDate>
```

The publication date is being utilized by more listing sites and directories as a way to show fresh content. Don't be stale; use the publication date.

The `<pubDate>` element must follow the RFC #822 guidelines (`asg.web.cmu.edu/rfc/rfc822.html`), which are simply:

```
[day of week], [day of month] [month] [year] [24 hour time] [time zone (GMT)]
```

Simple as that may be, you have to follow the correct naming convention for each of those elements. Table 9-1 shows how.

Table 9-1	Proper `<pubDate>` Elements
Day of Week	*Month*
Mon	Jan
Tue	Feb
Wed	Mar
Thu	Apr
Fri	May

(continued)

Table 9-1 (continued)

Day of Week	Month
Sat	Jun
Sun	Jul
	Aug
	Sep
	Oct
	Nov
	Dec

The day of the week is always expressed in double digits, adding a zero in front of any single-digit numbers (for example, 03 instead of 3), and the year is always expressed in four digits. (Well, at least it will be for the next 8,000 years or so, and then we'll just have to do something different.)

The big stumbling block with <pubDate> tends to be the time and zone:

✔ The time should always be expressed in 24-hour or military time, (HH:MM:SS). Again, add zeros in front if necessary (for example, 03:07:02 is correct).

✔ The time zone isn't represented by everyday abbreviations such as PST. Instead, it's referenced from GMT, or *Greenwich Mean Time*. (That's a city in England where the International Date Line passes through, not a small village on the east coast of the United States.) Podcasters in California are in either -0800 or -0700 (that's 8 or 7 hours earlier than GMT, respectively) depending on whether Daylight Saving Time is in effect.

Don't sweat the time stamp too hard. You should be changing the date every time you put up a new episode, but even if you had to hard-code the time stamp to 12:00:00 -0800, you wouldn't have a problem with it. Chances are, your RSS 2.0 is generated automatically, so time stamping should not be an issue.

<category> entry

Though the original drafters of RSS 2.0 had something very specific in mind, the <category> tag has become pretty much a free-for-all. If your podcast has an industry-recognized category, use that. If not, make it up! That's what we did in our example:

```
<category>Outdoors</category>
```

<image> tag

This optional RSS tag provides a graphical representation of your podcast. It actually contains several subelements that further describe the image. They are

- ✔ **URL:** The location of your image (in GIF, JPEG, or PNG format) on a Web server.

- ✔ **Width:** The width of your image, up to 144 pixels.

- ✔ **Height:** The height of your image, up to 400 pixels.

- ✔ **Title:** This text describes the image, but most people just describe their podcast again, because that's what the image should do anyhow.

- ✔ **Link:** The link to your Web site — just because you needed to put that in one more place. Can you say "overkill"?

All these elements, when used together, result in something very much like this:

```
<image>
  <url>http://mypodcast.com/images/logos/tDPWi100x86.jpg</url>
  <width>100</width>
  <height>86</height>
  <title>The Great Outdoors Podcast</title>
  <link>http://mypodcast.com</link>
</image>
```

<copyright> tag

Here's where you can list the copyright information about your podcast. It's free-form text, so you'll want to include all the narrative necessary to get your copyright information across. We use Creative Commons (more on that in Chapter 4) to retain some rights to our podcasts, yet allow for some additional freedom that is difficult with conventional "all rights reserved" notices.

```
<copyright>Creative Commons Attribution 2.5 License</copyright>
```

<language> entry

While the file itself is written in the RSS 2.0 flavor of the RSS language, the "human language" should also be declared:

```
<language>en-us</language>
```

If your podcast is not in English, see `blogs.law.harvard.edu/tech/stories/storyReader$15` for the appropriate code to use in this section.

<docs> entry

This is simply a link to the document that describes what RSS 2.0 is all about. This entry is optional, but including it is considered good form. In the unlikely event your feed is picked up by a developer who hasn't adapted his application to accept the RSS 2.0 standard, you're being a good global citizen and pointing him in the right direction. Think of this as the Rosetta Stone of your podcast feed.

```
<docs>http://blogs.law.harvard.edu/tech/rss</docs>
```

<itunes:subtitle> entry

This is what iTunes uses to populate the Description column of its application. It should be a collection of a few choice words about your podcast. We recommend simply mirroring the `<title>` tag.

```
<itunes:subtitle>The best podcast on the planet. Period. With your host,
            Me!</itunes:subtitle>
```

<itunes:summary> entry

Apple says you have up to 4,000 words in this entry. This content is featured prominently when your podcast is selected by someone interested in your show. Sounds like a repeat of the `<description>` tag to us.

```
<itunes:summary>This podcast blows the doors off all other podcasts that have
            ever come before or who will try afterwards. I'm not kidding.
            It's that informative and earth shattering. You'll see...
            </itunes:summary>.
```

<itunes:owner> and <itunes:author> entries

On the surface, it may seem we're repeating the same thing with `<webMaster>` and `<managingEditor>` described earlier in this chapter . . . no, wait. This *is* pretty much a repeat of that.

iTunes uses the `<itunes:author>` tag to power the Artist listing inside of iTunes. `<itunes:owner>` doesn't publicly display anywhere and is simply a way to identify who is responsible for the feed (much like the `webMaster` tag, again). `<itunes:owner>` has two subelements: `<itunes:name>` and `<itunes:email>`.

```
<itunes:owner>
    <itunes:email>evo@mypodcast.com</itunes:email>
    <itunes:name>Evo Terra</itunes:name>
</itunes:owner>
<itunes:author>Evo Terra</itunes:author>
```

<itunes:category> entries

Pay close attention here, folks, because this is another area that gets fouled up more times than we care to count. You can't make this one up — it has to follow Apple iTunes categories.

Look at the categories inside of iTunes and find out where your podcast belongs before starting this step. iTunes is a free download, and you have to install it in order to see what categories you have to choose from. Get it at www.apple.com/itunes/.

Some categories have subcategories, and both are handled a bit differently when it comes to tagging. If you find a subcategory you belong to, you have to identify not only the subcategory, but also the parent category as well. For this bogus feed we've built, we've selected a category/subcategory pair as well as a category that has no subs so you can see how each is coded:

```
<itunes:category text="International">
  <itunes:category text="Canadian" />
</itunes:category>
<itunes:category text="Sports" />
```

Notice how `"Canadian"` is nested between the beginning and ending tags for `"International"`. Because `"Sports"` has no subcategory associated with it, the tag has its ending / at the end of a tag, itself, just as you see with `"Canadian"`.

<itunes:link> entry

Continuing to do its own thing, Apple ignored the RSS `<image>` tag and came up with its own to better match the album art already used within iTunes.

This tag is made up of several different declarations, all of which you must follow if you want your artwork to show up inside of iTunes:

- `rel="image"`: This tells iTunes that the link in question is really an image file. It's not the most intuitive thing in the world, but you work with what you have.

- `type="video/jpeg"`: With this tag, iTunes knows that the image is a JPEG. Bet you didn't know that JPEG was originally used as a video format. Neither did we. If you decide to use the PNG format, you need to change the statement to `type="image/png"`. Regardless of your format, iTunes prefers images that are 300 pixels by 300 pixels in size.

- `href="[URL of your image]"`: This is a link to the image.

- Yet another title-like statement: Make it easy on yourself and just use the name of your podcast.

When it's all over with, you should have something that looks very much like this:

```
<itunes:link rel="image" type="video/jpeg"
          href="http://mypodcast.com/images/logos/tDPWI300x300.jpg">The
          Great Outdoors Podcast</itunes:link>
```

<itunes:explicit> entry

Apple has a kid-friendly reputation to uphold. And because it already has a huge 20-million-plus subscriber base, it doesn't want to allow any unsavory podcasts to fall into younger hands. Already having developed the `<explicit>` tag for songs designed for mature audiences, Apple simply extended that tag to the podcasting world.

Two possible values exist for this tag: yes or no. If you drop the F-bomb on your show, fess up and put a `yes` value in this tag. If you're so squeaky clean that people could eat off your podcasting rig, you still include the tag, but your value is `no`.

```
<itunes:explicit>no</itunes:explicit>
```

Loading up on <item>s

Now that the channel has been defined, it's time to talk about the individual items contained within the channel. An *item* is (in this case) an individual podcast episode. If you have three shows available for download on your Web site, you have three distinct `<item>` declarations in your file.

Chapter 8 sums up the pros and cons of making all your shows available. If you have the server space and the bandwidth to handle it, go right ahead. If not, you'll want to include only the most recent podcasts in your feed. You can control that with the items you include in your RSS 2.0 feed.

True to form, each of your podcast episodes starts off with the item declaration: `<item>`.

<title> tag

Much like your channel, each `<item>` element also has a title. In this case, it's the title of the episode:

```
<title>TGOP 013 - Ancient anglers, space age fishing gear and salmon gumbo from
          Alaska.</title>
```

Some podcasters prefer to put in some recurring text to identify their podcast (in this case, TGOP); others choose not to. It really is a matter of choice.

After you decide on a naming convention for your podcast episodes, try and stick with it. Listeners will grow comfortable with seeing your show display on their MP3 players or computer folders in a certain way. If you randomly change how you name your episodes, your audience may no longer recognize the files as yours. While there is no rule against changing, you might want to warn your audience before you do so.

<link> tag

Earlier in the chapter, we show you how to provide a link to your main podcast Web site. Here you're providing a link to the specific page where listeners can find your show notes and other information about this particular episode:

```
<link>http://www.mypodcast.com/tgop013.html</link>
```

<comments> tag

If you collect and display comments from your listeners on particular episodes of your podcast, provide a link to that specific page. For many, the <comments> URL is the same as the <link> tag. In our example, it's slightly different:

```
<comments>http://www.mypodcast.com/tgop13.html#comments</comments>
```

<description> tag

This tag works here in the <item> statement as it does in the <channel> statement. It is used to provide detailed information about the episode. This is the place for your show notes.

```
<description>Show Notes Cabin Fever Outfitters is the company that booked this
             trip. Can't recommend them highly enough! I had a great time
             catching fish and exploring the great Alaskan wilderness on a
             mountain bike. And you won't want to miss my review of the Tebo
             XR-123 Kevlar pole that I used to land the big one! Download The
             Great Outdoors Podcast Episode #13</description>
```

<guid> element

GUID stands for *global unique identifier*. Well, okay, *global* may not be the best word here, but that's what it is; don't worry — you don't have to pick something that's one-of-a-kind-in-the-entire-universe. But you should pick something that makes this entry unique to your RSS file. Here's an example:

```
<guid isPermaLink="false">1808@http://www.mypodcast.com/</guid>
```

In this example, a sequential, non-repeating number is added to the beginning of the URL of the Web site. Each time a new <item> goes in the file, the number is incremented by one. This helps the podcatching clients figure out whether a file is new. If a podcatching client has already seen the GUID for this particular podcast, it doesn't download the file. If it has never seen the GUID associated with this podcast, it downloads the show.

You can generate a GUID lots of ways. In reality, most people use a program to help generate the RSS file, and the GUID is automatically taken care of. In the event that it is not, you can just use the URL of the podcast media file for this episode, assuming you use a good filenaming convention, and you don't plan on repeating the filename anytime in the future.

<pubDate> entry

This tag shows when the podcast episode was published. Just like in the `<channel>` statement, make sure you follow the right convention. Assuming you have more than one `<item>` in your feed, each item has its own different `<pubDate>`.

```
<pubDate>Mon, 31 Oct 2005 12:02:28 -0800</pubDate>
```

<author> tag

This is simply the e-mail address of the person who created the content. For most podcasters, this is the same in each `<item>` in the feed. But if you're making a compilation where you repurpose content created by others, you may wish to put their e-mail address in here. The choice is yours.

```
<author>editor@mypodcast.com</author>
```

<enclosure> element

Chapter 2 provides a brief rundown of how the `<enclosure>` element makes podcasting possible — but now (finally) we come to that sacred piece of code. We hope you're not too disappointed when you see how simple it is:

```
<enclosure url="http://mypodcast.com/media/TGOP013_10312005.mp3"
           length="24849394" type="audio/mpeg" />
```

Hardly seems worth the fuss, does it? Believe it or not, this is the main thing that makes your podcasts automatically download to your listeners' desktops and MP3 players. The enclosure tag contains three elements:

- ✔ `url`: A link to the podcast media file.

- ✔ `length`: The length of the file. In this case, `length` is synonymous with file size, expressed in bytes.

- ✔ `type`: The standard MIME type of the media file referenced in the link. Podcasting works with a variety of media types. The example is for audio files saved in MP3 format. You can enclose video files (and even BitTorrent files), but to do that successfully, first you need to determine the appropriate MIME type for your preferred media file.

<content:encoded> tag

Earlier we show you how to put your show notes in your feed by using the `<description>` tag; this is just straight text, without any images, formatting, or hyperlinks. The most correct way to include these extras is to use the `<content:encoded>` tag.

Technically, the RSS 2.0 specifications allow you to place images, links, and even text formatting inside the `<description>` tag. However, there is some question as to how many of the podcatcher developers have allowed for that. Be safe. Keep straight text in your `<description>` and use this new tag to pass HTML.

You want good-quality show notes on your Web site and in your RSS feed — complete with URLs that lead to the various Web sites. So it's time to do something special (okay, sneaky) to avoid breaking any XML laws.

XML is pretty picky about which characters are allowed and which ones aren't. After all, show notes are written to be read by a human being, not an XML program — and human language just has a lot more stuff in it. If (for example) you want to put in quotes, ampersands, apostrophes, and other characters that are considered illegal inside XML, you have to use a Get Out of Jail Free card in the form of this statement:

```
<![CDATA[]]>
```

The `<![CDATA[]]>` statement informs the XML reader that the contents contained within the `[ ]` symbols are *not* XML and should not be treated as such. Some older XML readers just skip such contents altogether. But every RSS and XML reader we've seen switches over to HTML mode and displays the information properly — links, images, and all. As it should be.

So if you really want your description to read: "'There's trouble & danger ahead,' said the Cap'n" — quirky, isn't it? — you have two options:

XML-Encoded:

```
<description>&quot;&apos;There&apos;s trouble &amp; danger ahead&quot;, said the
          Cap&apos;n&quot;</description>
```

Using CDATA:

```
<content:encoded><![CDATA["'There's trouble & danger ahead', said the
          Cap'n"]]></content:encoded>
```

Now, which way are you going to choose? Both approaches give you the same results. One probably gives you a headache.

You can go about *escaping* or encoding illegal characters inside your XML in other ways. You can find more information about that in *Syndicating Web Sites with RSS Feeds For Dummies,* or at

```
www.w3schools.com/xml/xml_encoding.asp
```

For now, it's easier to tell the XML reader to lighten up and deal with the text as is.

<itunes:author> tag

You guessed it — yet another iTunes tag that looks amazingly like a standard RSS 2.0 tag. Hey, we didn't write the spec. We're just telling you how to implement it.

```
<itunes:author>Evo Terra</itunes:author>
```

<itunes:subtitle> and <itunes:summary> tags

The same rules apply here as did in the `<channel>` section. In this case, you are describing a single episode of your show in both short and long versions, respectively.

```
<itunes:subtitle>My recent trip to Alaska, plus my adventures.</itunes:subtitle>
<itunes:summary> Show Notes Cabin Fever Outfitters is the company that booked
            this trip. Can't recommend them highly enough! I had a great time
            catching fish and exploring the great Alaskan wilderness on a
            mountain bike. And you won't want to miss my review of the Tebo
            XR-123 Kevlar pole that I used to land the big one! Download The
            Great Outdoors Podcast Episode #13</itunes:summary>
```

<itunes:category> tags

Just as with the `<channel>` section, it's important to get this right:

```
<itunes:category text="International">
    <itunes:category text="Canadian" />
  </itunes:category>
  <itunes:category text="Sports" />
```

<itunes:duration> tag

Finally — something brand new with an iTunes-specific tag! Remember that iTunes was originally a music distribution system. As such, the length of a particular song displays next to the title. Podcasters too are asked to provide this information. It follows the HH:MM:SS format.

If you use software to help build your file, you may not be able to figure out the exact duration of your individual podcasts. iTunes has no way to verify this data, so both of us have just been hard-coding a ballpark figure of our average podcast length.

```
<itunes:duration>00:45:00</itunes:duration>
```

<itunes:explicit> tag

Here's an implementation from iTunes that makes a lot of sense. If your podcast normally doesn't include any questionable language or subject matter, go ahead and mark the channel with an explicit tag of `no`. However, if a particular episode does get a little on the raunchy side, you can use this tag to mark just the single episode.

Even if you know all your podcast episodes follow the same explicit label set forth in the `<channel>`, you still need to include it here:

```
<itunes:explicit>no</itunes:explicit>
```

<itunes:keywords> tag

Adding one more layer of information about your show, iTunes allows you to choose keywords that might pertain to your show. This can be very useful if you cover a lot of ground in your podcasts and find it difficult to sum things up in the `<itunes:subtitle>` tag.

Separate keywords by spaces and add in as many as you see fit:

```
<itunes:keywords>outdoors fishing Tebo salmon mountain biking</itunes:keywords>
```

Wrapping things up

As with any other markup language (and as indicated earlier in this chapter), you have to close those declaration tags. The closing tag looks like this:

```
</item>
```

This tells the podcatching client that the end of the episode has been reached. After you close your `<item>` tag, you can immediately add a second, and a third, and so on. There is no limit to the number of `<items>` you can have inside your RSS feed.

After you add all the episodes inside their own `<item>` `</item>` statement, it's time to finish the file:

```
</channel>
</rss>
```

These two lines of text bring to a close your `<channel>` declaration and mark the end of the RSS 2.0 file itself.

You should have no further text after these two statements. This really *is* the end of your file. If you have extra text hanging around after you close your `</rss>` tag, delete it. Or better yet, figure out where you wanted to put it in one of the elements listed here — and put it there.

Tweaking the Contents

The main function of your RSS 2.0 file is to distribute your media files to the various people who have subscribed to your feed. However, smart podcasters recognize that a well-formed RSS feed can be employed for a wider range of needs.

Making sure your episodes don't get skipped

Remember that subscribers to your feed have probably subscribed to other feeds as well. As their time grows more precious — perhaps because *somebody* subscribed to way too many feeds (who, us?) — they're going to start looking for clues from savvy podcasters to help them assign priorities to the podcasts already downloaded on their systems and set up their listening day.

RSS feeds also work to promote your feed to people who are potential subscribers. Various sites are now springing up to help podcast listeners find potential podcasts. PodRazor (`podrazor.com`) is one such site. PodRazor aggregates or combines RSS 2.0 feeds from as many podcasts as it can find and uses them to populate its search engine. Searchers then type in their keywords of choice, and PodRazer searches through thousands of podcast feeds to find references to the entered keywords.

This process is much the same as that used by Google and Yahoo! so it wasn't a surprise when Yahoo! announced the capability to search through podcast content. Google is probably not far behind. After all, searching is what they do, and they are well aware of podcasting and its potential for growth.

Adding descriptive keywords

While all the elements of a well-formed RSS 2.0 file are important, it's the `<title>` and the `<description>` content that are the most useful for listeners — be they current or potential. As a podcaster, your job is to create descriptions and titles that are both relevant to your content and intriguing to your listening audience.

As discussed in Chapter 8, keywords are important. Rather than making stuff up again, this time we use real-world examples to illustrate the point. One of your humble authors hosts several science-fiction-related podcasts. One of the shows features interviews with authors who create the popular science-fiction novels and short stories of today. Another show deals almost exclusively with science-fiction television and movies; yet another has loose ties with sci-fi but is really more about . . . well, whatever fits the podcaster's mood.

Understanding that each of these shows appeals to a completely different audience, the podcaster employs very different strategies when providing information about these shows. But as different as these strategies are, they follow a similar theme: Tell listeners what they want to hear.

No, we're not suggesting you lie or stretch the truth about the content of your podcasts. Instead, practice thinking like a listener. What do you think listeners want to hear? Then consider why you did this episode in the first place: Who would be interested in listening, and why? After you figure all that out, it's time to start writing descriptive keywords, and adding them to your `<title>` and `<description>` declarations.

Whether or not you heard it here first, the ability to change the contents of your RSS file is critical to your success as a podcaster. Before you select a hosting company or blogging software that manages your RSS 2.0 file for you, ask some important questions about modifying that file. (By and large, we'd say take a pass on companies that don't allow do-it-yourself changes to your RSS 2.0 file or template.)

Making Newcomers Feel Welcome

Think back to when you were a new podcast listener or, perhaps, consider the last time you added a podcast to your podcatching client. Did you know what you were getting yourself into? Perhaps someone recommended the show to you, and you already had a feel for what it was you could expect. But maybe not.

For a lot of new people just starting out as podcast listeners, there is a large gulf of uncertainty and concern they have to get over before subscribing to a new podcast. By subscribing to your feed, a listener is putting a significant amount of trust in you, the podcaster. Don't forget that podcasting means your subscribers automatically receive *any and all* podcast media files you make available, regardless of what's in them or how big they are.

How large will these files be? How often will they be coming down? What can I expect out of the content? Can I listen in front of my kids? Will the file size overload my hard drive?

These and a slew of other questions invade the mind of every person thinking about taking the plunge and subscribing to your podcast. And these concerns stay on the minds of those who bit the bullet and subscribed for at least the first few weeks. Your job, then, is to find ways to make those listeners feel comfortable so they keep listening. Stay tuned (as it were . . .)

Creating an introductory podcast

Congratulations. Either by way of your skilled listings in directories and listing sites (see Chapter 10) or from your incredibly good karma, a new listener has just subscribed to your feed and is about to receive a first-ever podcast media file from you.

Hold that thought a minute. Do you really want the most recent episode to be the first thing this new listener hears? Depending on the format of your show, that may not be the best doorway into the world of your podcast. It's like a new reader just discovering an author for the first time, with one big difference: In this case, the "author" releases the work one chapter at a time — and what if you (as an author) are currently on Chapter 12 of the saga?

Chapter 12 may not be the best place to start your podcast; a new listener may not have enough information to get the most out of it. Many podcasts seem to work in this "previously on . . ." format, where they grow comfortable with their listeners, assuming the listeners have been following along for some time. No knock there, just fact; personal attachment comes with podcasting, and it's one goal that many podcasters wish to achieve. We have no desire to see that involvement halt. But how is a new listener to catch up?

Rather than changing the format of your show, consider including an introductory episode to your podcast in your RSS 2.0 file. As of this writing, only a handful of podcasters employ this method of offering a guiding hand to new subscribers. (Look for that to change soon.)

Making this introductory podcast is simple. It looks like this:

1. **Record your welcome message.**

   Don't make this a major production; try to keep it short (ideally under 3 minutes). Discuss the major themes you cover on your show and why you do what you do. If you need to give listeners any warnings, this is the time and place to do it. Also, discuss how frequently you put out new episodes and what time length you try to hit for your show. And of course, give out your Web site address, e-mail, and any other contact information. Even though listeners may not write that information down, it shows you're happy to get feedback from your audience.

2. **Tag and upload this show as "Episode 000."**

   You want to properly ID3-tag everything you put up for download, and naming the show "000" or something similar sets it apart from your normal episode rotation. This practice is critical for your current subscribers because they're going to get this welcome message too.

3. **Create a static** `<item>` **in your RSS 2.0 feed as the first one in the list.**

   If you're using your blog or hosting provider to create your RSS 2.0 on the fly as you make new entries, you want to *hard-code* this item (type it in by hand) right above your dynamic code. Use the sample code from earlier in this chapter and modify the `<item>` elements as appropriate.

4. **Resave your RSS 2.0 template and rebuild if necessary.**

   Your new RSS 2.0 file should now contain the introductory `<item>` tag as a static element, always appearing ahead of your dynamic entries.

Understanding how it works

Because the `<guid>` tag is new, any podcatchers that check your RSS 2.0 file for updates automatically download the new introductory media files. Previous subscribers get the file as well. Some may listen, but most will trash the intro files — it doesn't matter, though. The new listeners are the ones you're especially interested in, and you've just given them a good understanding of what your podcast is about. With luck, your introduction fits with their assumptions of what your show was about, and they continue to subscribe.

And if they don't? No problem. You don't want to be wasting valuable (and expensive) bandwidth on an audience who isn't listening to your show.

"But won't they keep downloading the same file?" No, they won't — not if their podcatching client is doing its job right. The `<guid>` tag works to tell podcatching clients what's been downloaded already and what's brand new. After a file has been downloaded, the podcatching client ignores that file (assuming the `<guid>` and sometimes the `<pubDate>` don't change). The next day (or the next time the listener has the podcatching client check for new stuff) the intro cast is skipped over, and the next file(s) on the list is downloaded, never missing a beat!

Multiple-Show File Strategies

Some of you out there will catch the podcasting bug *hard.* It's so easy to create a podcast, you'll want to do more. Soon you may find yourself doing three shows a week, each with slightly different content and topics, each appealing to a different audience.

You begin to hear from your listeners that Monday's show is right up their alley, but Wednesday's coverage of different material isn't their cup of tea. You get plenty of e-mail and voice mail with the opposite viewpoint, and a good many listeners say they love everything you're doing. How can you make all these people happy? Simple. Multiple feeds.

Slacker Astronomy (`slackerastronomy.com`) is a great example. It didn't take long for the creators of this podcast to branch out into two different formats. Once a week, they create a podcast where they talk to the audience about something new and exciting from the world of astronomy. They make it funny and entertaining for anyone with even a passing interest in heavenly bodies.

Early on, the creators attempted to do interviews on the show. However, interviews tend to vary in length — and that's tricky to fit into a regular format. They started editing their interviews, using them as sound bites for their show. That worked at first, but the creators weren't satisfied for long. They had these long and interesting conversations with astronomers that just didn't feel right edited down to 45-second sound bites. But they also knew that shooting the cosmic breeze with an astronomer would be entertaining to a much smaller audience than their produced show.

The solution was simple: Produce two different feeds for the two different types of shows. Their main feed still contains their weekly show. The second feed, ingeniously titled *Slacker Astronomy Extra,* contains the occasional interview, planning sessions, and a variety of other audio content that doesn't fit the bill of the main feed — or that the creators deem less appetizing to their general audience but still worth putting out there. The hosts of *Slacker Astronomy* cross-promote each feed; they mention to the listening audience of one feed the current things happening on the other. The choice is now in the hands of the listener. Subscribe to one or both?

When you've figured out how to customize your feed, it should be easy to break out a second (or third) feed, isolating the content as appropriate. You need to check the documentation of your blogging software or RSS-generation tool to see what steps are necessary.

Part IV

Start Spreadin' the News about Your Podcast

THE PODCAST "LAMP TALK" WAS ABOUT TO BECOME "EXPLICIT."

"Sometimes these sockets need cleaning. First, make sure the lamp is unplugged, and then..."

In this part . . .

When you've finally managed to put your show "out there," you may find it's a cold, dark place. You need a beacon on your podcast that tells everyone you're here — and what your show is all about. In this part, you find the tips and tricks successful podcasters use to attract a wider audience. Additionally, you find ways to communicate better with your fans (yes, fans!) and keep your show fresh.

Chapter 10

Of Pings and Directories

*I*t's time to tell the world about you and your podcast — in other words, generate some publicity. Luckily for you, the podcast audience is typically pretty Internet-savvy, or at least has a broadband Internet connection, so you don't have to mail postcards, look for splashy photo-ops, or hire a personal consultant to keep track of your social calendar.

In the world of podcasting, publicity means notifying various listing sites and directories when you have new content available. Sometimes you can send the notification automatically (we call that a *ping*); other times notification requires some individual effort on your part. It's worth the effort; listing sites and directories are both critical to building your audience of listeners and keeping that audience engaged — and subscribed. This chapter gets you started using the available tools and offers tips for keeping the process simple *and* making sure your podcast gets noticed.

Publicizing Your Podcast

Though it may not be intuitive at first glance, three parties are involved in the "podcasting publicity triangle":

- ✔ You, the podcaster
- ✔ Potential listeners
- ✔ Directories or listing sites that list podcasts

Just like most Web searchers, potential podcast listeners are looking for fresh and recently updated podcasts. So this section shows you how to notify those directories and listing sites — and in turn, your potential listeners — not only that your podcast exists, but that you have fresh new content available for their listening pleasure.

Directories and listing sites explained

Directories and listing sites serve an essential purpose: They attract new listeners to your podcast. But each of them approaches the task in different ways:

- **Directories:** These Web sites keep a comprehensive database of podcasts. Podcast Alley (www.podcastalley.com) and Podcast Pickle (podcastpickle.com), for example, both employ an easy-to-use interface that allows potential listeners to browse through various categories of interest — as well as do searches on topics, interests, or podcast names.

- **Listing sites:** These Web sites — such as audio.weblogs.com or technorati.com — show the most recently updated podcasts or allow episode-specific searches. Listing sites generally lack the structure of a directory, and usually don't combine together podcasts into easy-to-browse categories. One listing service, Podscope (podscope.com), actually provides a way to search within the audio content of individual podcast episodes.

Some listeners prefer the categorization of directories; others favor the personalization of a listing site. Your job as a podcaster is to use both types of sites in the most effective way to bring potential listeners to your podcast.

Pinging for publicity

Pings are sent out by podcasters (or their corresponding Web sites) and are picked up by listing sites and/or directories. Think of the ping as working like a sonar blip from a submarine, and the listing site or directory as the receiving sonar operator. Pings are quite insubstantial, carrying a minimal amount of data to the directory or site listing in question.

When you ping a site, you're telling the computer or program that runs the recipient's site that you have something new to offer and that the listing site or directory should update its listing for your podcast. Sometimes this is handled by the information contained in the ping itself. If not, the receiving site may launch an agent or robot to investigate your Web site to discover what information needs to be updated.

You can only ping directories and listing sites that are designed to accept pings. It won't do you any good to send a ping to your local congressman or friendly media conglomerate unless the site has a directory specifically designed to accept pings. That's because pings update such directories and listing sites, which are in turn visited by potential listeners seeking your new or fresh content.

By themselves, pings won't do much to get you new listeners. But when pings work in concert with directories or other online listing services, they can be an invaluable way to let potential listeners know you exist.

Sending Pings to Directories and Listing Sites

The best way to send pings is automatically; you may even be able to ping a whole list of sites at once. But if the software you use to power your podcast doesn't enable you to send out automatic pings, you can still do it manually, which is a bit more time-consuming but gets the message out nonetheless.

The following sections help you decide which sites to ping and how to set up the process with the various podcasting software available.

Choosing which sites to ping

Legions of listing sites and directories accept podcasters' pings. For now, here's a list of places Evo pings every time he has an update for his podcasts or blogs:

- rpc.technorati.com/rpc/ping
- www.rpc.weblogs.com/RPC2
- ping.blo.gs/
- api.my.yahoo.com/RPC2
- rpc.blogrolling.com/pinger/
- www.syndic8.com/xmlrpc.php
- rpc.pingomatic.com/
- www.rootblog.com/Ping/

Technology changes at an ever-increasing pace, so it's highly likely that some sites we've mentioned have been modified since the printing of this book. Others will have been abandoned by their creators, and still more will have been created. Spend some time searching for places to ping — and consider joining a podcasting community (real or virtual) where you can ask others about the listing sites and directories they ping.

Totally automatic pings

Most blogging software supports automatic pinging of sites. (In fact, Movable Type comes preconfigured to ping many popular listing services and directories.) If you're using blogging software to maintain your RSS feed (Chapter 9) and/or show notes (Chapter 8), you can probably set it up to ping.

You'll want to set up your site to ping relevant sites every time you have a fresh podcast available. If you use show notes (which we highly recommend in Chapter 8) to accompany your podcasts, you'll want to set up your system to send out pings whenever you publish these notes. (We get to all that in a minute.)

If you don't use show notes, but still use a blog post to update your RSS 2.0 feed with the `<enclosure>` tag (see Chapter 9), the same process should apply. As a rule, you want to ping whenever you post and update.

When you update your blog, lots of moving parts come together, including the sending out of pings. Here's some of the automatic brouhaha that goes on:

- ✔ Text and links from the post are entered into the database.
- ✔ Templates assemble relevant database entries.
- ✔ Web pages are rebuilt to update all content with the information from the templates.
- ✔ Archives are created/updated.
- ✔ Pings are initiated.

To make sure your blogging software is set up to ping, look inside your configuration settings. Here's how to do that in some of the more popular programs:

- ✔ **Movable Type:** Choose Main Menu⇨the name of your podcast⇨ Configuration⇨Preferences. Then, on the Preferences screen, click the Publicity/Remote Interfaces/TrackBack link (shown in Figure 10-1).
- ✔ **Blogger:** You can find your configuration settings by choosing Settings⇨ Publishing, as shown in Figure 10-2. Note that as of this writing, Blogger is set up to ping only `weblogs.com`, which isn't much publicity but it's still better than nothing.

✔ **Libsyn:** This basic blogging/hosting provider specifically for podcasters is only moderately better than Blogger. You can configure settings by choosing Blog Settings➪Advanced Settings➪Auto-ping, as shown in Figure 10-3. Note that it's set to ping only `audio.weblogs.com`. (That's as of this writing; it may be upgraded when a new release comes out.)

✔ **TypePad:** This program allows you to set up customized pings, but it really puts you through the paces to find it. It's buried in Create a Post➪Customize the Display of This Page➪Post Screen Configuration➪Custom➪Trackback URLs to Ping.

Pings are sometimes called *trackbacks,* although technically (and strictly) a trackback is a different communications protocol used when someone mentions your post on his or her blog or Web site. But the concept is pretty darn close, and we're not splitting hairs over it.

Figure 10-1: Setting up Movable Type to send customized pings.

> **Publicity / Remote Interfaces / TrackBack**
>
> **Notify the following sites when I update my blog:** [?]
> When you update your blog, Movable Type will automatically notify the selected sites.
>
> ☑ blo.gs
> ☑ weblogs.com
> ☑ technorati.com
>
> **Others: (Separate URLs with a carriage return.)**
> `http://api.my.yahoo.com/RPC2`
> `http://rpc.blogrolling.com/pinger/`
> `http://www.syndic8.com/xmlrpc.php`
> `http://rpc.pingomatic.com/`
> `http://www.rootblog.com/Ping/`

Figure 10-2: Blogger can only ping `weblogs. com` automatically.

> `http://www.blogger.com/blog-publishing.g?blogID=5598944`
>
> Getting Started   ▾ Latest Headlines   VisibleHuman.java
>
> ← Back to Dashboard   ? Help   ✕ Sign Out
>
> **Ⓑ Ghost Writer**
>
> Posting   **Settings**   Template   View Blog
>
> Basic   Publishing   Formatting   Comments   Archiving   Site Feed   Email   Members
>
> **You're publishing on blogspot.com**
>
> Switch to: FTP (publishing on your ISP server) Or SFTP (secure publishing on your ISP server)
>
> **Blog*Spot Address**   http:// [azghostwriter] .blogspot.com
> Subject to availability.
>
> **Notify Weblogs.com**   [Yes ▾]
> Weblogs.com is a blog update notification service that many individuals and services use to track blog changes.
>
> [Save Settings]

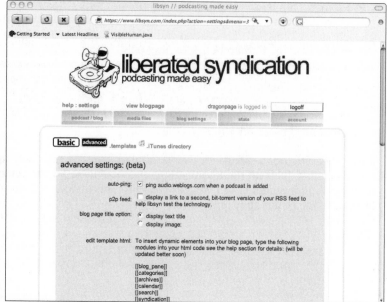

Figure 10-3:
Libsyn can
ping
audio.
weblogs.
com each
time you
post.

Be sure to follow the instructions for your particular interface for typing multiple ping destinations. Sometimes a hard carriage return (the Enter key) is required, sometimes they can be joined by a comma. Like we said, pay attention.

Pinging manually (if you must)

If you don't use a blog to run your site or your software of choice doesn't allow either automation or customization of pings, you're stuck with the method employed by the pioneers: manual pinging.

Most sites that accept pings have a form to fill out when you have fresh content available. Simple. Painless. But repetitive. Also necessary if you can't automate. Although the process differs for each site, here are the basic steps you follow:

1. **Go to the site that you want to ping and find the page where the ping form is contained.**

   Make a custom set of bookmarks in your browser to keep track of all the places you need to ping. That way you shave off as much time as possible when you make your posts.

2. Fill out the form.

Although each site has a slightly different form, most require the same information. You need the URL of your RSS 2.0 feed at a minimum.

You might want to copy the URL of your podcast feed (by pressing Ctrl+C or ⌘+C) so you have it ready to drop into those forms. All these sites require it, and if you're likely to mistype something, this will be it. Just don't copy anything else to the Clipboard as long as you need that URL.

3. Click Submit when you're done.

Most directories and listing sites validate all manual pings before updating the podcast listings on their pages. This helps cut down on errors displayed on their sites — and discourages spammers from sending out pings when nothing on a podcast has been updated. If the directory can't find your podcast feed because you've misspelled the URL or nothing in your podcast feed is new, then the directory or listing site invalidates your ping and doesn't update your listing. So be careful to spell (and type) the URL of your feed correctly. And (oh yeah) make sure you have something new in your RSS feed before you send out a manual ping.

You'll see various flavors of forms as you go about this process. Figure 10-4 shows the form on `audio.weblogs.com`, the granddaddy of them all.

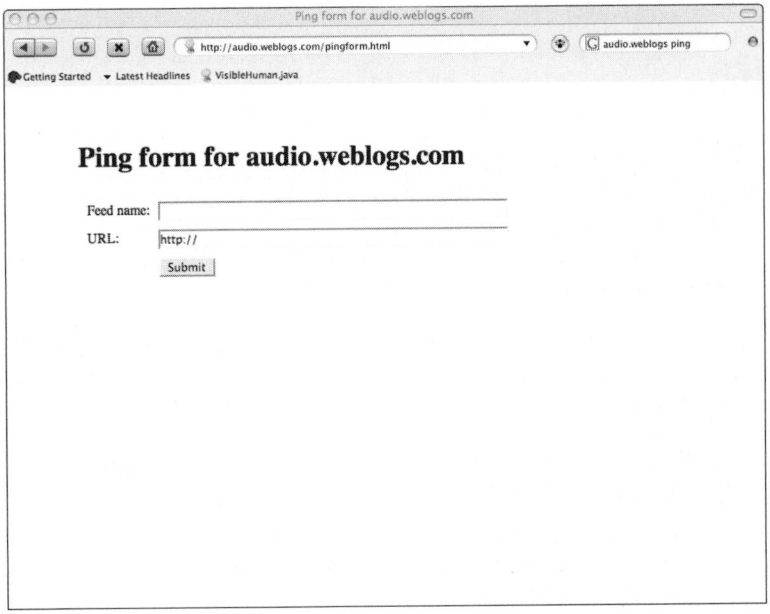

Figure 10-4:
Simple manual ping form for `audio. weblogs. com.`

Ping form for audio.weblogs.com

http://audio.weblogs.com/pingform.html   audio.weblogs ping

Getting Started   Latest Headlines   VisibleHuman.java

Ping form for audio.weblogs.com

Feed name: ☐

URL: http://

Submit

Technorati.com has an even simpler ping form, shown in Figure 10-5. Your RSS 2.0 feed should have a `<title>` listed in the `<channel>` declaration already, so Technorati pulls the information from there instead of having you type it. (If `<title>` and `<channel>` seem like a foreign language to you, head to Chapter 9 for the lowdown on using these tags.)

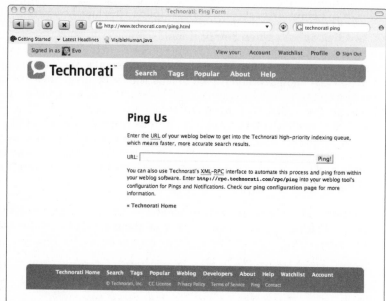

Figure 10-5:
Pinging
Technorati
manually.

Drawing In Listeners from Directories

Some directories get their information from pings to various sites around the Internet. Many others periodically check your feed to see whether you have any new podcasts to distribute. Regardless of which method a particular directory employs, first you have to let the directory know your site exists (well, yeah) and then do some basic maintenance on your listing from time to time. The following sections explain how to find directories, list your podcast, and keep your listing up to date.

Targeting your audience: Large or small?

Directories of all shapes and sizes, from uber-giants DMOZ and Yahoo! to a small sports-only podcast directory, make up the current landscape. When considering your approach to getting listed on various directories, think about your goals and why you want to be listed.

Podcasting is *narrowcasting* — which is distinctly different from *broad*casting. A radio station's livelihood depends on sending (some might say shoving) its message to the widest possible segment of the population. That's why radio stations invest in taller towers, buy bigger transmitters, and put up billboards over town — the more listeners they get, the more money they can make from advertising.

Podcasting is somewhat different. In our world, the more listeners you get, the bigger the drain on *your* resources and bandwidth. We're not saying that's a bad thing. But understand that the amount of money and resources necessary to maintain a subscriber base of 100,000 would break most of us, at least with the current technology we employ.

So rather than go after the biggest number of listeners, podcasters are better served by going after the biggest number of *targeted* listeners. You really want only *interested* people listening to your show as "their" show. Sure, broadcasters may say the same thing, but they might accept a fickle audience as long as it's huge (and tunes in enough to buy the sponsors' stuff). After all, listening to a radio program is as easy as clicking a button or turning a dial. (If only podcasting were that easy . . . well, maybe someday. . . .)

Finding the latest and greatest directories

New directories are popping up quicker than acne on a 14-year-old chocoholic, but with happier results: The creators of these directories have a vested interest in getting the word out to the podcasting community.

Because podcasting is an online thing, the community of podcasters tends to be an online thing, too. Various mailing lists, discussion boards (forums), and even podcasts exist for the exclusive reason of bringing the latest news and information about podcasting. To keep up on the latest happenings in the podcasting world — including the latest directories — we suggest subscribing to some of the resources listed in Table 10-1.

Table 10-1	Resources for Finding Directories	
Resource	*Where to Find It*	*What You Get*
Podcasters Mailing List	`groups.yahoo.com/ group/podcasters/`	This list has become the iconic watering hole for podcasters. If there is a new directory, chances are someone is posting about it here. This group is a great resource and is frequented by the founders, movers, and shakers of the podcasting sect.
Podcasting News	`www.podcastingnews. com`	Not only is it a great source for news, but it also contains a very active discussion group. Best of all, you can subscribe to XML feeds for both!
Adam Curry's Daily Source Code	`live.curry.com`	Adam, the podfather himself, spends a good amount of time on each podcast covering the latest in the world of podcasting. Getting a plug on Adam's show is bound to spike traffic, so any directory creator worth his salt is going to push hard for this to happen.

Listing your podcast with directories

As of this writing, most directories are edited and controlled by sophisticated wetware interfaces that come with their own inboard power systems, fuzzy-logic and synaptic processors, and tend to have a penchant for chocolate-coated goodies. (What's with the chocolate references?) We call them human beings, and they sit between you and your goal of getting listed in a directory.

Each directory has its own submission guidelines and processes. This early in the game, directories are happy to take as many submissions as they can get. But as podcasting grows in popularity, you can bet that many directories will become quite picky about adding in new podcasts.

Getting your podcast listed may be as simple as sending an e-mail to the editor of the directory. Others ask you to fill out an online form. Here's an example of one form-based submission you'll want to do right away: Podcast Alley. Take the tips and tricks you find out here and apply them to any other directory you decide to seek a listing from.

Follow these steps to submit your feed to Podcast Alley:

1. **In the upper-left corner of Podcast Alley's homepage (**www.podcastalley.com**), click the Add Your Podcast link.**

   Directory editors spend a fair amount of time cleaning up duplicate entries and deleting incorrect submissions. Please search the directory to make sure your podcast isn't already listed, and double-check your entries for accuracy before submitting the form.

2. **Enter the name of your podcast feed in the Title of Podcast box, as shown in Figure 10-6.**

Figure 10-6: Submitting your feed for inclusion on Podcast Alley.

   This is likely the same name you're using in your `<title>` feed in your RSS feed. If not, think of a good reason why. Or go back and change your title. Normally the two should match.

3. **In the Podcast Web site box, enter the URL of your Web site — not your RSS feed link, but the main Web site that houses your podcast.**

   This enables visitors to Podcast Alley to check out your Web site before (or after) they subscribe.

4. Enter the link to your RSS 2.0 feed in the Podcast Feed Link box.

Though we've said it before, it bears repeating: Double-check your link for accuracy! The folks at Podcast Alley aren't going to check your typing, and you don't want to send links off to the void, do you?

5. Enter the description of your podcast.

This is the area where a lot of new podcasters struggle. When writing your description, write for impact! Identify the key concepts your show is about — and write to them. You've got a limited amount of space to get your point across, so be careful of tossing in extraneous words that add more fluff than substance.

6. Enter your e-mail address.

This is useful in the event there are errors in the submission process, or so you can be notified when your show is listed. And when you get that e-mail, go back and make sure everything is correct!

7. Enter *relevant* keywords.

Not every directory allows this, but if yours does, take advantage of it. Just as you picked out the key concepts before, identify relevant keywords that people are likely to search on, and that you'd like to use to promote your podcast. Yes, "Barbie" is likely a popular search term, but if your podcast is about cooking mealworms for fun and profit, you don't want to target the audience that's likely searching on "Barbie." The searcher will be (at least) disappointed that your podcast isn't about Barbie, and you'll have just wasted precious (and expensive) bandwidth on a one-time listener you didn't really much want to attract in the first place.

8. From the Pick a Genre drop-down list, select an appropriate genre for your podcast.

In our opinion, this is the single biggest problem with directories: Genres are either too broad or too specific. And in most cases, you can only select one. So for now, grab the one you think comes closest to classifying your site (and pretend you *didn't* just get shoved into a box that doesn't quite fit).

9. Hit the Submit Podcast button, and you're in business.

That's it! Expect an e-mail in a few hours/days/weeks when your podcast has been listed. Remember that it's a good idea to return to Podcast Alley and check for any mistakes or omissions. If you find some, follow the instructions on the site to have them corrected.

Keeping your listing relevant

Every month or so (sometimes more, sometimes less), it's a good idea to revisit directories where you're listed and make sure the content displayed matches what you're doing. To give you an idea of what to look for, here are some reasons you might need to change your listing (or perhaps your categorization):

- ✔ You've expanded the focus of your podcast. For example, you started a podcast about fishing boats, but have now branched out to cover environmental concerns for lakes, streams, and waterways.

- ✔ You've added a regular co-host to your show and would like to include that person in your description.

- ✔ Your podcast has moved to a new server, and your RSS 2.0 feed has a different address.

- ✔ The directories have changed the way they handle your listing (this does happen). For example, perhaps your fishing-boat show was listed under Recreation, but now the directory has created a specific Fishing subcategory. Does your show belong there instead?

Make a set of bookmarks just for your directory listings. Then, when you pay your monthly visit to each of the sites, you'll have them all handy in your bookmark list.

Chapter 11

Speaking Directly to Your Peeps

C ommunication can be defined in a multitude of overly complex ways. For the sake of argument (and not to copy each and every dictionary entry we can find), we'll define the term as

The exchange of information between two points.

Note that last part — *between two points.* To us, this implies a bi-directional flow of information, to and from both parties.

If you've had the pleasure (note how well we can say that with a straight face) of attending any productivity or team-building seminars, the presenters really drive the message home: Effective communication is not a one-way street.

Here is one place where podcasting has a huge advantage over traditional forms of media. Radio and television, by and large, are one-way forms of information transfer. The show host talks, and you listen. *Live radio* (and a handful of TV shows) changes that paradigm, allowing listeners to call in to the show and be a part of it.

True communication is much easier for the podcaster than the traditional media producer. In the short time podcasting has been around, podcasters with experience in traditional broadcasting are reporting greater levels of interaction with their audiences, in a much more immediate fashion with greater quality of feedback. Chalk one more up to the podcasters — and the podcatchers.

In this chapter, we show you some real-world examples of how to foster communication between you and your audience, touching on a variety of methods and locations you probably haven't considered.

Gathering Listener Feedback

It must be a natural human emotion to fear the opinions of others. Perhaps it's insecurity, but we think it has more to do with our culture's constant reinforcement of the "How are you?" — "I'm fine. You?" — "Fine." meaningless chatter that precedes most of our conversations.

But something happens to that cultural crutch when it comes to podcasting. Listeners, for whatever reason, are compelled to actually give real and meaningful criticism. And podcasters, for the most part, take to heart those responses.

Of course, we're speaking in general terms. Yes, there are flamers and jerks out there with less than helpful answers at the ready. Podcasting can't change basic human nature for the ill-evolved, unfortunately.

Fostering good communication with your listening audience should be approached in a multitude of ways, such as

✔ Comments on your blog

✔ Online discussion groups

✔ Forums

The savvy podcaster is constantly on the lookout for additional methods of communication occurring outside his immediate control, such as forums, chat rooms, discussion boards, and mailing lists. All of these avenues are discussed in detail in the sections that follow.

Comments on Your Blog

In an ideal world, all communication, feedback, rants, and raves about your show would take place in a neat little box, keeping things nice and tidy for you. But because that won't happen, your best bet is to build a Web site that both enables and encourages the communication in your own backyard.

In Chapters 8 and 9, we demonstrate how much simpler adding show notes and generating RSS files is for those podcasters who use blogging software, rather than those who try to do everything by hand. Well, here's one more feather in the cap of Movable Type, WordPress, and even Blogger: Feedback mechanisms come pre-installed.

If you're already using a blog, you usually don't have to do anything special to turn on the "talk back to me" feature. In fact, it's a royal pain to make your blog not accept comments from the outside world. So relax.

In the world of blogs, this feedback mechanism is referred to as *comments*. Visit just about any blog you can find, read a post, and you're likely to find a small Comments link at the bottom. Figure 11-1 shows one example, though the treatment varies widely from site to site.

Podcasters use comments to gather feedback from their listeners about specific shows. Hence, comments are closely tied with show notes (you can find more on show notes in Chapter 8) about a particular episode.

Some podcasters get dozens of responses per episode; some get none. While there is some relation to the size of your listening audience and the number of comments you're likely to receive, it really has more to do with the connection users feel they have with your podcast.

There's an added benefit to enabling feedback about your episodes directly on your Web site: Communication develops amongst the listening community itself. Rather than talking to you, they start talking to each other, and the conversation takes on a life of its own. If this happens to you, don't fret over it; encourage it! Much like two co-workers chatting about last night's *The Daily Show with Jon Stewart,* two or more listeners using your Web site to talk to each other about your show speaks to the attachment they feel to what you have to say (or play).

Figure 11-1: The Bitterest Pill gets quite a few comments on each episode.

We recognize that not every podcaster is a blogger, and the technical requirements to install comment software on non-blog Web sites is well beyond the scope of this book. Fortunately for us, people have been using the Web to talk about the things they love (and hate) for much longer than blogs have been popular.

Online Discussion Groups

Community forums, groups, and discussion lists allow for easy virtual community building, enabling disparate people to share their thoughts and opinions on a wide variety of subjects. A podcaster can find many free services that help create places where listeners can post, share, and discuss their thoughts and ideas online.

As easy as it is to create places for these types of conversations to occur, it's likely that someone else has already done it. Spend some quality time searching the Internet for your name and your show. Maybe a devoted fan has already done the not-so-heavy lifting for you.

While the number of free online discussion groups is legion, we've decided to focus on two of the larger offerings: Yahoo! Groups and Google Groups. Both are free to join and free to create, but both are supported by various forms of advertising. There ain't no such thing as a free lunch, as Heinlein said.

Yahoo! Groups

Yahoo! Groups has the distinction of being one of the oldest and most widely used free discussion groups on the Net. While it may not have been first on the block, it has stood the test of time, and many consider it the 800-pound gorilla on the block. Yahoo! Groups also boasts of a huge user group, which could help your fledgling group swell in size rapidly.

Setting up a group is quick and easy; just follow these steps:

1. **Log in to Yahoo! Groups at** `groups.yahoo.com`**.**

   If you already have an account, enter your Yahoo! ID and password.

   If you don't have a Yahoo! ID yet, click the Sign Up link and follow the simple instructions to get your free Yahoo! account.

2. **To start a new group, click the Start a Group Now link in the middle of the page.**

   If you're returning to Yahoo! Groups, you'll find a list of all the groups you've either created or belong to on the left side of the page.

3. **Select the appropriate category and subcategory for your group. Then click the Place My Group Here button.**

   As you select categories, you will likely be presented with subcategories to refine your group's placement. Continue selecting links until you've found the appropriate categorization for your group.

4. **Enter the appropriate information in the Group Name, Group Email Address, and Describe Your Group text boxes. When you're finished, click Continue.**

   See Figure 11-2 for an example of a page that's been filled out.

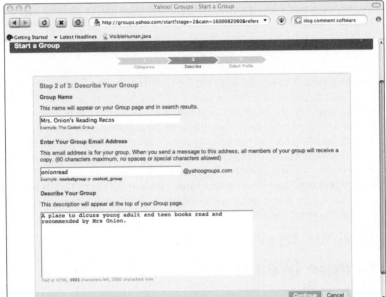

Figure 11-2:
Yahoo!
Groups
allows you
to describe
your group
with a little
text, or a lot.

The Group Email address is the e-mail address members of your group will use to send messages to the entire group. You get to make up the name of this e-mail address, though we suggest making it something simple and easy to remember. Acronyms are a good idea here, as are any abbreviations or secret words that your group members are likely to remember.

5. **Select which Yahoo! Profile and Email Address you want to be associated with this group.**

   Because you're setting up the group, you will be the *Owner* (which gives you phenomenal cosmic powers like kicking people out if they get out of line). If you have multiple Yahoo! IDs, you need to associate only one of those with this group. And if you have more than one e-mail address, the interface needs to know where to send the mail.

6. **In the Word Verification text box, type the letters that are displayed in the accompanying image.**

   Yahoo! Groups asks you to type the letters to help prevent e-mail spam — which is a good thing, right? Oh, and it's case-sensitive, so make sure you use capital letters where appropriate.

7. **When you're done, click Continue.**

   That's it! You've just created your group.

From here, you can set how much control and flexibility you wish to have over the group, as well as the ease at which others can join. Yahoo! leaves some things pretty open, yet locks down others. Be sure to follow the Customize Your Group link to make sure that the settings are to your liking. If not, change them!

When you're happy with your group, click the Invite People to Join link, and tell everyone you know about your new group. Well, maybe not everyone. But you should tell the folks who might be interested.

Most people don't "request" invitations. An invitation is something you send out to notify people about an event or new service, in this case your Yahoo! group. Sending an invitation to one or 1,000 people is likely an unsolicited e-mail. Chances are, recipients are not expecting this mail from you. That makes it look suspiciously like spam, and people are likely to just delete it. When you send out your invitations, don't send them to folks you don't know and make sure the mail is personal enough to let them know the message is not spam from some faceless person.

Google Groups

Not to be outdone, Google has recently released a service similar to Yahoo! Groups. Google is quickly becoming the dominant player in many online initiatives after its successful Gmail launch in early 2004. While Google Groups is currently in *beta* (which means it may not be fully functional), it's promising to be a fine product. Here's how to create a Google group:

1. **Sign in to your Google account at** `groups.google.com`**.**

   If you're already registered with Google, enter the e-mail address and password already registered with Google.

   If you don't have a Google account, the sign-up process is free and easy.

2. **Click Create a New Group on the left side of the screen.**

   Remember that Google Groups is currently in beta, and the position of elements on the screen may change in future releases. The wording of the link may change as well, but it should always be something easy to find and recognize.

3. **In the corresponding text boxes, type the Group Name, Group E-mail Address, and Group Description.**

   The group e-mail address is the e-mail address members of your group will use to send messages to the entire group. Google helps by suggesting an e-mail address based on the name of your group. You can change the e-mail name if you're not happy with it.

4. **Set the Access Level for your group.**

   If you want the maximum usage of your group, select the Public level. Of course, you may have reasons to select a more restrictive access level, and we're certainly not going to stand in your way.

5. **Click the Create My Group button.**

   You've now created your group and are all set to invite new members. Google Groups makes this an integral step in the creation of the group, whereas Yahoo! Groups makes it more of an option.

6. **In the large text box at the top of the page, enter the e-mail addresses of the people you'd like to have in your group. Then select the Add or Invite option button, depending on what action you want to take.**

   It's a better idea to invite people than to automatically add them to your new group.

   If you choose to automatically add the member to your group, e-mail messages from group members will show up unannounced in the recipient's mailbox, unless you told them to expect it. That's spam, pure and simple. Unless you know beyond a shadow of a doubt that the person you intend to add wants to be a member of your group, invite that person instead. That gives them the option to join or not, and makes you a better *netizen*.

7. **Select a subscription type and write a welcome message. When you're finished, click Done.**

   The default subscription type is to have e-mail sent individually to members that have joined your group. We suggest leaving this setting right where it is and allowing the members to change their own personal preference at their discretion. Some prefer the Digest Form option, and some prefer No E-mail at all. Leave it up to them.

Publicizing your group

After you create your online discussion group and send out your initial invitations, it's time to spread the word! In Chapter 12, we go into a longer conversation about publicizing you, your podcast, and everything you do to support that. But for now, here are a few tips on how to increase membership in your newly formed discussion group:

    ✔ **Publish the group information on your Web site.** Log in to your Google or Yahoo! account to find the URL for your group home page and/or your subscription e-mail address. Post this information prominently on your podcast's Web site.

    ✔ **Add the group information to your signature line on outbound e-mails.** Let each e-mail you send out act as a mini-advertisement for your discussion group. Provide a link to the home page as well as the subscription e-mail address.

    ✔ **Promote the group on your podcast.** Find time to mention the group on each episode of your podcast. Don't make an entire show about why you should join the group, but do talk about the ability to have stimulating conversations with other listeners as well as yourself.

Focusing on Online Forums

For all their usefulness, discussion groups have their shortcomings, especially when the topic of your show is complicated and multifaceted. This is compounded by the time-shifting nature of podcasting, causing your listeners to be a week or more behind schedule from one another. How are you going to handle conversations that span timelines and topics? We suggest giving forums a shot.

An *online forum* allows individuals to post their thoughts and ideas on a variety of topics — at their own choosing. Through a concept known as *threading*, multiple discussions can exist independently of all the others. Topics can get buried quickly in a mailing list like those mentioned in the previous section. Forums work differently, keeping all threads and topics available for clutter-free commenting at any time.

Finding free, hosted forums

Many pre-configured forum hosting sites exist, but Delphi has been around for about as long as any of them. Delphi makes it easy to create new forums and attract new members. Just follow these steps:

1. **Log in at** www.delphiforums.com.

    If you have a Delphi account, enter your username and password.

    If you don't have an account, it's a simple matter to create a free account with not much more than an e-mail address.

2. **Click the Create a New Forum link in the upper-left corner of the page.**

   Delphi may show you a list of forums you might be interested in. How the Delphi folks know this is beyond us. Do your best to ignore it and look for the Create a New Forum link instead.

3. **Enter the details of your free forum.**

   You'll provide simple things, such as the name, description, and keywords of your free forum.

   We suggest making your *Webtag* (the end of the URL that Delphi will build for you, like `http://forums.delphiforums.com/akfishing`) something short and relevant to your podcast. Abbreviations or acronyms would work well here. Also, don't neglect to add keywords to the Keywords section; completing it will help guide current Delphi members to your newly created forum when they search for it.

4. **Confirm your entries and then click the Continue button.**

   Check for typos and other errors before you click Continue.

5. **Edit your welcome message and send out invitations.**

   Delphi provides a pre-packaged script for you to send to interested people. You can leave it as is or rewrite it entirely, depending on your needs.

   Again, we raise the issue of how invitations might be seen as spam to some. If you missed that discussion, check out the "Yahoo! Groups" section, earlier in the chapter.

That's it! You can now customize your forum, start new posts, and spread the word about your newly created forum. Much like discussion groups, you can promote your forum by

- ✔ Posting the address on your Web site
- ✔ Adding the address to your e-mail signature line
- ✔ Mentioning the forum on each of your podcast episodes

Like discussion groups, forums take some time to build steam. Be persistent, post every day, and constantly encourage your listeners to interact with you and your podcast in this manner. But above all, be patient!

Purchasing software to take more control of your forum

After a time, you may find yourself wishing for more control of your lively forum. Perhaps you'd like to implement the look and feel *(branding)* of your Web site on the forum, eliminate the advertisements you get with the free service, or more tightly integrate your forum into your overall Web presence. When that happens, it's time to think about installing some forum software on your Web site.

Here we go with the tech stuff again. We're not going to go into great detail on how to install and configure forum software on your Web server. Hey, if we sidestepped the whole "Install comments on your blog" issue, there's no way we're going to open this can of worms. But we will give you some things to think about when wrestling with the decision of using free forum software or dropping some cash on one you can purchase.

There's the old saying: Why should I pay for the cow when I get the milk for free? Choosing between a free or paid solution depends on many factors, at the top of which are your level of technical prowess and tolerance for downtime. Like anything in life, there are tradeoffs with each option. Consider this checklist:

✔ Are you comfortable editing PHP or Perl scripts?

✔ Do you have the ability to create new MySQL databases?

✔ Can you change the permissions of files and directories on your Web server?

✔ Are you willing to continually seek out patches and updates to keep the hackers out?

✔ Can you handle having your forum down for days on end while you research the above?

✔ Do you want to field "I can't remember my password" questions from your listener base?

✔ What is the capitol of Estonia?

If you answered *No* to one or more of the preceding questions, you probably aren't ready to tackle installing your own forum software.

If you answered *Yes* to all the preceding questions — except for the last one, and, by the way, the answer is *Tallinn* — you don't mind getting your hands dirty. We recommend finding out what forum software your hosting company already has pre-configured on your Web server, if any. If your hosting company does not have a forum pre-configured for your system, start searching through the multitude of options out there ready for downloading and installing. Google is your friend. . . .

Seeking Out the Comments of Others

There's an old saying about the best-laid plans of mice and men (they often go awry). While there exists some doubt in our minds as to the reality of rodents podcasting, we can say for certain that listeners of your show, both fan and foe, will communicate about your show to others in a variety of formats and places of which you have absolutely no control.

There are likely existing forums, chat rooms, discussion boards, and mailing lists that deal with your particular podcasting topic. At some point, those people will find out about your show and start listening. Current research shows it takes these people exactly 3.7 seconds to post a review to the rest of the masses. Welcome to the community of the Internet.

There are a variety of ways to keep your eyes and ears on these groups and to find comments regarding your podcast. See the following sections for the details.

Trying a general search

Is it just us, or don't most people do a Google search for their own name at least twice a week? Could be just us. But that's a great way to see if people are talking about you. Google has a gazillion pages in its search database and constantly crawls a good percentage of the Web, finding interesting tidbits and adding more data with each pass.

When you search, try various combinations. If your name is a common one, such as *John Smith,* you're probably going to get a lot of hits unrelated to you. Try adding the topic of your show to the search for more relevant results. For example, if your name is John Smith and you're podcasting about underwater basket weaving, type **John Smith underwater basket weaving** in the Google search box. If your show name is unique, or at least uncommon, try using the name of your show as a search term.

We realize that there are other search engines besides Google. Yahoo! produces fine results, as do a few others. But for those who have neither the time nor the inclination to experiment with a dozen search engines, we suggest these two. Both syndicate their results to other lesser-known (but equally valid) search engines. Together, they cover the vast majority (by some estimates about 90 percent) of the indexed pages online. But as we've said countless times before, your mileage may vary. The same techniques we've outlined will work well on just about any search engine you prefer.

Using specialty search engines

Search engines are great tools, but sometimes they search a bit too far and wide for your tastes. Many specialty search engines have cropped up in the past few years to cater to the needs of people looking to search a more narrow set of criteria than "all Web pages on the entire planet." Researchers, academics, and students have had this level of access for a while. Now, several services have been made public that may be of use to the podcaster trying to find communications about his or her show.

Google News

In what might be the most narcissistic activity on the planet, Google allows you to easily do a daily check of who is talking about you and your podcast on the Internet with its *Google Alerts* free service. With this feature, you receive an e-mail when a news article within Google News contains text matching a text string of your choice, which is likely to be your name or the name of your podcast.

Here's how to set up a Google Alert:

1. **Access the Google News section at** `news.google.com`.

2. **Click the News Alerts link in the left navigation bar.**

3. **Enter the search terms for the topic you want to monitor, the type of results you want, and how often you want to receive results.**

   Just for example, you might wish to type in **evo terra**.

   If you want to search beyond news or more than once a day, you can change these default settings.

4. **Enter your e-mail address.**

   If you're already logged in to Google, you won't see this step.

   When Google finds matching terms, it sends you an e-mail notification along with a link to the article.

Technorati

Technorati (`technorati.com`) is really more of a "buzz engine" than a search engine. It focuses its concentration and power on blogs and news services and does an exceptional job of ferreting out conversations about hot topics of nearly any size.

With Technorati, you can search for keywords, key phrases, or specific URLs. Many bloggers have found ways to pass the URLs of their blog posts to the Technorati search engine, allowing them (and others) a quick way to take the pulse of the community reaction to their words. While Technorati won't search through podcast audio yet, it's a great way to find out if bloggers are discussing the ideas and comments you put forth on your show.

Podscope

As of this writing, many podcasts talk about . . . other podcasts. Many don't adequately use show notes, which makes it difficult for search engine spiders and bots to find the content.

Spiders and bots? Hey, Evo hosts a science fiction show, so this stuff comes natural to him. *Spiders* follow links around the Internet, much like real spiders follow the lines of silk on a web. Internet spiders report back on what they find, whereas real spiders wrap up their prey for a tasty snack later. *Bots* (derivative of robots) are automated scripts that act a lot like spiders, but usually don't "crawl" as far. Contrary to popular belief, bots do not have optional laser attachments and have no desire to send muscle-bound cyborgs from the future to *FIND SARAH CONNOR!*

But the fine folks at Podscope (`podscope.com`) have figured out a way around that — searching the actual audio entry of the episode. Figure 11-3 shows a recent result on searching for *Lance Armstrong* at Podscope. If the service finds any show notes, they are brought back as search results.

However, the true coolness lies a bit deeper. Click the little + button to expand your results, and then click the green "play" button to listen to a 10-second or so audio clip that contains the search phrase in question. How very cool! You can amuse yourself for hours with this little feature, puzzling over how we did it. And rather than spoil it for you with a technical description of the technologies involved, we're sticking with "magic" as the most relevant explanation.

Figure 11-3: Audio search results are displayed on Podscope.

Searching within a site or message board

As extensive and cool as search engines are, they can't cover everything on the Net. Not only are there physical limitations as to how wide of an area the spiders and bots can cover, there are also self-imposed limitations set up by Web site owners that inhibit a good indexing of the site.

Take forums for example. Earlier in this chapter, we mention that setting up and installing your own forum is complicated and beyond the scope of this book. By that same token, many who have managed to set up their forums have done so in a manner that renders their internal pages invisible to the spiders and bots of even the best engines.

When this happens, your only recourse is to hope that the forum has an internal search engine. Most do, though some require registration to access this feature. Figure 11-4 shows the search results we found by doing an internal search on a popular discussion board that prohibits spiders and bots from indexing its individual pages. None of these pages were indexed by Google or by Yahoo!.

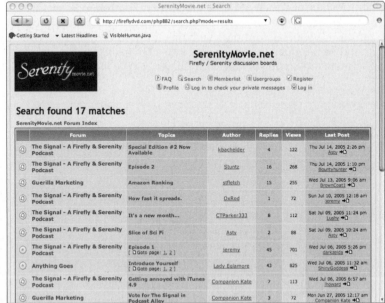

Figure 11-4:
Results of a search on "pod-casting" at Serenity Movie.net.

Checking your server logs

Many of the comments you find about your show on various other Web sites will contain a link back to your Web site, show notes, or even your XML feed.

When readers of those comments click the link left by the person who made the comment, evidence of that visit is recorded by your Web server in a *server log.*

Server logs are a nightmare to look at and really weren't designed to be read by human eyes. They contain massive blocks of text entries that record an exhaustive list of data about the visitor, including IP address, date and time of the visit, pages accessed, images seen, files downloaded, referring site, barometric pressure. . . . Okay, we exaggerated on the last one, but you get the idea.

Most Web hosting companies allow a more user-friendly interface to help site owners understand the information contained in the log file. Of greatest importance to this chapter is the *referrers* section, sometimes called site visits. These are the "footprints of others," if you will — evidence that someone visited your site after being *referred* (clicking on a link) from another site.

You are at the mercy of your hosting provider when it comes to your options for viewing server logs. Many of the podcast-specific and pre-configured blog options don't provide this level of detail. If you've configured your Web site from scratch, you likely do have access but are stuck with the tool your hosting company provides.

Figures 11-5, 11-6, and 11-7 show three of the more popular server log analytics programs (sometimes called Web stats) available from many hosting companies. Log in to your Web administration panel and look for any of these options. If all else fails, call or e-mail your hosting company and ask how to access your log analysis tools.

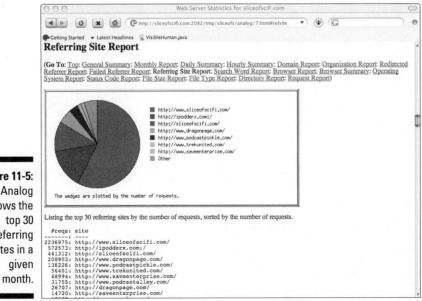

Figure 11-5:
Analog shows the top 30 referring sites in a given month.

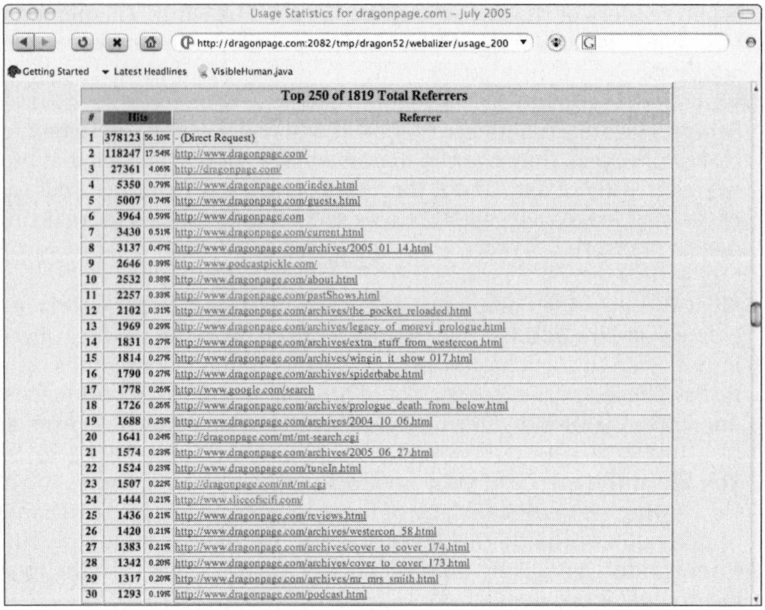

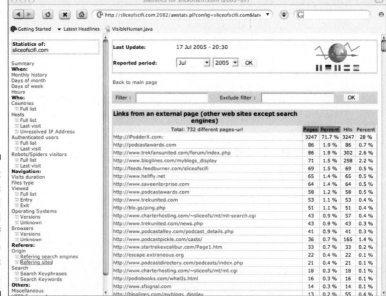

Figure 11-6:
Webalizer
shows the
top 250
referrers for
the month.

From here, simply click a link, and you go directly to the site with the link
that sent people to your site.

Figure 11-7:
AWStats is
considered
the gold
standard of
the free
analytics
software.

Some people spend hours every day looking over their server logs. Hey, that's your prerogative if you wish to head down that path. Be warned that obsession with Web stats ("the numbers") has been clinically proven to be detrimental to personal hygiene, interpersonal communication skills, and marital bliss.

Now that you've found the comments. . . .

Look, we're not your mother. We're just a couple of guys imploring you to actively communicate with your listeners, even if they comment about you in other places. So get to communicating already!

- ✔ **Blogs:** If the comment came from a blog post or a comment on a blog post, comment back! After that, make a note to come back and check a day or two later. A great feedback loop could get started, and the last thing you want to do is leave them hanging.

  Some of the blog comments allow you to subscribe to the comment thread, sending you an e-mail alert when someone posts after your post. We strongly recommend using this tool because that little note you wrote will likely get lost in the shuffle.

- ✔ **Forums:** The same advice holds true for discussion forums. We highly recommend signing up on the forum where they are chatting about you and becoming a regular poster. Most forums operate free of charge, so your only investment is time. Posting regularly keeps your show on the minds of the other people on the forum, almost guaranteeing that you'll gain additional listeners who are interested in what you have to say.

- ✔ **News stories, official reviews, and other comments:** Places that don't allow comments or additional direct feedback can be more challenging, but should not be avoided. Find e-mail addresses for the people who have written articles and let them know you saw what they wrote. Tell them you'll be mentioning their articles in an upcoming show. The more often they listen, the more good press you're likely to get from them.

When the comments are less than good

First, don't panic.

Second, don't respond. Not yet.

Third, let your blood pressure come down to a normal level.

Let's face it. Anytime someone has any critical comments about us, we get an emotional reaction. We call that being human, and it's perfectly understandable and quite literally impossible to suppress, unless you're one of those aliens from earlier in the chapter.

Once you're calm and feeling a bit more detached, reread the comment and plan your course of action. Here are some suggestions:

1. **Reflect on the comment.**

   What does the comment say, really? Does the person make a valid point? Is there an area of improvement you should make? If the comment was specific, go back and re-listen to the show in question. Did you say what the person said you did or stumble as bad as the person made it out to be? You may need a different perspective, so feel free to get someone else involved.

2. **Once you fully understand the criticism, decide if you want to respond or not.**

   Obviously, if a comment is in any way libelous, you may wish to seek legal counsel before proceeding. If a comment is simply pure vitriol, your best course may be to ignore it and go about your business.

   But if you feel it's necessary, reply. Just like any argument, it's best to keep things on a professional level with your words and mannerisms. While it may be hard to not put it on a personal level, try not to do that. It's not going to help the situation.

3. **If you decide to reply, consider how you will reply:**

   • **Send an e-mail.** If you send an e-mail, count on that e-mail being posted right alongside the negative comment. There's no guarantee the person will keep your correspondence private. In fact, count on the opposite. Whatever you say in a private e-mail should be something you would be willing to say in a more public forum.

   • **Get others to respond for you.** We caution against coaching their response, however. Instead, send your defender of choice a simple e-mail with a link to the offending post and perhaps a link to your episode in question, if applicable. Choose someone with a level head, not your older sister who'll punch anyone in the face who tussles your hair on the playground.

But more than anything, grow from the experience. Understand that anything you say in your podcast will be heard by a variety of people, with different backgrounds, experiences, and expectations of the world. We've been on both sides of this and can count many times where the negative comments we received turned out to be some of the best feedback. We think we're better podcasters for it.

Feedback, good or bad, is only as constructive as you make it out to be.

Chapter 12

Fishing for Listeners

. . . .

. . . .

As of this writing, there are over 10,000 podcasters. By some estimates, over 200,000 people listen to various podcasts, though we believe the actual number is somewhat higher still. However, that pales in comparison to the potential audience, somewhere in excess of 160 million people world-wide with a broadband Internet connection. While the audience is large, the options for listeners are legion. How do you attract an audience to your podcast?

In this chapter, we show you a variety of options that you may wish to use in an effort to gain a larger listener base. Some cost you money, others cost you time. But the end result should be exposing your podcast to the right people at the right time.

Getting Your Podcast Ready for Advertising

Whether you plan on spending real money or expending real energy, you need to do some prep work before you start your campaign. Advertising campaigns should not be rushed, but should be carefully planned and executed. Failure to do so can not only be a huge waste of time and money, but also may result in turning off potential listeners to your show, making it many times more difficult to lure them back for a second chance.

Polishing your presentation

Most podcasters need a few shows under their belts before they hit their stride. If you're on podcast episode number three, you likely haven't flushed out your show. Granted, you may have been planning this for months on end, or have previous experience behind the mic on another medium, or have nailed it from the beginning. If so, great. But understand you are in the minority.

While each person is different, we suggest giving yourself at least five full shows to find the sweet spot for your show. Experimentation is part of the format, so play with a few things along the way to see where your strengths as well as your weaknesses are.

Checking on your bandwidth

In Chapter 7, we talk about the negative aspects of too large an audience. Each new listener means more of your precious bandwidth is being consumed. For podcasters with limited bandwidth, getting more listeners can be an expensive proposition.

If you're using the services of Liberated Syndication (`libsyn.com`) or another unmetered bandwidth podcast hosting company, this won't be an issue for you. See Chapter 7 for more information about these very affordable services.

Figure 12-1 shows the bandwidth usage for one of Evo's shows, taken mid-July 2005. As you can see, his listeners have already consumed 256.65 gigabytes (GB) of transfers for the month. Your hosting company should provide a similar status report in your control panel. If you're unsure of where to look for it, call or e-mail your hosting company's support desk for more information.

Too many podcasters are often surprised when they run out of bandwidth. We're more surprised of how poor their math skills are. Suppose that you have 100MB of monthly transfers allowed for your site. On the 10th of July, you log in to your bandwidth stats page and see that you're already at 60MB for the month. Will you make it? Here are the formulas to figure this out:

Bandwidth consumed / number of days so far this month = Daily bandwidth rate

Daily bandwidth rate × the total number of days in the month = Total bandwidth needed

Now you plug in your numbers to find out your daily bandwidth rate:

60MB / 10 = 6MB

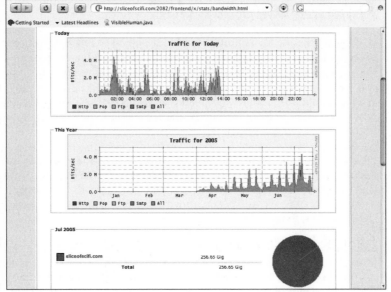

Figure 12-1:
A graphical
representa-
tion of
bandwidth
usage,
available
from most
hosting
companies.

You're consuming about 6MB per day. Now multiply this number (6MB) by the number of days in the month (31) to get the total bandwidth you need for the month:

$$6MB \times 31 = 186MB$$

No, you will not be able to stay within your 100MB limit. You will be roughly 86MB over your 100MB plan.

That sounds — and is — simple, but real world numbers might be helpful. In Evo's case, the math is

256.65GB / 17 days = 15GB average daily transfer rate for July

$15GB \times 31$ days = 465GB by the end of the month

As you can see, he needs 465GB of bandwidth to get through the month, assuming his traffic stays steady and doesn't increase. If his bandwidth ceiling was 500GB, he'd need to think twice before starting an advertising campaign, as he'd likely hit that ceiling, and his hosting provider would likely shut down access to all those brand-new podcast listeners he just worked so hard to get. Not a good way for anyone to spend his or her time.

As a good rule, you need to be utilizing less than 50 percent of your monthly allotment of bandwidth before starting an advertising campaign. If you're using any more than that, you'll run out of room and will have to seek alternative hosting options before proceeding. We cover some of these alternative options in Chapter 7.

Figuring out your USP

USP is a marketing term, and it stands for *unique selling proposition*. While you probably aren't charging money to listen to your podcast, make no mistake that you need to "sell it" to potential listeners if you're considering advertising.

Why should a potential listener listen to your podcast? And more importantly, how can you, as the podcast advertiser, present a message that makes a potential listener want to listen?

Plenty of books, Web sites, seminars, and post-graduate-degree programs are dedicated to the subtle nuances of advertising. We're not suggesting you go that far, obviously. But we do suggest you take a good, hard look at what you produce every week, and come up with a short, concise, and consistent message with which to promote your show.

Sometimes calling in help from the outside can be a good thing. Ask your friends and family, or even your listeners, to come up with some key points of why they listen to your show. We're not talking about a catchy slogan or jingle of the sort a Madison Avenue marketing firm might designate as the "perfect" thing to attract new listeners, but rather plain English (or your language of choice) ways to tell interested folks what your show is about and why they should be listening.

Here's an example. Evo produces three different science-fiction-focused radio shows. Each has its own flavor, and its own USP. The best example is his Dragon Page *Cover to Cover*. Early on, Evo and his partner focused on interviewing science fiction and fantasy authors. This set the show apart from other sci-fi shows that were interviewing various actors, discussing popular TV shows and movies, and generally skipping over the literary aspects of science fiction. In fact, they decided that that last sentence summed up the show: Literary concepts in science fiction and fantasy. And a USP was born.

We can't give you a step-by-step outline on this one. Spend a few days on it. Try it out on some folks first. When you find a message that fits, you're ready to proceed.

Exploring Various Advertising Options

In this section, we discuss some ways you can advertise to expose your podcast to a larger audience. Then later in the chapter, we talk about some additional opportunities that go beyond simply buying advertising space.

Is advertising right for your podcast?

Before launching your advertising campaign, apply some *Jurassic Park* logic. In that movie, Jeff Goldblum's character chastises the dinosaur-resurrecting mogul with "your scientists were so preoccupied with whether or not they could, they didn't stop to think if they should." Good advice for podcasters and mad scientists alike.

For many, podcasting is a labor of love and not a money-making proposition. As such, spending too much money or time on advertising may make a passion seem a heck of a lot more like a job — and you already have one of those.

Some of the podcasts we enjoy the most, such as Dave Slusher's *Evil Genius Chronicles* (www.

evilgeniuschronicles.org), are very vocal about not advertising and not working toward a huge listener base. Dave makes a podcast for one person — Dave Slusher. If other folks hear about the podcast and decide to listen, great — so long as they enjoy it and don't expect him to be something he's not. Fame is a double-edged sword — even the moderate fame a popular podcaster can achieve. Before long, e-mails and voice mails are flying in with ideas, suggestions, and even mandates of how you can make the show better — for them. Don't forget that *fan* is short for *fanatic,* and fanatical people don't always behave rationally.

Google AdWords

When it comes to exposing yourself to the largest possible audience, you simply can't beat the power of Google. More than just a search engine, Google allows you to reach over 80 percent of all active Internet users with targeted and relevant advertising. With Google AdWords (`adwords.google.com`), you need to keep your advertising costs under control and reach a very specific audience.

How it works

Google AdWords allows you to place text ads or *sponsored links* at the top and right side of Google search results pages, based on keywords that you (and others) bid on. Additionally, its content distribution network allows your text ads to appear on various Web sites related to the keywords for which you have placed bids.

Google charges advertisers on a cost-per-click basis, and the cost of the click is determined by how much Google is charging you for that click, not to exceed your maximum bid amount. You can spend $5.00 per day, or $500,000 per month on Google, showing the true scalability of the platform. Evo has been a power user of Google for years, both personally and on behalf of his clients, and has always found that Google delivers great results.

Google provides a Traffic Estimator to its AdWords clients, helping them understand what sort of traffic an advertiser might expect from a given set of keywords.

The signup process for the AdWords product is simple and straightforward, so we don't go in detail about it in this book. Simply access `adwords.google.com`, and Google takes you step by step through the sign-up process.

Using the service

When you first sign up for Google AdWords, start with a small investment. Even for representatives of large companies looking to start their own podcast, don't go overboard on spending real dollars on advertising campaigns right off the bat. Pick a modest number to start with, evaluate your results, and refine your technique. After you have it figured out, then you can go hog-wild!

After you decide on a budget, you need to find keywords that fit within that budget. Say, for example, your podcast is about fishing. For the keyword *fishing*, Google estimates approximately 2,600 clicks per day. That's a great traffic number that any fledgling podcaster would love to have hitting their site each day.

However, in order to get all those 2,600 clicks for *fishing,* Google says you'd need to set your maximum bid at $2.50 per click so that your ad showed in a good and competitive position against other people and companies advertising on the page. Google further estimates you would be charged an average of $0.62 for each of those clicks, making your total daily budget over $1,600 per day. Wow.

To help bring this cost down to a more manageable level, you need to get more targeted with your keywords. *Fishing* is a rather broad term, so try a few other combinations to see if you can find a cost within your budget. Here are a few examples you might consider:

- ✔ **salmon fishing:** If you enter salmon fishing in the Traffic Estimator, you get a more reasonable estimate of a total cost of $46.19 per day. However, at that price tag, you're only attracting 20 new people. *Salmon fishing* has a much higher cost per click than *fishing.*

- ✔ **fishing advice:** A more economical approach is to bid on *fishing advice.* Not as many big outfitters and organizations are willing to give advice away, so they aren't bidding on the keywords. Daily traffic isn't much more than 1 or 2 clicks per day, but the cost estimate is only $0.44 per click. Now you're into the world of reality.

All Google ads are bid-based, causing those who pay the highest amount of money for a click to rise to the top. If you only want to spend $0.25 to get a click, but the top bid on that keyword is already $4.50, you're going to be way down the list of advertisers.

Blogads

Advertising on blogs requires a different mindset than advertising on a search engine. Blog readers, for the most part, have little love for advertising. They're looking for content they can't get from the mainstream media outlets, or are completely caught up by the cult of personality surrounding their bloggers of choice.

Sounds like a perfect place to attract listeners to your podcast!

Blogads (`blogads.com`) is a fine example of one company that makes this easier on the advertiser. While you can find literally hundreds of thousands of blogs, Blogads has created a network of sorts, allowing you to place a single ad on a multitude of blogs. That's a whole lot easier than researching blogs, negotiating prices individually, and creating and tracking ads for each one.

According to Blogads: "Warning: ads you'd run on sites like MSNBC.com may underperform on blogs. Smart blogads join a community's conversation rather than shouting over it." If you're an independent podcast producer, you should have no trouble creating ads that really speak to why people should listen to your podcast. If you're podcasting for a corporation, getting your advertising department to speak in this language may be more difficult. Blog Ads has some great examples of what does, as well as what doesn't, work on its network of sites.

Signing up for Blogads takes only a few minutes. You're guided through the process of creating a compelling image and using supporting text within the ad. Prices range from $20 per week to over $5,000 per week, putting Blogads in a price range for nearly anybody who is ready to spend some money advertising his or her show.

Writing press releases

Some podcasters have had enormous success with press releases. When you write and release a press release, it's available to be picked up by a variety of news sources. On the plus side, you have a lot of room inside a press release to talk about your show. On the negative, you have no guarantee of who, if anyone, will pick up and run your press release.

Writing an effective press release is a true art form. It has to appeal to both the managing editor of the publication considering your release or building a story around it, and to John Q. Public who will be reading your release (or article built from your release) in the publication.

PR Newswire

PR Newswire (`prwire.com`) is the cream of the crop when it comes to online and offline distribution of your press release. PR Newswire has the ability to send your press release to thousands of media outlets, ranging from newsprint, radio, Web sites, television, and more.

The company also provides editorial services for your press release, as well as tips and tricks on how to write an effective release that is more likely to get results. If you're serious about getting the maximum exposure to your show and are thinking about using a press release as part of your strategy, PR Newswire is worth looking into.

However, many independent podcasters may find the cost prohibitive (around $300 to start) and the registration process somewhat daunting. In a world where online registration and upfront disclosure is commonplace, PR Newswire follows a more traditional approach. Gaining access requires you to contact your local bureau either via e-mail (`information@prnewswire.com`) or by telephone. You can find a list at `www.prnewswire.com/services/resources/bureaus.shtml`.

PRWeb

Considerably less archaic is PRWeb (`prweb.com`). This organization offers paid and donation-based services, and boasts of a good number of media outlets. The main difference between the two organizations (other than cost and the hassle-factor) is the quality of the distribution. PRWeb works to put your press release in front of thousands of online media outlets. Offline media sources may subscribe as well, but the primary distribution is online.

Not that that is a bad thing. After all, your podcast is an online service, and you're likely most effective reaching an audience who is already online. Both of us have had various write-ups in both online and offline media, and we've always received more traffic and attention to our Web sites from the online sources.

We don't want to make PRWeb sound somehow inferior to the traditional sources of press release distribution. Far from it, actually. While the service may not be as full featured, it can still be a great way to get your word out, and one that is quite cost effective.

For $80, PRWeb distributes your press release (among many other things) in Yahoo! News, a huge news source that is often referenced in the online community. Additionally, press releases at this level are reviewed by the PRWeb editorial team, providing valuable feedback on ways to make your press release more meaningful and more likely to be picked up by various other news organizations around the Internet.

Advertising without Spending Money

Before you start throwing money toward an advertising campaign, consider all the things you can do to spread the word about your podcast that don't require a financial investment. In fact, you probably should be doing these things even if you plan on tossing out some cash for effect.

Optimizing your site for search engines

In Chapters 8 and 9, we give you several tips on how you can make your RSS listings as well as your show notes more appealing to search engines. You can employ similar methods to your entire Web site, so that it receives the maximum exposure and visibility to search engines.

For more information on optimizing your site, we highly recommend *Search Engine Optimization For Dummies* by Peter Kent (published by Wiley Publishing, Inc.). Additionally, Cre8asite Forums at cre8asiteforums.com is an invaluable discussion board to keep up on the latest techniques on keeping your Web site search engine friendly.

Submitting promos to other podcasts

Podcasting has been called by critics (even us) a great hall of mirrors, as it seems that nearly every podcast spends a ridiculous portion of its time talking about . . . other podcasts!

We think this is normal for an emerging medium, and something that is, for the most part, accepted by the general podcasting audience. The podcasting landscape isn't shrinking anytime soon, and it's so fractured that many listeners are looking for their favorite podcasters to help steer them toward other podcasts they may find interesting.

Not all podcasters do this. In fact, the majority of the corporate podcasts must see other podcasts as competition, and are as likely to talk about another podcast as a traditional broadcaster is to talk about another station across town. Even some of the independent podcasters make a point not to talk about other podcasts, simply because they don't want to add to the hall of mirrors effect.

One of the more widespread ways podcasters talk about other podcasters is with promos. A *promo* is a short (or long) audio clip that describes your show. Other podcasts then insert this clip into their shows, or play it on the air so to speak, thereby presenting your message to their subscribed and downloading audiences.

Promos are a great way to let other folks know your podcast exists. Spend some time listening to other podcasts and see if they're playing promos. When you find one that does, see what the average time for the promotion turns out to be, and what type of content is being presented. Is it all serious business, or is more light-hearted humor involved?

Some podcasters are really good at making promos, and are even offering to make promos for free for other podcasters. A whole promo exchange industry is cropping up, allowing podcasters to trade time with other podcasters, each agreeing to run the other podcaster's promo for a certain number of weeks. Check out `kiptronic.com` and `podcastpromos.com` for details.

Recording your promo

Recording your own promo isn't difficult, and we tend to enjoy the ones that come from the voice of the podcaster. You've done the hard work by figuring out what makes your podcast special; now you need to sit down and record your promo. Here are a few tips:

✔ **Write out your script.**

Or don't. Some folks are happy flying off the cuff. But in the interest of time, we highly recommend putting some thoughts down on paper and running through them out loud to see how long it takes. Most promos are under a minute long, unless you have lots of great stuff to say.

✔ **Add effects and music from your podcast.**

If you use the same music (see Chapter 5) in your show each week, or have some special sound effects that brand the show as yours, include them in your promo. Effects are a great way to tie in your promotion to your show, giving new listeners assurance they have subscribed to the right place.

✔ **Don't forget your Web site URL!**

Too many podcasters provide the link to their podcast feed. Useless, in our opinions. Instead, repeat the URL of your Web site, where it should be painfully simple to subscribe to the RSS feed for your podcast. Now here's to hoping you picked an easy-to-remember domain name!

✔ **Include a link to the promo on your Web site.**

Recording a promo and sending it out to a few podcasts is great, but what about all the other folks who you inspire to make their own podcast? Chances are, if you put a link to your promo file on your Web site, others will grab that file and include your promo in their shows. It's also a good repository for when you find another podcast you think might want to run your promo. Save some e-mail bandwidth and send the link to the file, rather than the file itself.

One final note on sending out promos: Ask. Unless the show specifically says "submit your promos to us at . . . ," be a good podcasting citizen and send the podcaster a note asking if she'd like to run your promo. Requests that start off with "I listen to your show every week because you . . ." are likely to get a better response than those starting (and ending) with "Please run my promo."

Giving interviews

Don't forget that podcasting is the fastest growing medium we've seen . . . ever! If your podcast covers a brand-new area of the world or addresses an underserved market, folks are out there who want to talk with you about it.

Contact the publications, radio shows, Web sites, and other outlets that cover the industry your podcast falls under. Send them your press release, along with a personalized note telling them about your show and stating that you're happy to do an interview.

Interviews can be done in person, but most today are conducted over the phone. A handful are conducted via e-mail. Preparing for an interview can make the difference between a poor interview that never sees publication or airtime and a well-delivered interview that keeps the audience — as well as the interviewer — engaged and entertained.

Here are a few tips to make your interview go swimmingly:

✔ **Eliminate the BS factor.**

If you have only a passing interest in the subject for which you are trying to pass yourself off as an expert, you'll be quickly discovered, thrashed repeatedly, and left out for the buzzards. The people who are interviewing you likely are already experts in their fields, so don't try and come off as something you are not. Be open and honest about your experience, and focus on why you're doing the podcast.

✔ **Mention your Web site, over and over again.**

Remember that the listeners, readers, or viewers you are being interviewed in front of have no idea who you are and what you are about. This is your chance to sell yourself and your podcast. If your interviewer is good, he'll give you ample opportunity to mention your Web site and podcast. If not, it's up to you. Look for chances to drop the name and URL if necessary.

✔ **Stay positive.**

If the interviewer knows anything about podcasting, he'll likely ask questions on the future of podcasting, the death of radio, amateur versus professional, and all sorts of other controversial topics. Unless your podcast is about podcasting, we recommend rising above the din. This conversation doesn't serve you or the listening/reading/viewing audience well. Point out how your podcast addresses the issue, and resist the temptation to get into an argument. Unless your podcast is about arguing with interviewers, then go right ahead.

Generating buzz

All the processes we outline in this chapter are geared toward one thing: generating buzz for your podcast. The more folks you can get talking about your show, the better off you are. We don't buy the "any publicity is good publicity" line, but we do think that "Hey have you heard about . . .?" conversations amongst real people is the best form of advertising you can get.

Sometimes, you need to take the message to the masses. Find a discussion group or online forum germane to your podcast's area of interest and start posting.

Don't start out with "Hey, I'm new to the group and have this great podcast!" Instead, listen to the conversation, comment on a few threads, and get folks used to your voice before you hit them with the come-listen-to-my-podcast pitch.

In fact, the best way to pitch your podcast is to never utter those words at all. Instead, offer up things like "Last week on my podcast, I covered the very thing you were talking about, Jill." It shows you're paying attention to the conversation, and not just looking to spam a newsgroup or mailing list with your podcast URL.

As we mention in Chapter 11 regarding e-mail, a very fine line exists between tasteful self-promotion and outright spamming. Generating buzz is not the same as advertising. Advertising has its place, but most forums don't welcome it. If you can't decide if your post contains too much advertising or not, it probably does. Discretion is the better part of valor, in this instance.

Part V
Pod-sibilities to Consider for Your Show

The 5th Wave   By Rich Tennant

"You ever notice how much more streaming media there is than there used to be?"

In this part . . .

As you can see in the parts and chapters leading up to this one, podcasting is a breeze when you know the right steps. But now comes the moment of truth: We move away from the "how" questions and tackle "why" you might want to podcast. Fame and fortune? Strength and honor? Therapy and philanthropy? Fun with computers? An alternative to a real social life? These all sound like good reasons to us.

Chapter 13

Show Me the Money

*T*hroughout this book, we show you novel and interesting ways to toss significant amounts of coinage into the proverbial black hole of podcasting. Let's face it, this is a habit — and it likely should come with a warning from the Surgeon General, or perhaps your accountant.

Hosting fees, bandwidth overages, shiny new microphones, music royalties and licensing fees, phone charges, travel expenses . . . the hard and soft costs of this little hobby of yours just might add up quickly.

That's why this chapter shows you some ways to offset a portion (or all) of these costs, and perhaps even add a few dollars to your pocket while you explore your newfound passion. If you anticipate a large following, we'll cover some ideas you can use to make this your paying gig.

Being a podcaster is a lot like being an actor, writer, or movie star. A few select individuals may make it big, but the bulk of the masses will be just getting by. If you are reading this chapter first in hopes of getting a crash course in how to "get rich quick" with your podcast, you are about to be disappointed. If not, we can talk.

How Much Money Can You Make?

Most podcasters fall into one of three categories: small, medium, and large (well, yeah). Because of the very low barrier-to-entry — in effect, almost anyone can create a podcast — the smaller variety of podcaster will likely make up the bulk of the community for the foreseeable future.

Here's a closer look at the moneymaking opportunities for these three podcast categories:

- ✔ **Small:** Having a small audience size does not exclude you from drawing a revenue stream from your podcast. It likely limits the size of your potential revenues, but it doesn't mean you can't bring in at least some income.

  Small is a relative term, and we're not about to start tossing out audience-size statistics to draw a clear demarcation between small and medium. Small is also not a derogatory term; many podcasters enjoy the idea of keeping their cast small. There is a certain comfort in the small podcasts, a charm that some would say is diminished as the size of the podcast increases.

- ✔ **Medium:** Podcasters who find themselves (or claim to be) in the medium category may find that a larger listening audience affords them additional opportunities. For instance, corporations and advertisers may be more willing to consider placing ads or providing sponsorships to those shows with more than a handful of dedicated listeners.

  However, they also find themselves in a more competitive marketplace, as other podcasters start fishing for monies to help offset their costs. Stepping upward in the ranks also means stepping up the game, and many podcasters find themselves in an unfamiliar place — trying to develop media kits that boost their podcasts above the din raised by all those other podcasts chasing the very same advertisers.

  Creating an effective media kit, especially for a newly discovered marketplace such as podcasting, is actually a pretty important task (for more about the why, what, and how-to, see "Developing a media kit," later in this chapter). We highly recommend the *Podcast Brothers* (`feeds.feedburner.com/PodcastBrothers`) podcast to anyone looking for ideas and ways to make money with podcasting. Tim and Emil Bourquin produce this weekly show, covering the ins and the outs of making money with your podcast.

- ✔ **Large:** Breaking this barrier at the far end of the size spectrum is an elite set of podcasters who occupy the *large* category. When it comes to making money with your podcast, size really does matter. Podcasts with a huge audience base will likely find advertisers a lot easier to approach; they can present listener numbers that are more like what the advertisers are used to seeing in their more traditional media buys.

  There aren't that many really *large* podcasts out there — yet — so thus far the playing field is still fairly open. Still, it's no picnic for large podcasters; after all, they're still narrowcasting, and they probably won't rake in as much as a nationally syndicated radio program. Don't be surprised, however, if you see that paradigm change. Podcasters have much more flexibility than broadcasters, and arguably a closer relationship with the audience.

Does your podcast need to pay for itself?

"You spent *how much* on a new microphone?" You'll soon be hearing that, or a question just like it with a different gizmo attached to the question mark. Your non-podcasting friends, colleagues, and perhaps even family will gaze in wonder at your apparent lack of good judgment as you seemingly spend money as if it grew on trees, adding just one more piece to your previously professed "perfect" podcasting setup.

How can you, in good conscience, justify this outlay of cash without the financial backing of someone else? Surely if no one is willing to pay you to do this podcasting thing, you shouldn't be doing it at all, right?

In a word, wrong.

(Evo here.) As I write this, my 14-year-old son is busy bouncing back and forth between his PS2 and his PC, about $3,000 in total investments. My wife is on her laptop ($1,500) cropping recent images taken with her new top-of-the-line prosumer digital camera ($2,000). Next door, my neighbor is up to his elbows in grease, changing the rear seals (whatever those are) in his "family fleet" of ATVs before a trip to the dunes this weekend. He wins the prize, having no less than $15,000 invested in his passion.

Each of these non-podcasting individuals, all of whom are involved in the healthy pursuit of liberty and happiness, constantly spend money on their hobbies. My son thinks nothing of dropping $50 of his (read: MY) money on a game every two months. My wife now goes through at least two color ink cartridges every month. And Jerry next door has to burn through a few hundred dollars of fuel, parts, and doctor bills each month.

If I were to poll each of these people, asking them whether they had ever considered getting someone to help pay for their various addictions, they'd look at me as if I were from another planet. Well, except my son. He'd just grin and say, "But isn't that *you*, Dad?"

Think of the amount of money you spend eating out each week. Or for movie tickets, theater presentations, concerts, and/or bar tabs. These are things you love and enjoy, not things you're trying to find others to pay for. Most podcasters will spend no more than a hundred bucks a month on their show, and that's stretching it. And for such a small investment that has such a high personal payoff . . . do you *need* to be paid off in cold hard cash to do it?

(Tee here.) And of course, never underestimate the power and value of *SPUs: Spousal Permission Units*. Flowers, a surprise trip to a spa, and cooking dinner and cleaning house for a month. It will surprise you how many SPUs a little TLC can earn you for some killer podcasting hardware!

Convincing Advertisers to Give You Money

If the idea of begging for money sounds rather repulsive, good. If you have to resort to begging, you shouldn't be asking at all. People will only part with their cash if you give them a compelling reason. "Because I'm a poor podcaster" is not a compelling reason.

Whether your goal is to gain sponsors or sell advertising spots, you have to answer a very important question: What's in it for them? Why should someone else make a financial contribution to your show? There are a multitude of good reasons that you'll need to uncover, understand, and be able to explain if you hope to be successful in asking for funds to support your podcast.

Getting advertising money

Contrary to popular belief, there aren't nearly enough corporations so bursting-at-the-seams with unused advertising dollars that they'll welcome you with open arms when you approach them and say, "Hey! Wanna advertise on my podcast?"

Most corporations have an advertising *budget* (as in, limit on what they can spend). In nearly all circumstances, this budget is significantly smaller than the range of potential places they might be advertising — so they're looking for bang-for-the-buck. As one of the would-be venues for their ads, you're competing with other forms of media — including outlets that already have well-established pitches and presentations at the ready.

Before you start cold-calling possible advertisers, do a little homework: Spend some time, energy, and money developing something your potential advertisers can touch and see — a media kit, as described in the next section.

The big fish are very well armed in this pond. Large media outlets tend to have large media kits that were developed with the assistance of large advertising agencies that charged large sums of money for their expertise. The small- to mid-size podcaster need not go this far. But you need something more than just a burned CD of your latest episode.

Developing a media kit

A *media kit* is, in effect, a collection of marketing tools designed to awaken potential advertisers to their crying need to shell out big bucks to support your product (in this case, your podcast). The size of your media kit depends on many factors, among which are how much you want to spend and how much important stuff you think you have to say. It's not size you're striving for here; it's a compelling argument that you can present to your potential advertisers.

Media kits are most certainly not one size fits all. Your media kit should be representative of the actual feeling you try to produce on your podcast — competent, real, not over-the-top glitzy. Consider it like a job interview: It's okay to comb your hair and put on a fresh shirt, but you wouldn't send your good-looking-but-ignorant roommate as a stand-in, would you? (Look what happened to Cyrano.)

So here's a practical list of dos and don'ts to keep in mind when considering what to put in your media kit.

First off, the "Yes, go for it" list:

✔ **Include accurate listener statistics.** Well, as accurate as you can, anyway. Include the total number of subscribers to your podcast feed; estimate how many direct downloads an episode of your show attracts. If your podcast is seeing great growth, include a chart that shows the increasing numbers. (For more about listener statistics, see the handy nearby sidebar, "Can you ever really know the size of your audience?")

✔ **Display your show schedule.** If you update your podcast several times a week or once a month, put up a calendar or schedule of when your updates happen. If your show has no set schedule, be prepared to explain your methodology of updates. Many advertisers expect some sort of consistency (read: reliable exposure) from the places their ads are running.

✔ **Provide demographic information.** Some advertisers will want to know the general make-up of your audience. The more detailed you can get, the better. At a minimum, show a breakdown of gender, age range, and household income level. These statistics can be difficult to gather, but doing so increases your chances with many advertisers.

✔ **Showcase your popularity.** If you get 50 comments on each of your show note entries, talk about it. Technorati (technorati.com) and Google (www.google.com) can support any claims for the popularity of your site. Print out any great testimonials showing your knowledge and expertise in the field. Favorable comments from other known experts go a long way, too!

And in the "No, no, a thousand times no" corner, we have . . .

✔ **Don't artificially inflate your statistics.** Grandmother always used to say that lies just cause you to make bigger lies. Eventually you find yourself with an advertiser who wants you to explain how you came up with your numbers. Make sure you can support your claims.

✔ **Don't offer reduced pricing.** Podcasting is a new medium, and you likely haven't had time to put things on sale yet. Pick a price you're comfortable with and justify why it's worth it. Avoid discounting right off the bat; it simply implies that you're over-valuing your product. You can always negotiate the price, but don't try that in a media kit.

✔ **Don't include a copy of your entire show on CD.** People like to know what they are getting themselves into. Podcasters have a great opportunity to offer that courtesy to potential advertisers — to let them listen enough to sample the wares. Remember, however, that their time is limited. You may include entire episodes if you like, but you may find better success by stitching together "best of" clips from your show; these take less time to consume.

✔ **Don't make a halfhearted effort.** Okay, you don't have to create a full-blown presentation that would make the mavens of Madison Avenue envious of your skill set. But we're not talking Elmer's glue and crayons here, either. Treat it like a business; invest the right kind of time and money to make your media kit look (and sound) as professional as you can.

When you have your content figured out, go buy a nice pretty binder. Or better yet, order some custom ones online that feature your podcast logo, slogan, and Web site address. You can get them online from VistaPrint (`www.vistaprint.com`) if you want large quantities. For smaller runs, see what your local office-supply or copy center can provide.

Can you ever really know the size of your audience?

Tracking down listener statistics is elusive — and that's quite an understatement. While many of the podcasting pundits will tell you how important understanding your audience size is (especially when you're trying to attract advertisers and sponsors), it's difficult for them to agree on the best way to snag those numbers.

Web-server analysis tools are wholly unreliable in this regard; after all, they weren't designed for this purpose. They can tell you how many times your podcast episodes were requested, but not how many of those requests were successful. They can tell you how many times your RSS 2.0 file was accessed, but provide you with no tool to filter out requests made every five minutes by the same obsessed podcatcher.

The most widely used model of determining audience size is the *bandwidth-division method.* This requires you, the podcaster, to know two pieces of data: the average size of your podcast media files and the total amount of data transferred in a given month. For example, suppose your ISP reported that you transferred 350GB of data in the month of May. Convert that to MB by multiplying by 1024 (the numbers of megabytes in a gigabyte) to get 358,400MB of data transfer.

Okay, suppose that during that month, you put up four podcasts, each with a size of 10MB. Divide the total number of transfers (358,400) by the average size of your file (10MB) to get the "total" number of accesses to that file — in this case 35,840. Finally, divide that number by the total number of podcast media files released (4, in this case). The answer (in theory, at least): You have approximately 8,960 listeners to your show.

This number, however, does not take into account the data transferred by your Web server simply to run your Web site — say, images and text. Nor is it helpful when your podcast media files vary widely in size. And it still doesn't factor in those folks who downloaded 90 percent of your show before the connection broke.

Podcast-specific hosting plans, such as Libsyn, are trying out new statistical tools to get a better handle on determining audience size. Their calculations are much more complex than the division method, but are drawing considerable fire from the community of pundits.

Our advice is to find a method that seems to work for you and stick with it. It's the best you can do . . . for now.

Establishing a rate sheet

And you thought you were headed into uncharted waters by just creating a podcast? How about figuring out a fair price to charge for running advertising? That's by no means a science. Heck, it's not even an art form at this stage! It's total guesswork — picking a number, throwing it out there, and seeing what sticks.

Sometimes all you can do is put your best foot forward and make your pitch. Talk to the advertiser about your dedicated audience, and how loyal it is to your show. Breaking down the costs into per-listener numbers might help as well. Whatever your approach, don't try to compare your numbers with those of traditional outlets the advertiser is already working with. Instead, talk about how *adding* podcast advertising to the mix can enhance its current efforts, allowing the company to reach an audience that has turned away from traditional media sources in favor of this new medium.

Setting advertising limits

Podcasting is not radio, nor should it be. One of the many complaints about radio is that it has become too commercial-saturated over the years. Podcasting is currently being presented as an alternative to the same tired stuff you hear on the radio. Do your part to keep it fresh — and keep the commercial time to a minimum.

While no hard-and-fast rule exists (and some podcast audiences are more tolerant of commercials than others), one useful approach is to follow the 15/30 rule: For every 15 minutes of podcast content, you can run up to 30 seconds of advertising. No, people aren't sitting around with stopwatches ready to hand out demerits if you play an ad before the 15-minute mark. This is simply a general rule for trying to figure out how many commercials to run.

Of course, you can skirt this rule somewhat if you do something a bit different with the advertising you run. But at that point you're moving away from traditional advertising and entering into the realm of sponsorships.

Getting a sponsor

Sponsorship and advertising are often used as interchangeable terms, but they're actually distinct approaches with different requirements. For the purposes of this discussion, we consider sponsorship as a relationship you (the podcaster) have worked out with an organization that regularly funds — and has a vested interest in the success of — your show. (Obviously, you can't say that about all advertisers.)

Sponsorships were popular — almost to the point of exclusivity — in the old days of radio in the early 20th century. During that time, corporations would actually create the various radio programs as an advertising vehicle — they could even censor content if (for example) some writer goofed and had the villain using the sponsor's product. Modern-day advertising deals, which allow a station or program to drop a 30-second ad into its already-established programming, came into play much later; these days such deals dominate the scene.

Traditional media sponsorships have all but disappeared, and their last bastion can be found in the lucrative world of daytime television: They have morphed into . . . the dreaded infomercial. No, we're not suggesting that you turn your podcast into an infomercial for anyone. However, if you are catering to a very niche audience and a corporate entity can service the needs of your audience, that angle may be worth considering.

Understand that obtaining a true sponsor for your show likely means you give up some creative control. Instead of paying you a few dollars to run a pre-produced ad, your sponsoring corporation underwrites your entire show, or at least a significant portion of it. Rather than getting you to take a break from your content while you talk about its product for a few moments, your content becomes *dedicated to* talking about its product.

Two notable examples of this "pay-for-podcasting" model are the *Disneyland Resort* podcast (disneyland.com/podcast) and the (albeit short-lived) *Heineken Music* podcast (www.heinekenmusic.com). In both cases, the corporations underwriting the program are heavily involved with the content.

If you're thinking about approaching a corporation to underwrite your show, you need to provide much of the same information necessary for securing advertisers, as discussed earlier. In addition, you need to demonstrate how your show can help bolster the success metrics of the corporation. "It's a cool show that your customers will love" probably won't cut it.

There is no secret sauce that irresistibly attracts corporate sponsorship. Each corporation has distinct goals and objectives. Any podcast trying to solicit sponsorship would be well served to understand these goals and objectives inside and out, and be prepared to clearly demonstrate how sponsoring a podcast can help the company achieve those goals.

Asking Your Listeners for Money

There is one group of potential financial backers out there who could care less about your fancy media kit: your listeners. They couldn't give a hoot about your anticipated growth curve in subscribers or your ratio of direct download-ers to feed-based audience. They do have a vested interest in your continuing to produce the very best possible show, each and every episode — and they are (usually) content to let you take the show in the direction you feel it should go.

Sometimes your show is important enough to them that they're willing to pony up. That's why the following section discusses some novel ways you can go about soliciting your listeners for funds to help offset some of the costs of creating a podcast.

Please don't turn your podcast into a weekly telethon. Most people tolerate the time when NPR goes into pledge-drive mode, but no one looks forward to it. If you're going to ask your audience for money, do it tactfully and as rarely as possible. Please.

Gathering listener donations with PayPal

Some of your audience will so love your show that they'll happily hand over some of their hard-earned money — if you'll only ask.

Asking for listeners' support is a two-step process: First you ask for the money, and then you provide an easy and convenient way for your listeners to send you money. PayPal (www.paypal.com) has been handling small and large Web-based transactions for years. A PayPal donation link can be fully integrated in to your Web site with minimum hassle. Here's how:

1. **Log in to PayPal.**

   If you don't have a PayPal account, click the Sign Up link at the top of the page and follow the simple instructions. You need a valid credit card to sign up.

   As this book was written, PayPal modified the navigation of the following pages. This chapter has been edited to reflect those changes, but please note that the flow may be slightly different in the future. Regardless, the steps you need to follow are basically the same.

2. **From your Account Overview page, click the Merchant Tools tab.**

   The Merchant Tools section allows you to set up a variety of ways people can send you money.

3. **Click the Donations link in the Key Features box on the right side of the page.**

   You may also find this link under Website Payments elsewhere on the page.

4. **Enter a donation name and donation ID in the appropriate text boxes.**

   For the donation name, enter the name of your podcast, followed by `Donation` (for example, `Bob's Fishing Podcast - Donation`). Use the same information for the ID field.

You can also use the ID field to denote multiple types of donations, or donations for different shows in the event you produce more than one podcast. You can put anything you want in this field, but keep in mind that it will be visible to those making donations — so make sure it isn't something confusing.

5. **Enter a set donation amount if you want.**

   If you want your listeners to donate a set amount, chose that amount here. If you leave this field blank, your users will have to enter an amount before they donate. You decide which is best for you. Also, change the designated country if you'd like your currency to be something other than U.S. dollars.

   If you're familiar with using HTML forms, you can later add a suggested donation amount, and allow your listeners to change the amount if they desire. Get a copy of *HTML For Dummies* if you need help with editing forms.

6. **Select the style of Donation button you would like to use.**

   If you have a custom button, here's the place to change it. If you don't have one, don't worry. The default button works just fine on your Web site, and you can always change it later if you want.

7. **Set the encryption to No.**

   If you are confident you won't want to change any of the settings given so far, you may set the encryption to Yes. We prefer to leave it unencrypted, so we can later edit any options without having to re-create a button from scratch. Also, turning encryption off allows PayPal to create a simple-to-use URL for your donation page that you can add to e-mails and show notes.

8. **After you fill in the fields on the Donations page (as shown in Figure 13-1), click Create Button Now.**

9. **On the Add a Button to Your Website page, you have some decisions to make about the custom HTML code for your button:**

   If you're comfortable doing some minor editing of the HTML that makes your Web site work, then copy the HTML you see in the first box — and add it to your page.

   If you think editing HTML is a little beyond you just now, then simply copy the text in Link for Emails and include it in your show notes. You'll want to make it a hyperlink, so don't just leave it like this:

```
https://www.paypal.com/cgi-bin/webscr?cmd=_xclick&business=evo%40dragonpage
        %2ecom&no_shipping=0&no_note=1&tax=0&currency_code=USD&charset=
        UTF%2d8&charset=UTF%2d8
```

Instead, you want to enclose it with an `<a href=""></a>` tag and include some descriptive text, like this:

```
<a href="https://www.paypal.com/cgi-bin/webscr?cmd=_xclick&business=evo%
          40dragonpage%2ecom&no_shipping=0&no_note=1&tax=0&currency_code=
          USD&charset=UTF%2d8&charset=UTF%2d8">Donate to my show</a>
```

That should do it for the donation link.

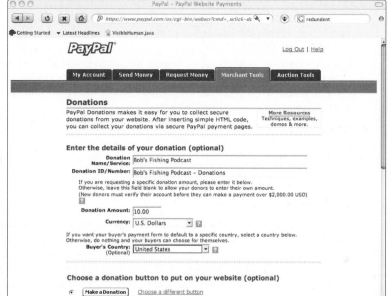

Figure 13-1:
PayPal
makes
accepting
donations
as easy as
filling out a
few fields.

Curious about what your donation page looks like to those who click the link? Cut and paste the link into your browser and press Enter. If you want to change the color scheme or add a logo, simply return to PayPal, choose My Account⇨Profile⇨Custom Payment Pages, and set up a new style. It's all very point-and-click.

Selling stuff

Some podcasters offer merchandise for sale as a way to support their show financially — T-shirts, hats, mugs, CDs, autographed pictures, you name it. If it's sellable, chances are some podcaster out there is selling it.

If you're contemplating selling stuff via your podcast, you fall into one of two groups:

- ✔ **Those who have stuff to sell:** Musicians, authors, artists, and craftspeople fall into this category. For these podcasters, offering CDs, books, prints, or other items to the listening audience can bring in significant revenue. (Down the road, there's no reason why it shouldn't be possible to make a living via podcasting — though nobody's doing that just yet, as far as we can tell.)

  Once again, PayPal (www.paypal.com) can be very helpful in taking away the technical hurdles for selling items online and integrating them into your podcast and Web site. If you can master the process for setting up online donations, you aren't far from having PayPal work as your entire online shopping cart. But this book is about podcasting, not about PayPal. Luckily for you, Victoria Rosenberg and Marsha Collier have already penned *PayPal For Dummies.*

- ✔ **Those who need stuff to sell:** For those podcasters who need stuff to sell, CafePress (www.cafepress.com) is more than happy to step in and offer its assistance. Remember the T-shirts and other stuff mentioned earlier? You can go to the trouble of making those yourself, carrying an inventory, and shipping the orders out as they trickle in — or you can let CafePress take care of all that for you.

  Setting up a CafePress storefront is a breeze, though it's a highly configurable task, and how you set it up depends on what you want to sell. A basic shop is free to set up and to use. Your listeners buy stuff with your logo or design on it from the CafePress store, and CafePress pays you a commission. It's very simple, and requires only some quick setup information from you to get started. Figure 13-2 shows a CafePress store for *The Dragon Page.* It took about five minutes to set this up; CafePress takes care of the rest.

Don't expect to make huge tons of cash via CafePress. Unless you can convince a large group of your listeners that they simply *must* have a $25 T-shirt with your logo on it, we wouldn't recommend quitting your day job just yet.

Fee-based subscriptions

Getting your listeners to donate a couple of bucks to you or buy your latest CD is one thing, but getting them to *shell out money for the privilege of listening to your show* is another matter altogether.

Not that it isn't a viable business model. For those of you with specialty content that people are already paying to hear, it can be a great way to expose your information to a wider audience.

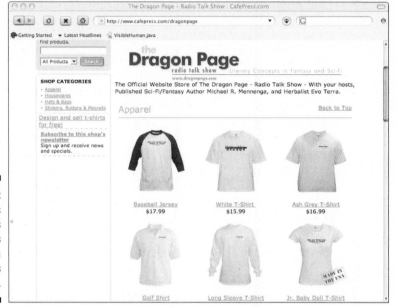

Figure 13-2:
Listeners
can buy lots
of goodies
from a
CafePress
store.

If you don't have a pre-established following, this approach likely won't help you. If you do have a following, but have never required anyone to give you money to hear what you have to offer, you may find yourself with less of a following afterwards. Use this option sparingly — and only if you really think others are willing to give money to listen to your podcast.

One problem with charging people to access your podcast feed is that not all podcatching clients support secure connections. Then not only do you have to convince folks to pay you for the right to listen to your podcast, but you also have to convince them to use a particular podcatcher so they can pay you. Not very open and friendly — or likely to work well.

In an attempt to circumvent the issue, some podcasters may try giving out the URL of the podcast feed only to those who have paid a fee. It doesn't take a rocket scientist to figure out how non-secure that option really is. An address for an RSS feed is simply a link — something that's pretty easy to pass around till it gets posted on all sorts of Web sites.

There are options for secure RSS feeds, however. Implementing them gets technical and complicated in a hurry, and goes beyond the scope of this book. Instead, focus on building your show and making it the best you can. After you have command of all the intricacies that go into creating a top-notch podcast, then you can consider charging your audience a fee to listen.

Chapter 14

Podcasting for Publicity

"*T*rue" podcasters bristle at the growing commercialization of podcasting. With iTunes stepping into the podosphere and spotlighting many corporate podcasts, the independent voices have voiced many concerns that boil down to one: A "true" podcast is done for passion, not for profit. The movement towards podcasting as a moneymaking venture goes against the grain of a "true" podcast. The words, opinions, and emotions should all be aimed for the listeners' hearts and minds, not their wallets.

Well, yeah — and even as we cheer the sentiments of the purists, we have to observe that sheer love of the medium isn't all there is to it. *Truth* be told, podcasting is the next great way to reach the consumer. It's economical, unobtrusive, and can be a great way to connect with your potential audience.

With time, patience, and nurturing, any mass-market technology — be it the Internet, blogging, and yes, even podcasting — can be applied to promotion. For example, Dave Slusher of the *Evil Genius Chronicles* (evilgeniuschronicles. org), while very much against the big corporate machine (which, as he observes, "dictates to the masses what they think they want to consume") is in fact a smaller-scale marketing machine for independent musicians, presses, and films. His podcast features the work of musicians and writers such as Michelle Malone, The Arts & Sciences, and Gentle Readers — and each artist has a strong individual voice with Slusher. After all, both his show and his show-related blog promote these artists' endeavors, offering listeners a whole new way to invest in their works.

Promotion and marketing in podcasting are still new to podcasting, and in the eyes of larger corporations, podcasting is an unproven medium. Because podcasting is "audio-on-demand," there is no formal way to measure numbers, feedback, and response in the same way radio and television advertisements are tracked.

However, with Apple iTunes and its podcast subscriptions going from zero to 1 million in *two days* — match those numbers, J.K. Rowling! (Oh, wait a minute, you did. Never mind . . .) — the corporate world is starting to take notice, realizing that some independent podcasts are actually discovering new audiences for their products (and broadening their existing audience) one MP3 at a time.

Podcasting and Politics

What some old-school politicians might once have snickered at, they're starting to take more seriously. The "podcasting fad" is beginning to catch the attention of major political players, including some who may have scoffed at blogging and even (if you can believe it) the Internet as ways to connect with their constituencies. They're starting to use podcasts to connect to the people, and more importantly, to the young voters who can easily make or break a victory at the polls.

What we're defining in this section as a political podcast is a podcast *hosted by a political figure or an individual seeking a political office,* not pseudo-journalists, former comedic actors, or convicted felons spewing their opinions for all to hear. Anytime a podcast goes public on the issues, its creator walks a fine line between public servant and political commentator. The following podcasts all keep their content focused on the issues and less on what they "feel" are the issues.

The first politician to use a politically themed podcast was John Edwards (shown in Figure 14-1), the 2004 Democratic vice-presidential candidate. Following the 2004 election, he launched *One America Committee Podcast with John Edwards.* Found at `www.johnedwards.com` (also accessible via `www.oneamericacommittee.com`), the podcast covers poverty, Internet law, and environmental issues and encourages youth involvement in politics. Also featured in this podcast is Elizabeth Edwards' update on her current fight against breast cancer and her efforts to raise awareness about the disease.

Edwards invited the world into his home with an intimate podcast that not only gets political, but personal as well: "Elizabeth and I are both sitting here at our kitchen table. The microphones are sitting on my four-year-old Jack's blanket that he sleeps with every night, so we feel very much at home, and I hope you enjoy this discussion!"

If you're a politician and you want to get in touch with the people (as a way to respond when voters complain about poor communication with their representatives or the candidates running for office), why not invite the country into your kitchen, offer them a cup of (virtual) coffee, and ask them to relax a bit? The Edwards's informal podcast humanizes them as public figures. Instead of dishing up prepared statements from professional speechwriters, they can offer American voters (and worldwide listeners) impromptu, candid, sincere opinions on issues facing the country and the world.

Figure 14-1:
Senator
John
Edwards,
podcasting
an inside
view of
Capitol Hill
and politics
with *One
America
Committee
with John
Edwards.*

Unlike other political *commentary* podcasts and talk-radio shows (for example, Al Franken's *Air America*, *The Donkey Hunter*, G. Gordon Liddy, Rush Limbaugh), the *One America Committee Podcast* is a perspective on politics from some-one with previous experience in *holding* an office, be it on Capitol Hill or in City Hall.

Podcasting has now caught the attention of the govern-ator himself, Arnold Schwarzenegger, who is now podcasting his weekly radio addresses (at `features.governor.ca.gov/index.php/podcast`). And the White House has joined the podosphere with President Bush's podcast (`www.whitehouse.gov/rss`) of his weekly address to the country. In an interview with *Business Week,* Democratic strategist Joe Trippi sees a time when podcasting will carry the same impact and influence as blogs. "Podcasting is growing even faster than blogging. I think podcasting is going to have a huge impact on the next election cycle."

When going political with a podcast (whether you're running for the U.S. Senate or podcasting your term as School Board representative), here are a few things to keep in mind:

> ✔ **Keep your podcast on a consistent *weekly* schedule.** Monthly podcasts don't cut it; the tide of politics is in constant flux. Because time-shifting (making use of the wee hours of the night) is part of what makes pod-casting work, daily updates are less than practical; however, weekly

podcasts work well for ongoing political issues, and you can shape their content to remain timely enough, week by week, to fit the podcasting medium. Set a day for delivering your weekly message and stick to that schedule.

✔ **Focus on the issues, not the opinions.** As mentioned before, a political podcaster will always walk a fine line between public servant and political commentator. John Edwards, Arnold Schwarzenegger, and President George W. Bush all keep their podcasts focused on the issues. If they were suddenly to start hammering away with opinion and commentary, they'd become more like Sean Hannity, Bill O'Reilly, or Al Franken (whom nobody elected). If you want politics as your podcast's subject matter, ask yourself whether you're looking to help listeners understand the issues accurately and take meaningful action, or whether you're just ranting and venting to entertain people who want their opinions reinforced.

✔ **Give your listeners a plan for action.** When you cover the issues in your podcast, provide possible solutions to the pressing matters of your community and your constituents. Whether you're detailing blood drives or fundraisers, or launching an awareness campaign for cancer research, increase that divide between *political figure* and *political commentator* by offering listeners ways they can get involved in the community and make a difference.

Telling the World a Story, One Podcast at a Time

The whole point behind promotion — be it for books, film, or other forms of entertainment — is to win prospective target audiences (or build on existing ones) with something new or a different take on a familiar commodity. For a fraction of the cost of print advertisements and broadcast-media commercials, podcasting opens up markets for your creative work — and can even start to get your name into an international market. If you are an established presence in the writing market (or any entertainment field), the fans you have nurtured, with time, will not only eagerly support your podcast, but also introduce your MP3s to reader groups, friends, and enthusiasts of the subjects you're writing about.

Allow us a personal account of the journey from podcasting fan to full-fledged podcaster. When *Podcasting For Dummies'* own Tee Morris was in the final rewrites of *Legacy of MOREVI* (shown in Figure 14-2), his publisher made contact online and said, "Okay, Tee, start thinking of neat promotional ideas for *Legacy.*" Around this time, Evo and Michael, proprietors of The Dragon Page (www.dragonpage.com), had started podcasting two shows — *Cover to Cover* and *Live Fire.* Tee thoroughly enjoyed their podcasts and appreciated that podcasting made the shows available *on his time.* As Tee considered all the things he liked about podcasting, he began to consider recording *MOREVI* for audio. After all, he'd been complimented several times on his live readings. And as an actor who loved playing around with his Mac's audio and video features, he figured . . . *Why not?*

So Tee called up Evo, and a plan began to form.

Figure 14-2:
Tee Morris takes his debut novel, *MOREVI: The Chronicles of Rafe & Askana* (cowritten with Lisa Lee), and adapts it for the podosphere.

Cover art by Sans Talbot

The week of January 21, 2005, the Prologue of *MOREVI: The Chronicles of Rafe & Askana* went online (www.teemorris.com/podcast) and so began a completely new kind of promotion, different from what The Dragon Page had ever done before: A chapter presented every Friday, as read by the author. Tee was unsure what to think at first. Did a download necessarily mean a *listener?* He wondered, "Who *is* listening? Is it generating interest in *Legacy*? Or in my other titles, for that matter?"

The answer came after *MOREVI's* conclusion — a review from SFFAudio.com, a Web site featuring the latest releases in audio science fiction, fantasy, and horror: "Swashbuckling action takes the main and heart-rending romance builds slowly culminating right at the end . . . but though it might sound it, *MOREVI: The Chronicles of Rafe and Askana* isn't a traditional fantasy novel, it is derring-do adventure set in a world that would fit well on a shelf next to Eric Flint's *1632verse* alternate-history series . . . "

A traditional writer's dilemma — balancing creative work against the work you do to get heard or read — had taken on a new form. With all that time and money invested in appropriate Web-host and audio equipment, could the time and effort invested in a podcast be better spent writing another book? The bigger question was, "Is a podcast of my novel really worthwhile?"

With a spike in sales (which included a few international readers) via Amazon, pre-orders for *Legacy of MOREVI*, and the sales at Westercon 58 in Calgary, Alberta, Canada, Tee had an enthusiastic answer: *Yes.*

Podcasting can introduce your writings or your music to audiences world-wide. For artists in more visual arts such as film, dance, painting, or sculpture, podcasting can serve as an audio journal leading up to the premiere of your work — or as a venue to promote your career. It's an instant connection with your audience, and a great way to build an audience by getting them to know you on however intimate a level works best for you and your work. Planning a strategy for this kind of promotion only helps your agenda:

- ✔ **When podcasting for visual media, briefly describe the action for the audience.** In his hourly podcast for the SciFi Channel, Ron Moore adds in his commentary on whichever episode of *Battlestar Galactica* happens to be airing (www.scifi.com/battlestar/downloads/podcast). He does not take for granted, though, that people will always be watching the episode along with its companion podcast. In only a few words and a few seconds, he sets the scene of what's happening in the episode, for the sake of listeners who may listen to his podcast independently.

  If you're documenting your visual art, it will only take a moment to describe what you're doing. For the painter: "I am using green with just a hint of black so we can make the eyes appear more unearthly, unnatural." For a dancer, "In reconstructing the Australian Aboriginal dance, you must remain grounded and deep in your squats, more so than what is normally seen in modern dance." You don't need to go into every minute detail. Only a few words are needed to create a picture.

- ✔ **For writers and musicians: edit, edit, edit.** Awkward pauses, stammers, and stumbled words are obstacles for a writer introducing his work to the podosphere: They've gotta go! The approach is no different from that of an independent musician who podcasts a rehearsal session or a recording: You don't want off-key instruments and vocalists missing the high notes. Your podcasts need to sound sharp and clean.

  Musicians, no matter if it takes five takes or 50 takes, should have their instruments in tune, lyrics clearly pronounced, and all notes sung on key. Writers should enunciate, speak clearly, and (most importantly) enjoy the manuscript. Each piece, whether music or printed word, should be a performance that serves as your audition to a worldwide audience. (While that may sound a bit nerve-wrecking, don't think of it as walking out on stage so much as building something fine to send out into the world. Just have fun, and your audience will enjoy the ride with you.)

And if you need a refresher on the basics of editing, skip back to Chapter 5 for the primers on editing with Audacity and GarageBand.

✔ **Open or close your podcasts with a brief, off-script commentary.** Scott Sigler always kept his listeners on the edge of their seats with his podcast of *EarthCore* (`www.scottsigler.net`), but he also connected with his fans at the beginning of each episode, addressing them directly with a brief message (less than five minutes). For example, he assured them he wouldn't hold the last chapter hostage, tantalized them with the promise of a new podcast in the works, and announced the release date of *EarthCore* in print.

While Sigler does have a knack for action-packed storytelling, this connection with fans also helped people relate to the author, which added to the intimate experience of a podiobook. Nothing is wrong with a quick "Thank you for listening," or even a brief "Here's where I will be in the future for signings . . . " Let your audience know who you are, and they'll show their appreciation through their support of your current and future works.

Keeping Good Company: Community and Soundseeing-Tour Podcasts

Slice-of-life podcasts that encourage community among listeners and among fans are podcasts for promotion. The promotion comes from word-of-mouth advertising ("buzz") that these podcasters generate from their thoughts, comments, and opinions on their subject — be it traveling across Spain, daily life in New York City, George Lucas's *Star Wars,* or Joss Whedon's *Firefly.*

Slice-of-life podcasts let the world into locations that listeners may be curious about. After a few podcasts, you can even encourage listeners to experience that corner of the-world-as-you-know-it.

Putting together a soundseeing tour of your favorite destination

Rich Pav is your average, ordinary blogger, making his way through the not-so-average or ordinary Land of the Rising Sun. In *Herro Flom Japan* (`www.herro flomjapan.com`), Rich frames his various travels and encounters with the history, culture, and people of Japan in his own unique point of view.

According to his companion blog, Rich doesn't consider his podcast to be a true *soundseeing tour* — but his glimpses into Japan were compelling enough for listeners to nominate *Herro Flom Japan* for the First Annual People's Choice Podcast Awards in that category.

Rich's blog also offers some supportive advice to new podcasters: "I'm sure there are lots of people who want to start their own podcast but a little voice in their head says, 'But what if people think I [stink] and they hate me?' There is no 'if.' Once your audience outgrows your circle of friends and family, someone out there is going to tell you just how bloody awful they think you are. And the bigger *you* get, the louder *they* get. That's the way it goes. You just have to get used to it."

Soundseeing tours are virtual walks down the sidewalks and side streets of a foreign country and can promote the community of a city, region, or country better than any brochure found in a travel agency.

Creating a podcast to bring together a community

Community and tourism can go beyond a city or country. It can be based on a shared interest. *The Mousepod* (mousepod.net), hosted by Jesse Obstbaum, is a podcast by a Disney fan, for Disney fans (see Figure 14-3). Jesse's 45- to 60-minute podcast is a journey into fond memories (and sometimes harsh truths) about the Walt Disney Corporation. He is not a fan who believes all is perfect with the Worlds that Walt Built, but Jesse does look back with reverence to the times when Walt Disney was still around, creating the characters that kids everywhere (and the kids still inside the grown-ups) can now look on and smile. Jesse also interviews Disney fans, asking about their favorite memories, which can include a favorite movie, a memorable *Wonderful World of Disney,* or a trip to Disneyland or Walt Disney World. What makes Jesse's podcast more of a community than the musings of one fan preaching to Goofy's choir are the listeners who are contributing content for the sake of the show.

On the 50th Anniversary of Disneyland, fans of *The Mousepod* recorded and submitted to Jesse's Web site some slice-of-life moments from the Opening Gala. Although Jesse was unable to be there to experience the celebrations, these Mousepod fans banded together to become part of the podcast.

Jesse is not consciously assuming a spokesman role, but he is encouraging other Disney fans to join him in his celebration of Disney fans — the same community of fans who visit the park properties, buy the DVDs, and tell their friends about their experiences.

Figure 14-3:
Jesse
Obstbaum
encourages
community
among
Disney fans
with *The
Mousepod.*

Another way of bringing a community together is to ask listeners what they think of various topics *before* recording your podcast, and then base your next podcast on that feedback. This is the strategy that hosts Kade Hutchinson and Kevin L. Pratt adopted for their podcast, *alienEthOS: The Ethics of Sci-Fi* (www. alienethos.com), a different kind of science-fiction-and-fantasy podcast. Instead of just talking about their favorite movies, books, or latest trends in the genre, Kevin and Kade explore the *ethical* issues in science fiction movies, TV shows, books, and comics.

Ethical issues? In science fiction and fantasy? Are these guys serious? Oh, yeah — but they do manage to get in a few laughs along the way. (Kade does a mean Dame Shirley Bassey impersonation.)

alienEthOS explores issues raised throughout science fiction and fantasy. For example, how humanely should the human race regard — and treat — the "new" Cylons on *Battlestar Galactica*? (It's another way of asking, "What is human and how should we treat each other?") Or, for that matter, can Harry Potter's House Elves handle equal rights and freedoms — can a society have a servant class and still be considered ethical?

The show also looks at the relevance of such questions to current headlines and society and then extrapolates the message and meaning that fans can take from it. *alienEthOS* describes itself as "a community-driven show with comments and voice mails from our listeners," which the hosts pull off by petitioning responses from their audience on topics posted on their Web site. From here, the podcast is built. Eventually, the hosts foresee Skype interviews with authors, producers, and celebrities of the genre contributing content, as well as simultaneous podcasting with one show podcasting the topic from their perspective and *alienEthOS* taking its own slant on the same topic. But no matter how far or fast this podcast evolves, the community and its opinions will always remain its core focus.

Soundseeing tours and community podcasts cover a wide range of audiences. Both approaches share a mindset and some "sound" production principles:

✔ **Don't rely on the environment to *be* the podcast.** Part of a soundseeing tour is the ambient noise. The atmosphere of a marketplace, the rumbling of a train and various announcements to its commuters, and even the traffic passing by builds the world (or the part of it you are presently occupying) around you. But a soundseeing tour should not be you simply walking through your local downtown or social hot spot, recording the world passing you by. There should be commentary accompanying your podcast because even though it is a window to your world, the podcast centers on *you* as a walking frame of reference. You are the host. Your thoughts, opinions, and observations are driving this podcast, and the environment is working with you to create a complete picture. Feel free to comment on what you see and allow yourself a chance to explore. Always remember, the podcast is driven by, guided by, and centered around you.

✔ **You are the host, but it's not all about you.** This may sound like we're contradicting the previous bullet point, but we are merely reminding you that community-based podcasts should be *about the community*. Yes, there is room for personal thoughts and commentary, but in small doses.

The podcast is about the community and how it interacts with the world around you; that is what the content should focus on. Your podcast can feature other members of the community who share the same opinions as yours or even take opposing viewpoints (a spirited debate can liven up your show). Just remember that the community-based or soundseeing tour is not about you personally, but about how you see the world, how that connects with the people around you in the community, and how all that comes together in the pursuit of a common interest.

✔ **Avoid the negative.** Particularly with community-based podcasts such as *The Mousepod* and *The Signal* (`signal.serenityfirefly.com/signal.php`), it would be easy to turn a podcast into a gossip column or a personal rant against the very concept that brought the community into being. While there is no law or ethic barring you from speaking out or voicing concerns, a community is based on support. Whether you consider yourself a fan of Harry Potter, Apple Computers, or Prince William County, your goal in a community podcast is to remain positive and celebrate the benefits of being part of the cooperative spirit. If there is a matter of concern in your community, then there's room for debate and action, and as with a political podcast, be sure to offer some possible solutions to these issues.

Regardless of the kind of community you're chronicling, your podcast should work much like glue — helping to keep supporters together in the face of problems (instead of just crying in your collective beer) and celebrating what gives them joy. Reinforce that sense of community and keep your podcast strong.

Chapter 15

Podcasting for Passion

*O*ur mission from the beginning of this book has been to fill you in on what a podcast is, demystify the technical aspects of getting your voice heard on MP3 players around the world, and assure you that anyone with the drive can get their message across with the right tools. But a podcast is empty if you don't have that drive or that passion to get your podcast up and running and keep it running — whether the episode goes out every week, every other week, or monthly. We drop that word a lot in the previous chapters: *passion.* What do we mean by "podcasting with passion"?

Okay, if you take the dictionary as a starting point, *passion* means *a keen interest in a particular subject or activity,* or *the object of somebody's intense interest or enthusiasm.* You can have state-of-the-art audio equipment, hire the most engaging vocal talent, and employ the best engineers, but that isn't what makes a podcast a podcast. The artists and creativity behind a podcast make an investment — not simply financial or physical — and collect the windfall in listener feedback and download stats.

Yes, a podcast can make money, promote a cause, or bring attention to social issues, but without that passion, you might as well sit behind a microphone and read the instruction manual to your mobile phone. Passion is what motivates relative unknowns to slip on the headphones, step up to the microphone, and let their words fly.

This chapter won't presume to show you how to create, cultivate, or conjure your own passion. It's something you have, or you don't, for a given topic — and we suspect everybody has it for *some* topics. Instead, we offer some real-world examples of how others apply their passions to podcasts — and some tools to apply a little passion-power of your own.

The Philosophical Question for All Podcasters: Why Do We Do It?

It's going to come up sooner or later: Someone will question your motives, rationale, and even sanity at your investment of so much time and energy into this newfangled thing called podcasting. We highly recommend deep nonsensical answers such as "It's because of the cheese" be returned to these people. Then watch their eyes start to twitch. That never stops being funny.

Gaining perspective on passion

Mur Lafferty does not make a penny off her popular podcast, *Geek Fu Action Grip* (geekfuactiongrip.com). Her plan — as a freelance writer for magazines, gaming companies, and other print venues — is to make a living at writing, eventually selling her first novel for publication. In addition to her contribution to the Dragon Page's *Wingin' It!* (dragonpage.com), *Geek Fu Action Grip* (shown in Figure 15-1) delivers original (and playfully witty) essays that bring a smile to your face — along with a slightly *different* perspective on the world.

Figure 15-1: Mur Lafferty (inset) gives her perspectives on the world in *Geek Fu Action Grip*.

Logo created by Angi Shearstone

These essays showcase a unique and refined voice — and Mur is giving these essays away for free! For free? What is she thinking? Wouldn't Mur be making a fortune selling these essays to magazines and newspapers? Conventional wisdom (such as it is) would say so; some writers would scoff at her for giving away quality work, or think it smarter if she "threw a bone" out for free and saved her *really good* work for paying markets.

While it is always good to make money at what you love, what good is it to offer your work for sale if no one knows what you're capable of? Following the same ethic, Mur offers original essays for *Wingin' It* and then writes her own for *Geek Fu Action Grip.* "I wanted to contribute something to the podosphere that wasn't there already," Mur says in response to the inspiration behind *Geek Fu Action Grip.* "No one was reading essays, much less geek-oriented. I've gotten a lot of good feedback, and now I like to take that feedback and make the podcast better. I podcast because it's a good outlet for my thoughts and my writing. I've met some awesome people and it's made my writing better."

By offering to the world her essays, Mur not only sharpens her craft, but also lays the groundwork for a *fan base* — a devout group of listeners who will happily invest in her future works if they're ever offered for a price. Her name is also beginning to become more known in the writing and gaming circles, and now her talents are attracting editors, landing her opportunities to write for one of her favorite publications, *Knights of the Dinner Table,* and read short stories aloud for *The Escape Pod* (`escapepod.info`).

But is future opportunity the only reason Mur podcasts?

Hardly. What makes *Geek Fu Action Grip* a delight to listen to is Mur's enthusiasm behind every podcast. For the Durham, N.C. mother, gamer, writer, and all-around-geek, her podcasts serve as a catharsis for the random events in life that catch her attention: "The knowledge that there are people who are looking forward to my podcast really means a lot and does a lot to motivate me. I know a lot of podcasters have had the problem of not receiving sufficient feedback. A nice e-mail here and there really means a lot to keep people going. Also there's just the old ego thing — if I think I have something to say, I'll podcast about it."

Her "audio blogging" comes across more like a portable, personal, stand-up comic — making light of something that the world is paying way too much attention to, or poking a little fun at herself when she contradicts herself. This enthusiasm comes out in her writing and in the delivery of her writing, and it's what makes Mur's podcast an enjoyable ride with every new upload.

Whether Mur's wisdom was planned from the start or not, it offers some good take-aways for the budding podcaster:

- ✔ **Always look for a unique angle.** The last things we need are carbon copies of other podcasts or (perish the thought) wacky morning DJs. If your passion is commonplace, focus on a niche or small aspect that you have the most knowledge about.

- ✔ **Step beyond your comfort zone.** No one expects you to be a trained voice actor. All they expect is for you to talk about your passion with authority and sincerity. Remember, you're only trying to appeal to people who care.

- ✔ **Don't get preachy.** Passion and authority are fine, but don't cross that line into assuming you know more than everyone else. Unless you're putting together a sermon or series of lectures, speak in the common tongue and with respect to your audience. If we want to be talked down to, we can always tune in certain talk-radio hosts.

Podcasting passion with a purpose

Speaking of fun and exciting (and, okay, escapist) rides, the *EarthCore* podcast (`scottsigler.net/earthcore`) might have escaped notice had it not been for the passion behind its production. True, its author (shown in Figure 15-1) found a terrific hook when he described his science-fiction thriller as "*24* meets *Predator*" — but even his promotions convey the edge and vitality in his voice.

Scott Sigler — whose novel-in-installments is, hands down, the most successful of the podiobooks initially offered by `www.podiobooks.com` — set out to show that a book in audio format did not have to be a guy in a soundproof booth simply reading the manuscript. "I podcast because it's the perfect vehicle for serialized fiction," Sigler says of his decision to podcast his debut novel. He seeks not only to hook listeners with the format, but also to keep them in suspense till next week's episode: "My novels are long, with cliffhangers at the end of each chapter. That's designed to keep you turning the pages. With podcasts, you just have to wait for the next episode."

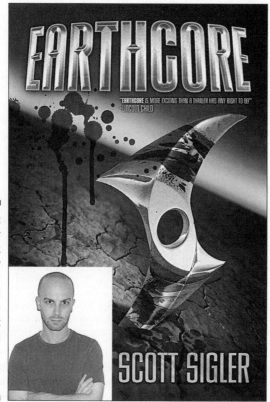

Figure 15-2: Scott Sigler (inset) took his "nearly published" novel *EarthCore* and went from podcast to print, all in one year.

Scott's nostalgia for radio-style serials is not the only motivation behind his podcast. "The amazing reaction I get from the listeners is the motivation," he adds, acknowledging his loyal fan base. Scott Sigler's avid listeners affectionately refer to his podiobook as *EarthCrack* (probably because they're hooked), and keep him meeting those delivery deadlines for uploads and even resort to bribes as they try to get a sneak peek at what's coming up next before other subscribed listeners hear it. "To know that my fiction has entertained thousands of people, helped them escape from their day-to-day lives, and just plain have some fun means the world to me. Is it a power trip? Sure! But knowing that I've delivered a great story and entertained someone is a fantastic feeling."

Even if you aren't putting out a podiobook (which we highly recommend), Scott showcases some excellent attitudes and approaches that would serve many podcasters well:

- **Cultivate feedback.** Don't sit on your heels hoping someone will e-mail you. Put together a contest, solicit information, and generally get out there and ask people what they think.

- **Respond in a timely manner.** If you're going to ask, you can't ignore the responses. When someone takes the time out of his or her busy schedule to e-mail you feedback — positive or negative — be sure to respond. Sooner rather than later, please.

- **Have your audience spread the word.** Who better to seek out people who might like your podcast than those who already love what you do? Assuming these people have friends, have them toss a little love your way by getting their friends to listen. Ask them to burn your show onto a CD and pass it around. Make it easy for others to listen!

Practice makes perfect passion

Then there are podcasters like Nicole Simon. No essays. No whirling blades of blood-splattering death. Her podcasts are podcasts-for-the-sake-of-podcasting — which make her voice (and others) familiar, if not yet wildly popular, in podcasting circles. Embracing her title as "one of the sexiest voices in podcasting," Nicole Simon of `www.useful-sounds.de` sends out her occasional musings on technology, podcasting, the Internet, and just about anything else that grabs her attention. There is no agenda here. She does not have a book to promote, a writing career to launch, or even a desire to internationally network herself. This native German speaker merely wishes to practice her English.

In episodes that last from 30 minutes to an hour, Nicole practices her skills of grammar and vocabulary with her honest and open commentary. For Nicole, her modest exercise in the English language was merely that: a modest exercise. Then came the 2005 Reboot — a yearly conference (held in Copenhagen, Denmark) that focuses on advances in the Internet, unconventional thinking centered around communication, and new advances in telecommunication. Suddenly Nicole found herself an unexpected celebrity among the keynote speakers, many of whom recognized her — and a few of whom were regular listeners to her podcast.

Another aspect of *Useful Sounds* that keeps Nicole Simon podcasting is not the notoriety — or even the bilingual feedback from her English- and German-speaking listeners. It is merely the desire to broaden her own communication skills. There is also a sincere joy in sharing with the world a look into *her* world, voicing opinions on things that matter to her.

If you plan to use a podcast to practice something, here are a few tips to keep in mind:

- ✔ **Stop apologizing, already.** Mention early in your podcast that you're new at this language/game/career and then get on with it. The idea is to podcast about it, not belabor the fact that you are new.

- ✔ **Don't pretend to be something you are not.** No one has all the answers every time, and when you're learning a skill, you're going to make mistakes. Embrace them, laugh about them, and podcast them. But for heaven's sake, don't try to cover them up because the real experts out there will call you on it every time.

Passion comes in all shapes and sizes

Also never short on opinions — or providing glimpses into his corner of the world(s) — is science-fiction author Paul S. Jenkins. (Or would he call what he writes *speculative* fiction?) His bimonthly podcast *RevUp Review* (www. rev-up-review.co.uk) — launched in March 2005 — provides listeners with a review of books, movies, podcasts, and music. The *RevUp Review* is not only a review of all things speculative, but also a revue of music available at the Podsafe Music Network, soundseeing tours around his village and around his home, and even a serialized presentation of his previously published short stories. Is Paul trying to generate new interest in his own published works? Does he have an agenda in promoting the Podsafe Music Network? There *has* to be an agenda here, doesn't there?

Well, we don't believe so. The *RevUp Review* (or "Revue," depending on your take on Paul's approach) comes across as an hour with an old friend over a pint at your local pub. Paul Jenkins' passion comes through in the sincerity behind his podcast — seasoned with a whimsical, almost mischievous, approach. In one recent episode, Paul presented an alternative to the beer-cast: a breadcast. The RevMaster (as he calls himself) welcomes the world into his kitchen for a ten-minute segment of baking fresh bread, starting from the beginning with measuring of water and breaking out the flour. Paul knows this kind of soundseeing theater may not rivet action-addicts, but he isn't pressured to be aggressively entertaining all the time. You can hear in his voice a genuine delight — in not only recording this culinary experience but also sharing it with the world.

Paul's approach to podcasting is easily adaptable for many:

- ✔ **Don't be afraid to explore new areas.** Just because your podcast is about fishing, it doesn't mean that you can't meander to rock climbing, pickup-truck repair, or even the secret to marital bliss. Exploring new areas can breathe new life into stale podcasts and even help you find new areas of interest and expertise you didn't even know you had.

- ✔ **Keep it personal.** If you're going to go off on a tangent, make sure "you" go along as well. Podcasting is as much a cult of personality as anything, and your audience will forgive your wanderings if you take yourself, as well as them, along for the ride.

Universal love for the podcast

What Paul, Mur, Scott, and Nicole all share in common is a true love for the podcast. Mur could easily put her podcast on hold to finish writing. Paul could give the *Rev Up Review* a hiatus if he wanted to go backpacking across his own country or take the Chunnel and enjoy a holiday in Europe. Nicole might want to pay a visit to the States, take in a bit of touring of her own. And Scott . . .

Well, in the case of Scott Sigler, we suspect that if he had stopped his podcast of *EarthCrack* (oops, that's *EarthCore*) before reaching the final chapter, the legions of fans dedicated to his weekly adventure would have very well crafted their own whirling blades of death, hunted him down, tied him to a chair, and hit Record for him! (When you've got a jones, you've got a jones.)

But even if those fans weren't there, Scott — along with podcasters like the ones showcased here — would continue to record, produce, and upload shows simply for the love of the podcast. These podcasters stand out in their dedication — they apologize if a podcast doesn't meet its promised schedule, make the effort to improve production quality, and infuse enthusiasm into every new show. It is this passion that brings the podcaster back to the microphone and invites new podcasters (like you!) to take the host's chair.

Holding Interest: Keeping a Podcast's Passion Alive

You have your podcast underway. You are planning to have a weekly show. The first month in, you feel strong, confident. But this is all in the first four episodes. How do you keep the momentum going?

In the early days of a podcast, you can easily see yourself continuing banter a year from launch date — but remember, it's *52 episodes* you're planning. Have you taken into account sick days? Vacation? The occasional stumbling block of inertia ("Do I really want to do a podcast today?"). Even the best bloggers need to step away from their keyboards, recharge their own batteries, and then jump back into their journaling. Personal health, well-being, and time to edit postings if your postings need editing (and if you're human, sometimes they do) are factors you also must consider. Add in dealing with conditions such as background noise and having to tax the strength of your voice, and podcasting can become less of a joy and more like a chore or a second day job. Plenty of podcasts begin strong out of the box, only to have their feeds go silent, and remain so.

Even with passion, momentum is difficult to sustain. How do podcasters keep that spark and drive alive? Well — as with the answers to "Why do we do it?" — podcasters have a myriad of opinions and thoughts. Each show applies different approaches and tactics to keep each new episode fresh; even amid diverse topics, common threads can be found between all podcasts that provide the momentum to forge ahead 50 episodes later.

Podcasting on puree: Mixing it up

After you rack up a few episodes of your podcast, take a look at its format. How do you have it set up? Is it all commentary? What can you do to vary the content?

Just because this is your first, second, third — or seventeenth, eighteenth, or nineteenth — cast, it doesn't mean you have set yourself in stone. (That's where you find the fossils of all sorts of creatures that didn't manage to evolve.) In this section, we look at ways to dodge that asteroid and keep your show from suffering an extinction-level event.

Don't be afraid to try different things with your podcast's format. For example, you might:

- ✔ Talk about a product, service, or idea that is only loosely related to your normal focus.
- ✔ Interview a guest with a unique perspective on the focus of your show.
- ✔ Experiment with adding a co-host, even if only temporarily.
- ✔ Podcast from a "remote" location or from a "studio" if you normally do remote shows.

The Dragon Page, hosted by one of your illustrious authors, has been in a near-constant state of evolution since its inception nearly four years ago. It started with a single host and acquired a second after eight shows. Things stayed constant for a while, and then the hosts added a news segment to the show.

But news is too often (and too easily) boring, so one of the hosts ferreted out the strangest news that was only loosely affiliated with the topic at hand — science fiction and fantasy — and that was always a shock to the other host (which tended to wake the episode right up). If that wasn't strange enough, they created a goofy little segment called "Feed the Dragon" where Michael, Evo, and the occasional guest serve a person, organization, or even a concept up for a sacrifice to an "in-studio dragon."

Fast-forward through the years (time travel saves belaboring the point), and we present a show that's survived Internet radio, broadcast radio, live remotes, and even podcasting. Your show may not have to go to elaborate lengths to stay fresh, but it does need to heed the creed: *Evolve or die*.

Starting from scratch

Keeping the passion alive and well in one podcast can be found in variety — and in allowing yourself to follow another passion in a second podcast. Okay, that may double your workload, but it also keeps your perspectives fresh and excited about what to focus on in upcoming podcasts.

If you have enough content to warrant a second podcast, don't overload one podcast with this new content; why burn out? If your gut instinct is telling you to begin a second podcast, go for it. Variety, not only in a podcast's original content but also between the different podcasts you create, can benefit both shows. Now, instead of the same old podcast every week, you can allow yourself different avenues to explore — and maybe a whole new audience.

Two real-world examples show how this can be done effectively. After focusing on books and authors for so many years, Michael and Evo were looking for new areas on which to focus and new listeners to attract. They found a willing audience with — oddly enough — an unfilled niche (more like a huge podcast hole): sci-fi TV and movies.

Attaching themselves to arguably the most enthusiastic of all fan crowds — *Star Trek* geeks — Michael and Evo created *Slice of Scifi* (`sliceofscifi.com`), a podcast-only show that quickly grew into an overnight success.

If you're thinking about branching out with a new show, consider these tips:

✔ **Take your audience with you.** If you're podcasting about lawn bowling, yet hold a secret passion for seventh-century Gaelic text, expect only a handful of folks to subscribe to both shows. However, if you move from lawn bowling to a podcast on sports medicine, they may find the new topic an easier pill to swallow.

✔ **Cross-promote.** Even if your podcasts are quite close in scope, there will be listeners to one who aren't aware of the other. Although we caution against turning one podcast into a giant commercial for the other, plug the heck out of your other show. Within reason.

✔ **Keep trying.** Don't expect to hit your stride in the new show by Episode 2. You'll have to try different formats, flavors, and ideas over there, just the way you did to make your first show perfect. (Or is it? Maybe it's getting a little stale. Time to spruce that one up, too.)

It's pretty safe to say that Mur Lafferty has carved out a niche for herself with *Geek Fu Action Grip,* but even Mur is discovering that need to branch out. Even as broad as her show is, certain topics in her life just don't fit comfortably into her audio blog and essay show. In fact, she is finding one aspect of her life — her daily pursuit of finishing her novel and landing a publishing contract — difficult to cover in her current podcast. But the content for this particular topic was accumulating, so Mur started up the *I Should Be Writing* (shouldwrite.blogspot.com) podcast, which serves *two* passions: podcasting and writing.

I Should Be Writing is for writers who are all in the same boat as she is, rowing like mad toward that elusive publishing contract while struggling to finish that first novel. Here Mur addresses writers who feel her pain — and other listeners who may be curious about people who write novels (and the process behind the book) — and imparts what she's learning in her quest to complete that first draft. It is not a podcast on how to publish a novel but a way of documenting the road to a publishing contract. Hopefully. Listeners will keep track with Mur on daily word count, and (no doubt) will help keep her honest about setting aside time for writing. Writers also working toward that contract will benefit from hearing the true-life struggles of another writer on the same path and may provide some insights. The balance among passion, creativity, and community is worth thinking about.

Mur's efforts bring up two points especially worth mentioning:

✔ **Your next podcast may be closer than you think.** Keep a close eye on your feedback; look for recurring themes that your audience likes to hear. If it's a broad enough topic and you can speak on it with authority, you may be able to craft a show around audience suggestions instead of having to sweat bullets to come up with something brand new every time.

✔ **Look for the niche within the niche.** If your main topic is broad, break it out into chunks and see what needs further exploration. Granted, a deep dive into the minutiae of a niche topic may reduce the size of your listening audience. But so what? This is about exploring your passion, not about gaining market share. And (we promise) there's always someone else out there who will want you to delve even deeper into the obscure topic you've just built an entire podcast around.

Reinventing yourself

Apart from inventing a new podcast to keep the passion alive, another option is to continuously reinvent your podcast to where audiences have no idea what will be coming up next. Here are some ways that you can do that:

- ✔ Feature a different guest host each week
- ✔ Have contributors develop content for you
- ✔ Ask your listeners for topics

If you subscribe to *Area 51* (`area51show.com`), you know what to expect — splatter-style, envelope-pushing, completely bizarre commentary from the cast and crew of this comedy review. When you plug into *Requiem of the Outcast* (`www.requiemoftheoutcast.com`), it's a safe bet that you'll get an earful of silliness, sarcasm, and satire, some of it inspired by adventures in the *Star Wars* community. Listeners come to your podcast with a certain level of expectation even though the content is new and fresh every time.

And then there's the podcast *Cyberpunk Radio* (`www.mental-escher.net/cyberpunkradio`), a podcast that continues to define, challenge, and then completely reinvent itself on every cast. From the hosts of *Mental-Escher,* who are based out of the San Francisco Bay area, *Cyberpunk Radio* is an intriguing goulash of science fiction, virtual reality, surrealism, audio montages, and social commentary . . . or is it? Even after several episodes you may not know and like it anyway for its edgy and original take on podcasting, or you may find the first few episodes a complete waste of space on your computer. It's not a podcast for everyone — a few episodes are hardly what you'd call family-friendly — but how many creative minds are this committed to creating a world in the distant future of next week? The artists at *Mental-Escher* conjure another world, another time — an alternate reality where machines rule over man (though sadly they don't look or act like the pretty people in *Battlestar Galactica*).

The passion behind this podcast is the challenge to constantly reinvent the content, creating unpredictable programming for the subscribers. Of course, the risk in alienating your listeners who are seeking normalcy and standardization in a podcast (to an extent) is ever present, but then again a podcast like *Cyberpunk Radio* might not be for them. This type of podcasting is podcasting for podcasting's sake, and the podcasters themselves keep their passion alive by continuously changing the format of their own show. Along with delivery of new content, it's an entirely different presentation of new content, part of what makes *Cyberpunk Radio* an intriguing, if not mysterious, listen.

Re-invention for the sake of re-invention isn't a bad idea, but it's so twentieth-century. You may find it a better idea to move forward with a plan. So here are a few dos and don'ts — with the don'ts first.

What NOT to do (ack! run away! run away!) . . .

- ✔ **Don't use shock-radio techniques.** Hearing a podcaster drop a few words that would make most grandmothers blush isn't anything new, and it's a cheap way to get a laugh and attention. Neither of your authors has any moral compunction against the more colorful aspects of the English language, but try to use them sparingly, okay?

- ✔ **Don't go from kid-friendly to adults-only.** If you're unhappy being a family show, give some advance notice so folks can unsubscribe. Hell hath no fury like a mother scorned (or even unpleasantly surprised) . . .

- ✔ **Don't get angry when you get dissenting e-mail.** Not everyone will be happy with your decision to change things around or to add a new segment. Deal with it and move on. You can't please everyone — or "correct" their opinions — so don't even try.

What to DO with all your might . . .

- ✔ **Cast your net wide.** Be open to a variety of new ideas and concepts, and don't be afraid to try them out on your audience. Your loyal listeners will likely forgive you a few miscues along the way.

- ✔ **Have a purpose for the change or addition.** Find the common connection with what your show has focused on before and talk to your audience about it. You can do this before or after the "newness" goes in the show, but your listeners will enjoy knowing the method behind your madness.

- ✔ **Encourage feedback about the change.** When you do this, ask more than "do you like it?" Find out if your audience feels differently about your show, if they think it's "fresher" or perhaps more appealing — and why. The changes you put in place are designed to give your show a boost; be sure and ask for confirmation that it actually happened!

If you find yourself in need of a break, there's nothing wrong with taking some time out. As a courtesy to those who are listening, however — whether it's 20 or 20,000 — let them know you're holding off on new episodes for a few weeks so you can reorganize priorities, goals, and the whole momentum of your podcast to make it even more rewarding for them to listen to. The same courtesy applies when you've had an unexpected illness: Give your listenership a quick update on what happened; reassure them that your voice is back and that your podcast is back. As passionate as you may be about a podcast, always remember your health and your voice must come first. There's nothing wrong with missing a week or two of a podcast while you get back up to par.

Truth and Honesty in Podcasting

"To me, ultimately, martial art means honestly expressing yourself. Now it is very difficult to do. I mean it is easy for me to put on a show and be cocky and be flooded with a cocky feeling and then feel, then, like pretty cool . . . and be blinded by it. Or I can show you some really fancy movement — but, to express oneself honestly, not lying to oneself — and to express myself honestly — that, my friend, is very hard to do."

—Bruce Lee, from an interview on *The Pierre Berton Show*

When Tee was writing the first draft of this particular chapter, he had playing in the background *Bruce Lee: The Way of the Warrior,* a (really cool) documentary featuring recently discovered footage from his work-in-progress *Game of Death,* rare commentary from The Dragon himself, and interview footage. In one of the interviews came the preceding quote — a compelling moment when Bruce Lee sums up, in his own words, what martial arts means from his perspective. As Tee pondered his words, it struck him that Bruce was basically saying, *Martial arts is all about keeping it real.*

And (for whatever reason) he blurted out loud, "If Bruce Lee were alive today, he would have a podcast!"

Part of the passion in a podcast is cultivating honesty with yourself and your audience, and that honesty in your podcast is what keeps listeners coming back. "To thine own self be true . . ." — one of Shakespeare's most-quoted lines from *Hamlet* — holds as true for podcasting as it has for every other intensely personal creative activity; let it serve as a mantra that fires up your drive to produce a terrific podcast. Honest passion, and honesty in general, cannot be faked in a podcast as many podcasters are producing their audio content without any other compensation save for ratings on Podcast Alley and Podcast Pickle, some feedback from listeners, and perhaps the occasional donation. On the larger scale, podcasters, regardless of their agendas or goals, are on the podcasting scene because they want to be there, and if that honesty in wanting to deliver new content is even remotely artificial, listeners will pick up on that and also lose interest in your podcast.

It's okay to ask yourself, before hitting Record or getting that first take into Audacity or GarageBand, *"Do I know for sure what I'm getting into?"* — or (more to the point), *"Do I really want to do this?"* — but never ask yourself whether you *can* do this. That is not even a question to consider. Podcasting encompasses and welcomes voices of all backgrounds, all professions, all experience levels (be they professional, semiprofessional, or amateur). You can do this — and you have as much right to as any of us. All you need is the mic, the application, the feed, and the host. From there, it all rests on you.

Podcasting is a commitment of time and resources — to yourself and to your listeners. It's a promise you make to bring to the podosphere the best content you can produce — and with the right support, passion, and drive, your podcast will evolve, mature, and move ahead with the same zeal that inspired the first episode. Accomplishing this feat rests on remaining honest in your desire to sit behind the microphone and produce your next show. If you're not sure about the answers to *"Do I know for sure what I'm getting into?"* or *"Do I really want to do this?"* ask yourself, *"If I don't want to be here, then why would listeners want to download and hear my latest episode?"*

"To express myself honestly — that, my friend is very hard to do." Oh yeah, Bruce Lee would have produced an incredible podcast.

Part VI
The Part of Tens

In this part . . .

*L*ike any *For Dummies* book worth its weight in compressed MP3 files, this book contains a Part of Tens.
Because podcasting is likely to change drastically in the
next few years, this particular Part of Tens provides lists
of ideas, thoughts, and philosophies from the authors to
take along on your podcasting trek. Chapter 16 helps to
guide you in your selection of podcasts to listen to for
ideas, inspiration, and fun. Chapter 17 covers some of the
most influential people in podcasting. Chapters 18 and 19
are diametrically opposed views of how podcasting will, or
will not, influence the future of traditional radio. (Isn't life
on the unexplored frontier exciting?)

Chapter 16

Top Ten Types of Podcasts to Check Out

Ah yes, narrowing down the thousands and thousands of podcasts out there to an elite ten: the Top Ten Podcasts You Should Be Listening To. The Best of the Best. In the podosphere, these higher planes are commonly referred to as The Pod Squad, Podcast Pickle's Favorites, and Podcast Alley Top Ten List.

Where to begin? Where to begin? We sat down, and each put together our own top ten lists of podcasts. What we found was that one of us swore by some podcasts the other had never heard of, and vice versa. We started wondering, "How are we going to narrow this list down and eventually get it to ten?" Then we took a closer look at our lists and realized "Hey, we've got a pattern going on here!" Between the two of us, we had a solid cross-section of *types* of podcasts, not just in the way of genres but in production values. So with a quick edit of the outline and a change of mindset, we present the Top Ten Types of Podcasts to Check Out.

There are other kinds of podcasts that were, perhaps, not showcased here, but with these ten kinds of podcasts as a starting point, you can easily begin to fill playlists and MP3 player space. Once comfortable with what you hear, you can then follow the "Favorite Podcasts" links that your podcast's companion blog offers. From this list given here, you can sample a wide cross-section of audio content. Relax, download, and give your ears a treat.

Tech Podcasts

If you're thinking about podcasting, you likely have a comfortable knowledge of computers, Web-surfing, and blogging. But regardless of how technologically savvy you are, you can never stop learning. That's why your aggregator should be catching at least one *tech podcast.*

The agenda for a tech podcast is (surprise!) technology — usually computer-oriented. All geek, all the time. Geeks, nerds, wizards, and Tech Help gurus sit behind a microphone and pull back the curtain on how your computer works, how to make a podcast's RSS feed better, and how to make your time behind the keyboard more efficient.

Tech podcasts come delivered to you in a variety of skill levels and on a variety of topics:

- ✔ **Macs:** Some excellent podcasts for Mac users include *MacCast* (shown in Figure 16-1 and available at www.maccast.com), *Your Mac Life Podcast* (www.yourmaclife.com), or *MacPhilly Almost Live* (www.macphilly.com).

- ✔ **PCs:** *Typical PC User* (typicalpcuser.biz/tpcu/) and *Darn PC* (www.darnpc.com/wordpress/) focus on the Windows environment and its latest updates and upgrades.

- ✔ **General computing:** Many of the tech podcasts out there like *This Week in Tech* (or TWiT, as it is so lovingly referred as by its hosts and listeners, available at www.twit.tv/) or *HomeNetworkHelp.Info* are generic in their approach to operating systems, following a mindset that a computer is a computer and the rest is mostly bells and whistles.

- ✔ **Technology perspectives:** *The Girl on Tech* (girlontech.blogspot.com) or *The Chris Pirillo Show* (www.thechrispirilloshow.com) give personal perspectives on technology in society and go beyond the geek-speak, giving their own perspectives on issues and how technology can affect just about everything.

Whichever podcast you feed into your podcatching client, find a tech podcast that is right for you and either enjoy the new perspective, or allow yourself to grow into your geekdom. There is a lot to learn out there about computers, PDAs, Bluetooth, and other cool Q Branch gizmos that are available at your local electronics store. When you have the basics down, these podcasts allow you to unlock their potential and go beyond your expectations.

Logo by Tim Madden, courtesy of Adam Christianson

Figure 16-1: *MacCast* is one of many podcasts offered to Mac users to get the most out of their iBooks or Power-Books.

Independent Music Podcasts

Podcasting is audio content on demand, and after taking a listen to what is being offered on the radio, that is a very good thing. Maybe it's a hazard of getting older, but some of us just aren't hearing anything on the air that's all that interesting or exciting . . . unless we happen to find an alternative station that has a few up-and-coming bands we've not heard of, or independent musicians who are looking for the big break.

The good news is that those maverick sounds are alive and well and doing just fine in the 21st century, and they're finding a new promotion channel with podcasting.

Independent labels, where the artists also work as promoters, producers, and holders-of-all-rights, have control over where their music plays, how often it is played, and how much it costs you. Many indie musicians who are having trouble getting exposure and radio airplay can grant permission for podcasters to use their music. What does this cost the podcaster? A few moments of time and a spot or two, such as, "This music is brought to you by . . ." and "Visit this band online at w-w-w-dot . . . ." And in return, the musician is exposed to a worldwide audience.

Musicians such as The Gentle Readers (featured on *Evil Genius Chronicles* at `www.evilgeniuschronicles.org`), The Transfer (featured on *EarthCore* at `www.scottsigler.net`), and Fumitaka Anzai (featured on the *Rev Up Review* at `www.rev-up-review.co.uk`) have all enjoyed the benefits and windfalls of associating themselves with a podcast. Now indie musicians are turning to podcasts that not only are dedicated to the broadcast of podsafe music, but also spotlight independent musicians whose sound goes against the corporate music industry's notion of "what the public wants." Here are a few such podcasts you may want to check out:

- ✔ **Bandtrax** (`www.bandtrax.net`): *Bandtrax* serves as a radio station for the independent label. Artists are invited to submit music and sell CDs on the Bandtrax Web site.

- ✔ **The tartanpodcast** (`www.tartanpodcast.com`): Podcasting from Glasgow, Scotland, Mark Hunter showcases unsigned or independent label music in order to win an audience for these new artists.

- ✔ **LoveHouse Radio** (`www.lovehouseradio.com`): Based out of Richmond, Virginia, host P.D. Love took his love of music, his appreciation for the independent artist, and his everyday life and turned it into a podcast that highlights featured artists on the Podsafe Music network.

Many of these podcasts work together on the Podsafe Music Network (`music.podshow.com`) to offer the podosphere a one-stop location to find postcasts that showcase the innovative and creative minds of independent music.

Science Podcasts

The approach to science made popular by scientists like Carl Sagan and professional experts Adam Savage and Jamie Hyneman (hosts of the Discovery Channel's *Mythbusters*) is rampant in the podosphere. Here are some science podcasts that we recommend:

- ✔ **Slacker Astronomy** (`slackerastronomy.com`): If you have always wondered about what is really going on beyond our atmosphere, take a listen to a podcast descendant of the Carl Sagan *Cosmos* concept. For those who would never leave the planet without their attitude, Aaron Price, Pamela Gay, and Travis Searle dubbed the show *Slacker Astronomy*.

- ✔ **Skepticality** (`skepticality.com`): This podcast looks deeper into the news too weird for mainstream media, and takes a critical microscope to the pseudoscience of the paranormal, the supernatural, close encounters, and urban legends.

✔ *The Science Show* (www.abc.net.au/rn/science/ss/): Australia's Robyn Williams looks at all aspects of science, ranging from biology to chemistry to everyday applications of scientific achievements.

Science shows are good for you — like vegetables, only better. Not only can you learn something new or broaden your scope in a field you may regard as a hobby, but you can marvel at how the hosts demystify concepts once comprehensible only to Ph.D.s and keep the ideas easy to grasp.

Educational Podcasts

Why not broaden your horizons with educational podcasting? For example, say you've always wanted to learn Spanish. You could shell out some bucks for the "Teach Yourself Spanish" series, or you could to listen to the free podcast *Really Learn Spanish* (its companion blog is located at radio.weblogs.com/0142338/). Instructor Johan van Rooyen takes his unconventional teaching methods (mastered over a seven-year stint with teaching English in Spain) and turns them into a podcast that features "star pupils" as special guests who are looking to become more comfortable in the language many of us take in high school but forget by the time we leave college! (Imagine ordering at a Mom-and-Pop taqueria . . . and getting it right.)

If you are not interested in learning another language, take a look at some of the other subjects offered in the podosphere. Here are just a few examples of what's available:

✔ **History:** *HistoryPodcast* (historypodcast.blogspot.com) is completely devoted to history for the lovers of history. This is a feed you will want to subscribe to. Or if you do wish for a more specific era of discussion, my most gracious lord, check out the *Medieval Podcast* (podcast.medievalstudies.info/).

✔ **Money management:** If you're looking for advice on managing your money, check out *Radio Economics* (www.radioeconomics.com). Or if you have a friend or family member getting ready for that next step in education, try *Student Financial Aid News* (www.financialaidnews.com/blog/index.htm).

There is a lot to learn from the world, and whether you're tuning in to one of the numerous podcasts sponsored by universities and colleges or to an enthusiast who wants to share and swap resources with you, all this continuing education is available online, in audio, and at no charge.

Comedy Podcasts

There are times in life when you just need a good laugh. One of the joys of podcasting is having those good laughs categorized, digitized, and waiting for your call, whether it is on the computer or your favorite MP3 player.

Humor, though, is in the eye of the beholder — or in this case, the ear of the listener. Performing a search on "Comedy Podcasts" offers you many, many choices, ranging from kid-safe comedy to adults-only. Some of the earlier podcasts cited (such as *Slacker Astronomy* and *Skepticality*) pepper their podcasts with humor (always good to add), but straight-up comedy podcasts are not intended to do anything other than entertain and perhaps make you think.

These podcasts cover a wide spectrum of humor. Here are a few comedy podcasts that we enjoy:

- ✔ *The Bitterest Pill* (thebitterestpill.com)**:** Perhaps you like your humor dry, witty, and maybe just a touch smarmy. Dan Klass and his podcast, *The Bitterest Pill,* should do the trick. With his background in stand-up comedy, Dan's delivery is edgy and relentless. He takes a hard, cold look at the world and makes observations that you might think but would not have the courage to express openly. Dan not only gives you his opinions but also podcasts them for the world to hear.

- ✔ *Requiem of the Outcast* (www.requiemoftheoutcast.com/ wordpress/)**:** If you're looking for something closer to family-friendly and pleasantly geeky, give Rich Sigfrit's *Requiem of the Outcast* a listen. While it's mainly a podcast by *Star Wars* fans for *Star Wars* fans, Rich's slightly twisted talent in comedy sketch writing appears and manifests itself as wacky, goofball fan humor that can make even the casual fan of science fiction chuckle. If it ever wanders beyond the realm of family-friendly content, Rich and his cohorts Ron and Jamie Garner let folks know about up-and-coming situations that are not for the young or the squeamish.

- ✔ *Area 51* (www.area51show.com)**:** This podcast comes at you with guns blazing, and if you're not wearing Kevlar, then you're going to feel it the following morning. Making *Monty Python* seem like *Bear in the Big Blue House*, *Area 51* strides up to the boundaries of good taste.

  Area 51 is not about alien conspiracies or science fiction. It's a completely irreverent, slapstick, and sometimes-graphic comedy show that is many things, but family-friendly is not one of them. If you like your comedy in-your-face and intense and challenging notions of what you can and can't get away with, then you have found a friend in *Area 51.*

Husband and Wife Podcasts

Comedy is prevalent in all the various genres of podcasting, especially with husband and wife podcasts. After all, sometimes you need humor to deal with your spouse. You can find a variety of husband and wife podcasts, and here are a few we recommend:

✔ ***Honeymooners*-type humor:** "Playfully blunt" is a great way to describe this kind of husband-wife podcast for it is a glimpse into how spouses interact with one another, and there is a spirit of fun shared between the genders. It's as if you were listening to *The Honeymooners* being podcast, and no matter what is said, no matter what jibe is hurtled, no matter who scores the most lethal blow to the ego, it always ends with a heart-felt "Baby, you're the greatest," a dip, and a kiss. Here are a few you may want to check out:

- *Croncast* (`croncast.com`)

- *He Said / She Said* (`www.hesaidshesaidpodcast.com`)

- *Illinoise* (`www.illinoise.net`)

✔ ***Married with Children*-type humor:** While the love is still there (after all, the couple that podcasts together stays together), the conversations in these podcasts can turn to extremely detailed tangents on nocturnal activities, embarrassing moments with ex-girlfriends, and other subject matter that could be considered racy, raunchy, and just plain wrong on many levels. Here are some fun podcasts that fit this bill:

- *The Dawn and Drew Show!* (`dawnanddrew.podshow.com`)

- *Keith and The Girl* (`www.keithandthegirl.com`)

Always check the listings to see how "playfully blunt" couples (in either list) can get in their podcasts. Dawn and Drew do give a disclaimer on their home page, a brief and simple warning that maybe, just maybe, they will dare to tread paths that few choose. Many podcasts that deal with mature themes (a nice and proper way to say "sex") post disclaimers on their podcasts' Web sites or in their blogs' show notes.

Soundseeing Tour Podcasts

Podcasts offer their listeners (as well as their hosts) an audio gateway to the world. In a *soundseeing tour,* the world is depicted in the (described) sights and live sounds around the host, offering listeners a virtual visit. Usually armed with an iRiver, podcast hosts take their listeners for a trip out into a familiar environment, hold conversations, and interact with the world around them, recording events in the same way a tourist fills up card upon card with digital photos.

For example, Japan sports several soundseeing tours. Together, these five podcasts span every corner of The Land of the Rising Sun:

✔ *Planet Japan* (www.planetjapan.org/podcast.html)

✔ *Kobe Beef* (kobe-beef.blogspot.com)

✔ *Kyoto Podcast* (homepage.mac.com/japanpodguides)

✔ *Herro Flom Japan* (www.herroflomjapan.com)

✔ *Tokyo Calling* (www.tokyocalling.org)

Part of the appeal in this handful of feeds is how each takes place in the same country, but remains unique in its perspectives. With podcasts from Kobe, Kyoto, and Shiraishi Island, subscribing to more than one podcast located in the same country can give you a wider perspective than just one.

Other soundseeing tours include countries where hosts open the door to their homes and take the world on a trip to the grocery store, a quick errand into town, or (for the really lucky ones) a quick stop-off at the pub. Here is just a sprinkling of these types of podcasts:

✔ **Amsterdam:** *Bicyclemark's Communiqué* (www.bicyclemark.org/blog/)

✔ **Canada:** *Island Podcasting* (radio.weblogs.com/0145147/)

✔ **Great Britain:** *The Definitive London Podcast* (www.learnoutloud.com/ Catalog/Travel/-/The-Definitive-London-Podcast/6925) and *Perfect Path* (www.perfectpath.co.uk)

✔ **New Zealand:** *Kat's Kiwi Podcast* (katskiwipodcast.blogspot.com)

And in the same spirit of soundseeing tours comes its offspring: *beercasts*. In a beercast, hosts fire up a recorder and capture for posterity and podcasting purposes a night out with friends. Especially when everyone podcasting orders a different brew, beercasts feature some of the most unique and hard-to-find microbrews along with insight on "what makes a good beer." Mmmmmmm . . . beeeeeercasts.

Serialized Novel/Short-Story Podcasts

When Tee stepped into podcasting, no author had yet set out to do what he was planning: to serialize a novel in podcasts, from beginning to end. Twenty-two chapters of *MOREVI* and a preview of *Legacy of MOREVI,* over a period of 23 weeks. But would anyone really want to listen?

Wow — people did want to listen and continue to do so months after its conclusion! And now, other authors are beginning to discover the potential of
this exciting new way to promote their works, their unpublished material,
and (of course) themselves.

Podiobooks are podcast novels with the authors recording their works from
home. Alongside Tee's swashbuckling epic fantasy, MOREVI (`www.teemorris.
com/podcast/`), others have come on board:

- *The Pocket and the Pendant* (`markjeffrey.typepad.com`)**:** Mark
  Jeffrey joined the podiobook genre with this young-adult science-fantasy
  adventure.

- *EarthCore* (`www.scottsigler.net`)**:** Scott Sigler performed this jugger-
  naut rock-and-roll/science-fiction thriller.

These podiobooks led the charge that eventually led to Podiobooks.com (`www.
podiobooks.com`), a Web site (founded by your humble authors) dedicated to
offering podcast novels (and even nonfiction titles) from one reliable source.
Now, Podiobooks.com (shown in Figure 16-2) offers Paul Story's *Tom Corven*
(`www.dreamwords.com/TomCorven.htm`), a podcast live from the Scottish
highlands. And it continues to field many queries from authors, both known
and unknown, in how to join the ranks of podcasting authors.

Figure 16-2:
Podiobooks.
com
presents
novels, one
chapter at a
time, one
podcast at a
time, each
read by the
author.

Logo created by Zaphire

But what if podcast novels are too big a commitment? You can still get in a fast "fiction fix" with these podcasts:

- ✔ *Escape Pod* (`escapepod.info`): This podcast offers its subscribers a wide variety of previously published and brand-new short fiction, including five-minute flash-fiction podcasts.

- ✔ *The Seanachai* (`goodwordsrightorder.com`): This podcast continues to spin yarn upon yarn, tale upon tale, and moral upon moral in the Irish tradition of storytelling.

Since the success of the first three podiobooks and the launch of *Escape Pod* and *The Seanachai,* more and more writers are turning to podcasting for promotion and distribution of their work. So curl up with a good MP3 player and enjoy the free fiction that the podosphere has to offer.

Passionate Podcasts

There it is again! The *P* word — passion. Yes, yes, yes, there should be passion in every podcast you listen to, but some do their thing simply as a celebration of something — a salute, dedication, or just plain declaration of love for a sport, TV show, or another interest that (for whatever reason) *matters* to a group of people. Here are some podcasts around such interests:

- ✔ *The Signal* (`signal.serenityfirefly.com`): If you take a look at Podcast Alley's Top Ten podcasts, you find a show up there called *The Signal.* This podcast is a celebration of the prematurely cancelled sci-fi-Western-adventure television show *Firefly. The Signal* is a podcast from *Firefly* fans, for *Firefly* fans, and for people curious as to what the fuss is all about. Eagerly counting down to the release of the television show's feature film, *Serenity, The Signal* continues to show support for an out-of-this-world Western, its actors, and the crew behind-the-scenes.

- ✔ *Zencast* (`www.zencast.org`): This podcast explores Buddhist and Zen teachings, features new age music artists, and teaches techniques in meditation, aligning bio-energies, and spiritual enlightenment.

- ✔ *Cubscast* (`cubscast.com`): If you are less into achieving inner peace and more into screaming from the cheap seats at Wrigley Field, then *Cubscast* may be what you're looking for. As of the writing of this book, podcasts are available for the Boston Red Sox, the New York Yankees, the Oakland Athletics, and the new kids in the sport — the Washington Nationals. There are podcasts for professional wrestling, football (both American and European), and NASCAR, many of them fan-based, fan-sponsored, and fan-hosted.

✔ ***Catholic Insider*** (www.catholicinsider.com): But what if your passion is more rooted in the spiritual growth of your faith? Does God have a podcast? (Pretty deep question, we know. . . .) Well, God does have someone on the payroll, not only making the Top Ten lists but winning the People's Choice Award for Best Religious Podcast. The *Catholic Insider* (shown in Figure 16-3), podcasting from The Netherlands, is hosted by Father Roderick Vonhögen, Catholic priest of the Archdiocese of Utrecht. Not only does he answer questions concerning faith, religion, and everyday values, he also offers up commentary on *Harry Potter* and *Star Wars*.

A man of God. A sci-fi geek. Now *that's* the makings of a fun podcast!

Figure 16-3:
Want the inside scoop on the Catholic faith? Tune in to the *Catholic Insider,* a podcast that looks at life from the Archdiocese point-of-view.

Podcasts about . . . Podcasting

It may sound redundant and feel a little odd to listen to a podcast about podcasting. It would be like tuning into an interview show for interviewers interviewing other interviewers, or having an electrician come over to an electrician's house to fix faulty electric wiring. But why not?

✔ ***podCast411*** (podcast411.com): On this podcast about podcasting, Robert Walch picks the brains of podcasters from every genre, every recording method, and every work ethic, and asks them "So how do you do it?" and "Why do you do it?" The goal of *podCast411* is to answer just those questions — and to keep podcasters informed about what is currently playing in the podosphere. Featuring these podcasts lets other podcasters tune in, listen, and use what they hear to make their own podcasts grow and improve.

✔ *Podcast Brothers* (www.podcastbrothers.com)**:** This podcast keeps the podosphere informed on the various trends and the really cool developments of podcasting. Tim and Emile Bourquin focus on the state of the world of podcasting, the portable media that offer ways of taking podcasts on the road, and future trends that podcasting is leading businesses into. Again, two podcasters keep their attention on their passion of podcasting, and keep their listeners and show producers in the know about what people are doing in this exciting medium.

Chapter 17

Top Ten Most Influential People in Podcasting

*I*n just over a year, the number of podcasts grew from a few dozen to over 10,000. Even if you're running on "Internet time," you have to consider that a meteoric rise.

If you're reading this book, you're likely new to podcasting and might have missed out on the trials and tribulations that went along with that huge growth spurt. As with any sudden rise, select individuals proved themselves to be instrumental to podcasting, as well as to other podcasters, during those formative times all those long months ago.

The following list suggests ten (or so) of these individuals who will likely continue to influence the shape of things to come in the podcasting world. As you read these names, try to remember that these are regular people like the rest of us. True, some of them may seem larger than life (even in a field this new), but all of them put their pants on one leg at a time — unless they're wearing skirts.

While we encourage you to make your own decisions, a wise budding podcaster or future podcast star would do well to take a listen to the wisdom/information/rants put forth by this group. Often controversial and usually informative, each of these people has a unique outlook on the world of podcasting. We've found each of them to be helpful guides in our own growth in podcasting. But (as we've said probably way too many times in this book for our editors' tastes) your mileage may vary.

Dave Winer

Podcasting really wouldn't be podcasting without the capability to enclose files inside an RSS feed — and Dave Winer is the one who made that happen. Without that extension of RSS, we'd all be downloading files in real time, wondering why anyone in their right mind would put up a 65MB file.

Dave is one of the more interesting characters in the world of podcasting. In addition to his technical contributions, some would argue that Dave's contributions to the spirit of podcasting are every bit as important.

As of this writing, Dave continues to produce *Morning Coffee Notes* (morningcoffeenotes.com). This podcast sticks with relatively rough-and-ready production values, but it's worth checking out as a pioneering approach. The use of music is pretty casual, which brings up an important point for you ahead-of-the-curve types out there . . .

If you wind up incorporating a lot of music into your podcast — especially if your ambition is to provide programming for a commercial market — make sure you have copyright clearance for the music you use. (That clanking chain you hear is The Ghost of Napster Past.)

Dave's show features Dave, a portable recording device, and his surroundings. Sometimes it's a discussion about a piece of technology; sometimes it's a conversation with an interesting individual. But listeners to *Morning Coffee Notes* are always treated to thought-provoking opinions and ideas from one of the progenitors of podcasting.

Dave is very much a "polarizing" individual with strong opinions he's not afraid to share. He doesn't pull any punches, and you always get the truth as he sees it. As is often true of strong opinions, the result is that some technologists bristle at the mention of his name, while others welcome his ability to look at challenges and conventional wisdom from a new perspective. Yes, he rambles — sometimes in directions that escape our personal interest or clash with our opinions on various topics. But he's Dave Winer, a voice worth listening to. You can decide what to do with the information after that.

Adam Curry

In 1987, both of your authors were freshman in college and MTV (the icon of the generation that remembers when they actually *played* music videos) hired a new VJ named Adam Curry. Almost 20 years later, despite life experiences, diplomas, and other strange changes and artistic ventures, it's still baffling to think that the same guy who was introducing the latest Madonna video is now "the Podfather."

Adam Curry's importance to the craft might be the single best example that illustrates the "just-do-it" nature of podcasting. It was Adam Curry, not some highly trained programmer, who hacked together the first podcatching client program to harness the power of the recently created enclosed-media files in RSS 2.0 feeds — and made them download during the computer's off hours.

Since that time, Adam has become the most recognized (and arguably the most popular) podcaster around. He continues to produce the *Daily Source Code* (`dailysourcecode.com`), which was probably the first "podcast about nothing." Listeners never know quite what to expect; Adam could take them on a tour of his kitchen, or discuss the latest round of talks that his company, BoKu Communications, is having with some technology or content partner that will change the shape of podcasting in the future. The proverbial potluck show that contains its own inside joke.

Adam is definitely at the forefront of podcasting as a valid means of distributing content — and is attracting attention as a business model and an agent of change in our world. It's worth making time to listen to "the DSC" — even if you fast-forward through the parts that don't appeal to you — but we've all received special permission to do just that from the Podfather, so you won't be swimming with the fishes anytime soon.

Steve Jobs and Bill Gates

To the best of our knowledge, neither of these two gentlemen have podcasts, and you may be wondering why we're listing them as influential. For those who don't collect the Mega-Corporation Trading Card set, Steve Jobs and Bill Gates are the brains and founders of Apple and Microsoft, respectively.

The actions of their companies, via direct and indirect hardware and software applications, have a distinct and unquestionable impact on the future of podcasting. It's not a big leap to assume that without the huge consumer adoption of the Apple iPod (which arguably has spurred sales of other portable audio-file players), podcasting would not have spread at the incredible rate it has. As of this writing, the latest version of iTunes is causing yet another explosion, as more folks are discovering the simplicity (and joy) of listening to podcasts.

Because podcasts originate from, are transferred through, or wind up on a personal computer, Microsoft is involved. However, its reach goes much farther than the ubiquitous operating system — and could have a profound impact on podcasting in the future. Microsoft products are *everywhere* — from cellphones and PDAs to entire media centers and game consoles. Look for this company to continue to turn out products that not only make use of podcasting technology, but also to extend it in directions that directly benefit its bottom line.

As much as podcasting has been a bootstrap movement, the big guns are coming. Heck, they are already here, changing the game as it's forming. But such is the nature of all technology. Of course, other technology companies will exert their influence as well — but it's worth remembering that market forces are in play already, and will continue as podcasting progresses.

Doug Kaye

Doug Kaye is the driving force behind IT Conversations (www. itconversations.com), a collection of podcasts and programs that stay at the cutting edge of technology and innovation. With show hosts talking about everything from blogging to digital rights and new-media trailblazing, it's easy to stay informed (though sometimes a challenge to keep up) if you listen to one or (gods help you) all of the programs Doug helps produce.

But Doug's contribution to podcasting goes beyond simply assembling the best high-tech people to create the latest conversations about IT innovation — and providing them a vehicle for their thoughts. He's actively seeking to capture as many speakers, panel discussions, and conversations from various events and expositions all over the world. There's a vast amount of knowledge shared in these venues, and Doug's opinion is that too few people get a chance to hear about it. He's working hard to change that, by capturing those discussions as they happen and making them part of the IT Conversations family of offerings. In essence, he'll be archiving this knowledge for future interested people. (Should be quite a future.)

It's a great plan, and one that takes an incredible amount of dedication. Doug works closely with each of his show hosts to make sure their podcasts are engaging, sound great, and are a joy for interested people to listen to.

Rob Walch

Every day or so, Rob releases another edition of *podCast411* (podcast411. com), each of which features an interview with another podcaster about . . . podcasting. While that may sound a bit like high-tech navel-gazing, you might be surprised at how worthy the content is to add to your already overloaded subscription list.

Podcasters should be listening to Rob's show because it's about what they do. Who better to learn new tips and tricks from than the people actually doing it on their show every week? Most of the conversations stay focused at a fairly high level, avoiding the "detail dump" that would turn most people off.

Rob talks with other podcasters not only about how they podcast but also *why* they do it. For every question about a microphone or particular piece of hardware, Rob digs deeper into the goals of the show, the way the hosts approach their craft, and what their hopes and dreams are.

It's a fascinating show for anyone interesting in learning from others who are constantly refining their shows. If you're podcasting, you should be listening to this one.

Nicole Simon

The denizens of middle management yearn for the day when they are handed the key to the executive washroom. For podcasters, that day comes when the first e-mail from Nicole Simon arrives.

Nicole has an insatiable appetite for podcasts, consuming so many that we're convinced she has multiple copies of herself listening simultaneously, and then downloading all of them into one giant uber-Nicole. When the uber-Nicole finds a podcast that she enjoys or thinks has promise, she's more than happy to give the podcaster some *suggestions* on ways to improve it.

Not only does she provide honest and direct feedback to the podcasters she listens to, she helps keep the podcasting community in check — making sure every podcaster considers the international component of what is said or done on his or her show. Too often we get caught up in what "the government" might do, or state that "new shows will be posted in the morning" without specifying the time zone we occupy. Nicole is there to ask tough questions such as, "to which government are you referring?" and "would that be your morning, or my morning?"

She also produces her own podcast called *Useful Sounds* (`www.useful-sounds.de`) and has what is commonly referred to as the sexiest voice in podcasting. (Both of your authors agree.)

Dave Slusher

Dave Slusher is another early adopter of podcasting, creating the *Evil Genius Chronicles* (`www.evilgeniuschronicles.org`) from Conway, South Carolina. With a varied background that includes working with various IT startups and hosting a nationally syndicated talk-radio program in the 1990s, Dave may be the perfect blend of technology and talent. But that's not what put him on this list.

Dave is the single best person at "keepin' it real," to borrow a "street" cliché. When podcasters get too caught up in ratings, tracking downloads, various awards, and whether they're being fairly judged in their community, Dave Slusher is right there to say, "Why the hell do you care what anyone else thinks?"

Dave advocates the power of passion-for-what-you-do as the single biggest motivation for podcasters. Podcasters should take that position to heart; it's easy to forgive a few technical miscues, or to turn the other cheek when a podcaster is experimenting with a new format. But listeners can tell when a podcaster is trying to be something "more" than he or she truly is, and that's a big turn-off. Heck, there's already an entire radio spectrum dedicated to that sort of thing.

Brian Ibbott

We put Brian on this list for two reasons. First, he's one of the original music podcasters and many of you readers are likely thinking of starting a music podcast of your own. (Hey, lots of us wanted to be DJs when we were kids.) More importantly, Brian is a music podcaster who is doing it right — and doing it the legal way.

As mentioned in Chapter 3, podcasting licensed music legally is a challenge. With his podcast *Coverville* (`coverville.com`), Brian has worked directly with ASCAP, BMI, and other various organizations that hold the rights to major-label music and songs. While many music podcasters are just a process server away from a major lawsuit, Brian is sitting pretty.

Brian also serves as an example of how to create a niche podcast out of the music you love and fill a void not covered by the traditional outlets. Brian has a passion for cover songs, and has built a show completely around songs that fit that bill. Not only that, but he's taken it a step further, featuring groups of cover songs that have a common thread and producing *themed* episodes of his podcast. Simply brilliant — we don't know of any radio stations or programs that provide this service.

So before you rush out to make the next hot music podcast, consider the legal ramifications. And while you are pondering that, also ask whether your future podcast sounds like the same stuff anyone can listen to over their radios. Follow Brian's lead, and give the world something *different* with your podcast.

Ray Slakinski and August Trometer

Some folks might argue that when iTunes became a podcatching client, the rest of the companies making alternative podcatching clients were doomed. Well, though we don't have a crystal ball or unlimited credit with The Psychic Friends Network, we'd say hold the phone on that one.

Ray and August are more than just the creators of iPodderX (`ipodderx.com`). These guys genuinely care about propelling podcasting forward, and they walk the walk by building the tools and services necessary to keep up (and help shape) the continually shifting nature of podcasting. These two guys are true innovators and see their role in podcasting as something more than just helping you pull MP3 files out of podcast feeds.

Historians tell us it was not the miners who made the gold rush of 1849, but the companies that provided the picks and the shovels. Keep your eyes on these guys; the picks and shovels they make are about to get very interesting.

Dave Chekan, Matt Hoopes, Marty Mulligan, and Dave Mansueto

Podcasting sucks. Bandwidth, that is. A lot of it, as we discuss in Chapter 7. Without these four guys (DMMD, as we like to call them), many podcasters would have folded up shop long ago because they couldn't afford to pay their hosting bill.

DMMD gave the podcasting world Liberated Syndication (`www.libsyn.com`), providing unbelievably cheap hosting and serving of podcast media files at a time when subscribers were flocking toward podcasts like lemmings off the cliff.

Libsyn is helping to change the paradigm of bandwidth and media-file delivery systems. Okay, nontechnical types may find it boring, scarily technical, and incredibly complicated — but it's a complete necessity for any podcaster who receives a modicum of popularity. Luckily for everyone, these four guys make it a breeze to keep your podcasts going when the wave hits.

As with any small company, they've weathered some rough spots along the way. But DMMD are committed to sticking it out, and we hope podcasters continue to stand by them or other companies like theirs. Because the thought of paying for incremental bandwidth is simply too scary to consider unless you win the lottery.

Chapter 18

Top Ten Reasons Why Podcasting Won't Kill Radio

In This Chapter

▶ Freedom from the FCC: good and bad

▶ Too many choices

▶ Independent music versus pop music

▶ Staying in touch

*A*nyone remember when you tuned in to MTV and actually saw music videos? Good times, good times. If you ever want to throw out some fun trivia, ask, "What was the first video to ever play on MTV and what group performed in it?" The answer is the video for the song "Video Killed the Radio Star" by the Buggles.

As goofy, chintzy, and utterly new wave as that song is, there was a bit of a panic when MTV went on the air. All musicians suddenly had to contend with something only a few performers — like Elton John, Meat Loaf, and ELO — had ever considered: image. Record labels and producers had to add into their budgets payrolls for directors, set designers, and scriptwriters. Radio stations suddenly had to compete with television over — rock stars! Listeners were listening to music on their TVs! What will become of the music industry as we know it?!

Well, it's 23 years later, and radio is still here. MTV now shows a variety of programming, and very little of it includes music videos. Radio — much to the contrary of what bean counters and consultants convince program directors — has survived MTV, Napster, Internet radio, and Howard Stern's announcement that he is jumping to satellite radio.

Now comes podcasting, and once again what many in the broadcasting industry dismissed as the next wave of Internet radio is beginning to gain ground. In less than six months, podcasting went from a feature in the *Washington Post Express* (a free, sample newspaper distributed at rail stations) to a front-page feature in *The Washington Post!*

For a new medium so easily disregarded, the radio industry is taking notice and regarding podcasting as a threat. While it would be neat to think that yes, podcasting is the people's radio and will bring about the downfall of the radio execs who believe they know what listeners really want, the radio industry will not be closing its doors nor will it suffer multigazillion-dollar losses on account of this grass-roots movement that is podcasting. No, the corporate radio business will continue to stand strong and still smell as pretty as a red rose in full bloom.

The Undiscovered Country: Podcasting Awareness

Podcasting has celebrated a one-year anniversary (and what a lovely party it was) and yet with coverage from the media, it is not uncommon to hear this question: "What's a podcast?"

Something like this happened to Evo when a mechanic at his local auto body garage spotted his license plate, which reads, simply enough, *PODCAST*. The mechanic asked, "What's a podcast?" Evo went into the bare-bones explanation of what a podcast is, how it works, and said, "It's so simple to do, you could go home, create a podcast, and have it online tomorrow!"

The mechanic's reply: "Why would I want to do that?"

Podcasting is still in its infancy and will remain the great unknown until more people realize:

- You don't need an iPod to listen.
- It's not dangerous to download an aggregator like iPodderX or Doppler.
- Once feeds are entered, it's easy to collect and listen to podcasts, either on your computer or your MP3 player.

When you use the word *radio,* even with the word *satellite* tacked in front of it, people understand the concept and know what you are talking about. For some, podcasting sounds too much like something geeks do for fun, but we're here to tell you that even geeks don't know what podcasting is!

Radio has decades of history, ranging from Orson Welles's *War of the Worlds,* to Abbott and Costello, to FDR's Fireside Chats, to Edward R. Murrow bringing the news from London during World War II. Podcasting's history includes socialite Paris Hilton, The Shocker (from *The Dawn and Drew Show!*), and a former MTV VJ who now refers to himself as "The Podfather" and his favorite casts as "The Pod Squad."

It is the newness of podcasting, along with the comfort level and familiarity of the general public (geeks included), that will keep radio in the forefront of broadcasting audio content. Perhaps marketers see a potential here, and so they should, but it will be a few more feeds, a few more articles in print media, and a little more innovation before podcasting can truly unhinge radio.

Are You Sure You Want to Say That?: Benefits of the FCC

The origins of George Carlin's famous rant "The Seven Dirty Words You Can Never Say on Television" stems from a routine appearing on the album *Indecent Exposure*. The monologue was played on Pacifica radio station WBAI-FM, bringing on the wrath of the Federal Communications Commission. Since then, the FCC has kept a watchful eye on what is said and done on the public airwaves of both television and radio.

Podcasting has remained out of the reach of the FCC, which gives podcasters and their listeners carte blanche to say and do just about anything they want. Some podcasts focus on sexuality of all kinds, and other podcasts let the occasional obscenity slip by the producers. Across the podosphere, though, there is an understood protocol that if you are doing a podcast that is meant for adults and not young Web surfers, it is a good idea to let people know.

The lack of restraints and restrictions of the FCC, allowing podcasters to go far beyond what is considered by the government as decent, is not only podcasting's greatest strength but also its greatest weakness. Part of the appeal of on-air personalities like Howard Stern is watching how far they are willing to go in order to challenge the FCC. We have no doubt that Howard is going to be a huge hit on SIRIUS satellite radio, but we also believe a good chunk of his listenership and an even greater chunk of his appeal and mystique will disappear. Without the restraints of the FCC, Stern can now cuss like a sailor, go way above and beyond what can be heard on conventional radio, and not care what he does or who he offends.

But here's a more obvious way the FCC gives broadcast radio an advantage over podcasting: You know that what you will listen to is deemed family safe (within reason). That can't always be said for podcasting. On your podcast, if you're swearing and producing content that's nothing better than prerecorded locker room talk, then you're probably in the clear because people know what to expect. However, if your podcast is on hobbies, politics, or sports, don't blindside your audience with profanity just because you can.

For mature audiences

Working blue is a term from stand-up comedy where your subject matter and vocabulary are strictly for adults. A great way to see the differences between working blue and not is to watch, back to back, the stand-up films Bill Cosby's *Himself* and Eddie Murphy's *Raw*. If you are working blue in your podcast, it would be a good idea to put in a disclaimer in the beginning of your podcast. Another option is to give your podcasts ratings similar to the ratings assigned to films. For an example of a podcast directory that implements a movie-style rating system, go to Podcast Pickle at www.podcastpickle.com. With the freedom to rant, rave, and swear, few podcasts out there work blue. An understood rule of podcasting is not to swear just for swearing's sake, and in many instances, editing out cuss words with sound effects can add a bit of humor to an already funny podcast.

So Many Podcasts, So Many Choices

An incredible thing about podcasting is how many choices listeners have in the way of content. Podcasting offers thousands of various feeds (as shown in Figure 18-1), ranging from general topics of interest to narrower topics that appeal to more specialized audiences.

Figure 18-1: Podcast Alley gives a rundown of podcasts by genre.

Conventional radio, however, has to vie for available airwaves and signal strength as well as fulfill a specific demand in the area. Sure, you may have choice in your listening area. For example, in the Washington, D.C., area, Tee can either listen to DC101 or Arrow 94.7 if he wants to hear classic rock. If both stations are playing music he's not keen on, then Tee must weather the storm and wait in the hopes of better programming. Podcasting, on the other hand, grants the freedom to choose from a variety that radio, be it public airwaves or satellite, could never deliver.

But is it possible to have too many choices? From a marketing perspective, yes, there can be so many choices offered to a consumer that the brain can't process that much information all at once. Then there is an issue of time. Do you have that much time in the day to listen to however many podcasts you register for? When you are searching for the right sports channel, you can more easily narrow down which show is best suited for your interests if you have 20 sports shows to choose from on satellite radio, as opposed to 188 various sports podcasts.

So while choice and variety are good things, too much can be a little overwhelming.

Quality Versus Quantity

Podcasts cover a variety of topics with a variety of personalities. Some podcast hosts are genuine, warm, and caring, giving you a glimpse inside of their world. Other hosts are wise-cracking, crass, salt-of-the-earth loud-mouths who are poking fun at the world while turning the mirror on themselves and dealing their own fair share of ribbing. So with the variety of subject matter comes an even wider variety of approaches and delivery. The same can also be said for the audio quality of these podcasts.

Broadcast radio, including AM stations that lack the quality and power of FM stations, can easily brag that its signal strength will always outperform the power of the MP3, and to an extent that is true. It's true until you start to travel outside of the transmission area, and the signal begins to fizzle. Weaker. Weaker. Then, much like a tense moment in a science-fiction movie as the escape pod slowly tumbles into deep space, the signal eventually disappears in a sea of static. If you have your favorite MP3 player plugged in to your car, your signal will never fade!

Still, when in the signal range with broadcast radio, you have a strong, powerful transmission with terrific audio quality. As mentioned in Chapter 6, there is no set standard for podcasts. Podcasts are produced with anything from professional-grade audio software and recording equipment to a 20-dollar microphone and Audacity software. The producers of the podcast, usually the hosts themselves, will compress the MP3 to provide the most efficient download. Many times, this will mean the podcast itself is difficult to listen to.

Without set standards for audio quality, you may find one podcast that covers sports the way you like and how you like it, but it may also sound like the hosts are talking in a tin can. Then you have the Official Curling Podcast — curling is a sport that many people know little about (or barely understand) — but man, does this podcast sound sweet! So until there are audio standards set in podcasting, it will be crap shoot as to how good a particular podcast will sound.

1 Can't Name That Tune: Music in Podcasting

Music is a popular topic in podcasting. In fact, it is the most popular podcast topic. At the time of this writing, 1,631 podcasts are listed in the Music/Radio genre, with Technology coming in second at 1,001 registered podcasts. As impressive and diverse as this may sound, hold your applause. As it was said in *The Hitchhiker's Guide to the Galaxy:* "Things are not always as they seem."

The Recording Industry Association of America (RIAA) is about as happy about podcasting as it was about Napster. With recent lawsuits following file-sharing technologies and the swapping of music files, legal teams are merely waiting to hop into their fleet of Tumblers (thank you, *Batman Begins*) and hunt down copyright offenders, and podcasting (in particular, music podcasts) has the potential to be a favorite target of the RIAA.

If you want to podcast a tribute, for example, to Billy Joel — call it the Big Shot Podcast: All Billy Joel. All the Time. — then you have to pay licensing fees to the RIAA just as radio stations across the country do. These licensing fees can be costly to the average podcaster. You can, however, play independently published and produced music, provided you have permission from the parties who hold rights to the music. In some cases, it is the record label, and other times it is musician. With many independent musicians, the record label and the musician are one and the same.

So if you want to play music that you don't hear on the standard radio airwaves, podcasting is a venue for you and your original music to be played to an international audience. If you want to play the hottest new releases from Coldplay, Switchfoot, and U2, you won't be able to do it for free. Because radio stations have the backing of corporate entities like Viacom, these fees are simply chump change for them. For the podcaster, that fee could be spent elsewhere . . . like rent.

A Prerecorded Show, Recorded Live: Live Remotes Versus Remote Podcasting

There are podcasts that you could consider slice-of-life podcasts. They're simply ambient noise of the world around them, recording a day in the life of the podcaster and sharing it with the world. These remote podcasts can be anything from a trip to the supermarket to the more-popular (and quite fun to participate in) *beercasts,* where friends just sit around and sample the beers of whatever establishment they are visiting. However, this is what separates podcasting from streaming audio: Podcasts are all prerecorded.

Radio will always have the advantage of *immediate* content. Radio broadcasts can bring live concerts, sporting events, and news to listeners as they happen. Sure, podcasting can serve as an archive for legendary moments of sports or history, but — while it is neat to hear Al Michaels scream out, "Do you believe in miracles!?" — nothing can beat the moment itself, whether you are watching it on television, listening to it on the radio, or fortunate enough to be there. The same thing can be said for the climax of Roger Waters's *The Wall Live in Berlin* concert or the 2004 Boston Red Sox breaking the curse.

Companion podcasts are the closest we come to live podcasts. A companion podcast is similar to Director's Comments found on DVDs, commentary that is meant to be listened to when either reading principal text or watching a television show. Such is the case with Ronald D. Moore, creator and head writer of the new *Battlestar Galactica,* and his companion podcast. Before each episode, Moore hosts a show that you can listen to while you watch the episode that is currently airing. You could claim this is live, but the true event itself *(Battlestar Galactica)* is prerecorded.

Radio will always have the advantage of transporting audiences to history as it happens, keeping listeners in the know of current events, and delivering content at that very moment. Satellite radio now solves the problem of limited reception. Subscribers to satellite radio never have to worry about losing a signal, staying with the live coverage from the beginning to the end.

Advertising: Show Me the Numbers

Because podcasting is such a new medium, potential advertisers will ask podcasters the same question they ask a radio station's sales representative: "So, what kind of numbers does your show pull in? How can I justify the cost of running ads on your morning show?"

The radio executive can pull out a ratings chart for his or her morning show and tell the perspective advertiser that the show pulls in a 12 share, which means 24,000 people are listening to the show. He can also break down the ratings points into age and gender groups, to give the executive an idea of what kind of listener tunes in.

The same situation with the podcaster is a slightly tougher sale. The podcaster says, "We measure how well a show is doing by bandwidth and downloads." Already, the podcaster has probably lost the potential advertiser with the word *bandwidth.* So the advertiser asks, "How many downloads do you have a month?" He looks at the numbers and asks, "Is that men and women, 18–25?" The podcaster doesn't really know for sure. "Well, these folks are downloading the show, but are you certain these people are listening?" Again, the podcaster can't answer for certain.

Advertisers want to know who your audience is and how your podcast can make a difference in getting people to their business. True, a podcast — unlike radio — reaches a much wider audience. A global one, in fact. But for many businesses, reaching a global market is less important than reaching a local market. You can measure your podcast's downloads many different ways, but when it comes to target groups (also known as *demographics*), radio holds an advantage with the ratings system in place.

Podcasting will eventually refine the various methods of measuring listener-ship and subscribers, and there are various scripts available that can be downloaded and incorporated into feeds and Web pages and can produce accurate numbers. But they are a far cry from the sophisticated ratings books generated for radio stations and their programming. Until computer programmers can come up with something more in-depth and easier for non-technical types to understand, it will be radio's ratings shares trumping the podcast downloads.

My Corner of the World: Local News

It's early morning rush hour and time to head out with a cup of joe, a break-fast burrito, and your newspaper. You get into the car and plug in your MP3 player and listen to the latest installment of *The Daily Source Code,* a change of pace from the local news station that is your usual morning fare. Only ten minutes into your commute, you run into a traffic jam. Thirty minutes later, you haven't moved. So you switch to your radio and hear:

> "And as we have been reporting all morning, the tractor trailer spilling biohazardous waste has caused some strange mutation spreading from car to car now trapped on the interstate. And it appears that some of the drivers closest to the tanker are eating the other commuters . . ."

You look up, just in time to see a small group of grey-skinned commuters with freakily glowing eyes walking toward you. What a different morning it would have been if you had listened to the radio and not your favorite podcast.

Broadcast radio has the potential to keep listeners informed with up-to-the-moment local news, a distinct advantage that podcasting falls short in fulfilling.

If you're trying to entice listeners to visit your community, traffic reports and local headlines might not be what you want to use. Add to this the problem of podcasting being unable to perform true live remotes, and the immediacy and urgency of local issues, traffic reports, and weather forecasts is lost. Local commercial and community-sponsored radio continues to fill a demand that podcasting cannot: late-breaking news in the area.

So before plugging in your MP3 player for your morning drive, you might want to tune in to your local news radio station first, just to avoid any apocalyptic backups on the interstate.

10-4, Good Buddy: Satellite Radio versus Podcasting with Professional Drivers

Satellite radio (XM and SIRIUS leading the charge) exclusively holds one advantage over podcasting: continuous content.

At present, the biggest subscribers to satellite radio are people in professions that involve driving — in particular, cross-country driving. Satellite radio solves the problem of traditional AM/FM radio in that the signal is clean, clear, and constant from one coast to the other. It is 24 hours of content that continuously refreshes itself.

In a 14- to 16-hour nonstop trek across the country, satellite radio can offer new and original programming. To achieve the same thing with podcasting, you would have to program into a podcatching client at least 28 podcast feeds (provided the podcasts are an average of 30 minutes in length), download them, sync them with your portable MP3 player, and then take it on the road.

It is not impossible to have podcasts take you from one coast to the other and back again, but as far as keeping the content original and new from beginning to end, you are looking at an impressive collection of feeds numbering in the 30s to 40s. There is also a bit more work involved with podcasting in programming in the feeds, downloading, and then syncing the casts. With satellite radio, the consumer simply has to turn on the unit.

Audio for the People, By the People . . . but Not Necessarily Embraced by the People

To listen to a radio broadcast, you need a simple transistor radio, a power supply, and a strong signal. Anyone can tune in, and you can listen anywhere within the transmission signal.

To listen to a podcast, you need the following:

- ✔ A computer
- ✔ A power supply
- ✔ An Internet connection
- ✔ An aggregator/podcatching client to subscribe and automatically download the audio content
- ✔ An MP3 player on the computer

All this is for listening to podcasts in the comfort of your own home. If you want your podcasts to go, you need to invest in a portable MP3 player. Not only is it an investment to podcast your own program, it can be an investment to just listen to them.

Finally, the sad truth and reality of a podcast is that you can put one together and tell your family about it, but that doesn't mean that they'll listen to it. If your grandmother is particularly savvy, then she might download and have a listen, but that is if your grandmother is really up on her latest Internet trends. Otherwise, she'll miss your podcast.

An advantage of radio is that you tell your family about your radio show. You give them the station and broadcast time. They tune in.

Listeners need to have some familiarity with technology and some Internet know-how to be able to set up their computers to receive feeds. While iTunes has opened the door for podcasting to reach the general public, podcasters are still working against the technophobia in receiving a podcast versus turning on a radio, tuning in, and listening.

Chapter 19

Top Ten Reasons Why Podcasting Will Kill (Or Seriously Dent) Radio

. . . .

In This Chapter

▶ Reasons why podcasting rocks

▶ Reasons why radio doesn't

. . . .

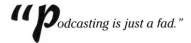*odcasting is just a fad."*

"This is nothing more than streaming audio, and that didn't go anywhere."

"I've listened to a few podcasts, and I'm not impressed."

The poo-pooers of podcasting (hey, that sounds like a great band name) have a plethora of reasons why podcasting will fail or never grow beyond the few thousand shows we currently see. And even if the numbers of shows steadily rise, radio and other forms of traditional broadcasting have nothing to fear. Or do they?

Chapter 18 gives you many reasons why radio will continue to be radio for the foreseeable future. In this chapter, we take the opposite vantage point. While the title may be a bit — okay, a lot — of an exaggeration, we honestly believe the powers-that-be in charge of the large corporate media conglomerates (radio, to you citizens of the world) have been observing the podcasting phenomenon for the past year with a weary eye.

Here are a few (ten, to be exact) reasons why.

Podcasters Don't Need No Stinking Transmitters

The distance a terrestrial radio station can transmit a signal is dependent on three things: tower height, transmitter strength, and FCC (or other appropriate government body) regulations. The first two are physical limitations that control how far a signal can travel. At some point, geography gets in the way, or the signal-to-noise ratio simply gets too low to allow for continued reception. The latter controls the competitive environment, ensuring that stations in different cities transmitting on the same frequency don't have to worry about their signals crossing over one another.

Podcasting is free from all those trappings. Instead of traveling in relation to the topography of the land, podcasts travel along the topography of the Internet. A signal released as a podcast in Arlington, Virginia, is just as easy to pick up in Perth, Australia, as it is for someone 20 miles away in Washington, D.C.

Syndicated radio programs rely on network relationships with various radio stations, each one picking up and rebroadcasting the program to its local area to achieve nationwide or sizeable regional coverage. Satellite radio naturally doesn't have those same limitations, but even it can't boast of global coverage unless it adds a few more multimillion-dollar satellites to its arsenal.

A podcast of exceptional quality and high personal appeal produced out of northern Scotland, for example, can (and occasionally does) enjoy worldwide distribution the moment the podcast is available online. Even the most popular programs on the largest radio networks in the world cannot make this claim.

 Reality check time: Just because folks all over the world can listen to your podcast doesn't mean that they will. And even if they all decide your program is the best thing since sliced baklava, listening to your program still requires a computer connection and device. So simmer down and get your head out of the clouds.

Podcasting Is Outside of 88.1 and 107.9 (And 530 and 1690)

The FCC (or other regulating government agency) allows a radio station to transmit on a specific frequency. That frequency falls somewhere between the end points of the AM and FM radio dial. In other words, you can't tune in to 87.3 or 108.7 FM, and you wouldn't hear anything if you could get your little orange stick to move to 450 or 1710 AM.

Really boring physics that you probably didn't pay attention to in high school tells us the number of frequencies has a limit between those two end points of the spectrum. Rather than make you do the equations, trust us that no more than about 200 radio stations are in any given area, split between the AM and FM spectrum. Two hundred may sound like a lot of radio stations, and it is. But due to a host of other incredibly mind-numbing physics issues and the hard facts of economics, you'll unlikely find that many choices in your area.

But pretend for a moment that money wasn't an issue, and that station owners were willing to take any slot they could get on the spectrum. Two hundred stations is a drop in the bucket when you consider how many podcasts you can access on a local basis.

Can you say "unlimited"? Seriously. The Internet wasn't designed with a hard limit on the number of connections. When network traffic gets slow, the companies that rely on those connections find ways to add more capacity. To our knowledge, we aren't in danger of filling up the Internet anytime soon.

Satellite radio and other forms of digital delivery change this, obviously. However, while satellite radio allows for many more channels than terrestrial radio offers, it still has very real limits. Ah, the freedom of zero spectrum!

The Rats Are Leaving the USS Commercial Media

Though the mega-corp media companies will squirm to hear us say it, the populous is spending less time with their radios, televisions, and newspapers. It's not that these staples of news and information are somehow less effective than they were 50 years ago. People are discovering new, improved, and more interactive ways to get their content and are making the switch.

Do a quick Web search (hey look! another interactive media), and you can find all the supporting documentation you need. In a 2004 report created by the investment firm Thomas Weisel, researchers predicted the only media channels with significant growth potential through the year 2007 would be interactive television (barely off the ground today), online (podcasting fits here), home DVDs, and video games. Traditional media is all in decline or flat at best.

We can toss out a host of reasons for this exodus, but it all boils down to one thing: more choices. We're still stuck with a 24-hour clock, and try as we might, we just can't cram any more hours in the day. Leisure time for most people is decreasing, so the ability to listen on the go is critical to many. Podcasting will become even easier to listen to as the technology advances, leaving the other forms of media consumption contemplating innovative ways to become more portable. Maybe that's why we are seeing so many radio programs and newspapers starting to podcast.

Podcasters Don't Have to Care That Most People Don't Care

Because of all the physical, legal, and economic limitations on traditional broadcasters, they have to make every second of their programming day count. And the only thing that counts is getting as many ears listening as they possibly can.

When you try to appeal to the greatest number of people, the content often gets watered down. You trade intensity for density, and are willing to sacrifice important and compelling programs for those that require a little less thought and are easily digestible.

As a natural result of this homogenization of radio, specialty and niche programs get pushed to the fringes of the clock, when listenership is already low due to the human body's sleep requirement. The station owner needs to fill the time with something, and it's a convenient way for him to say, "See? I carry cutting edge and meaningful content." He leaves out the ". . . at 4:00 a.m." end of the sentence.

But podcasting is all about the niche, because Podcast Land has no prime time. No one has to make hard decisions about putting great, but laser-focused, programs in a bad time slot. Whether a show has 100 listeners or 100,000, it makes no difference to the non-existent programming lineup. It's a matter of personal preference in the hands of the people listening, and no sacrifices are required to appeal to anyone other than those who are interested in tuning in.

We Now Pause This Commercial for a Word from Our Sponsor

Commercial radio exists for a single purpose: to make money for the owners. That's what *commercial* means. It's not about bringing more stimulating talk, playing the best music, or doing something for the greater good. Now, if the station owner can provide quality music, compelling conversations, or somehow give back to the community while making money, great.

Radio stations make the majority of the money they need to pay the utility bills and to provide employees a salary in one way: advertising. You might think the on-air talent is the lifeblood of a radio station; we know it's the sales department.

In the United States, one hour of clock time spent listening to commercial radio gets you somewhere between 45 and 50 minutes of content. The other 10 to 15 minutes are spent trying to get you to buy the latest car, switch your laundry detergent, or convince you to have a heart-to-heart with your doctor about that unmentionable problem.

As radio listeners, we're caught between two realities: The stations must run commercials to pay their overhead, and we've become accustomed to an oversaturation of commercials in our everyday lives. A few years back, most talk and music stations made an effort to reduce the number of commercials that aired in an hour. Did you notice? We didn't either.

Podcasters, by and large, are more sensitive to the perception of too much commercialization. Make no mistake — many podcasters want to get sponsors for their programs and to run commercials to not only pay the bills but also to make them money. But because advertisers have not yet flocked to the podcasters, podcasting has been more about the content than the sponsorships. For now.

But honestly, we think this trend is likely to continue for a few reasons:

- ✔ Podcasting is a personal experience, and listeners can easily unsubscribe and find something else if they perceive a podcaster is going overboard with the commercials.

- ✔ Many podcasts will likely focus on narrowcasting to their audience. This naturally limits not only the audience, but also the companies and organizations that wish to reach said audience with their particular message.

- ✔ The podcasting community demands it. Already we're seeing commonly agreed-to standards of acceptability on how many commercials to run and how often to run them. The current standard of acceptability is a 30-second commercial for every 15 minutes of programming. Of course, no official body makes sure all podcasters adhere to this standard, and certain podcasters exceed this limit.

But the community as a whole has seemed to have adopted a less-is-more approach, and is very cognizant of the detriment over-commercialization of this medium can have on a podcaster's ability to reach a wider audience. That may change in the future, and you'll likely see corporate podcasts completely ignore any standards the independent podcasts develop. But that's okay.

Podcasting Can Extend Public Radio

Mention public radio to many people, and minds immediately turn to endless classical music, dissertations on the status of the local wastewater treatment plant, and in-depth analysis of the current political situation in Uzbekistan. It seems that public radio is acting as a counter balance to the extreme sensationalism that is commercial radio by being anything but.

Say what you want about public radio, but we happen to like it. Unfortunately, much of the special interest programming we enjoy isn't on at a convenient time. Similarly, we've heard great programs on other stations while traveling around the country that simply aren't available in our local area.

Podcasting can extend public radio, whether you take that literally or figuratively. Already, we're seeing many public radio stations provide some of their programming in podcast form, allowing listeners the freedom of time-shifting. Additionally, we're seeing many NPR-esque podcasts appear, again spreading the feeling and spirit of public radio, minus the radio.

We're sure plenty of sensationalistic and commercialized podcasts are in the near future. But those are going to be in direct competition with the sensationalistic and commercial radio programs already on the airwaves. Because public radio is less about competition and more about cooperation, you'll likely see a mutually beneficial relationship develop between the public broadcasters and podcasters.

John Q. Public — Program Director

Program directors are the people responsible for what you hear on a station. If it's a music station, they pick (sometimes with lots of help and guidance from the larger corporate body) the genre of music that's played, and sometimes the individual tracks and artists. The same goes for talk radio and sports radio. In a nutshell, if something makes it on the air, it passed across the director's desk for approval.

We've known quite a few program directors. Many of them have an uncanny knack for selecting the hosts, programs, and style of entertainment that resonates soundly to the listeners in their community. But so far, none of them have made a station we can listen to for more than a few hours straight.

This isn't a negative comment about program directors, just an observation about programming for one versus programming for many. While podcasting networks have developed to provide listeners and subscribers with similar or related content such as The SciFi Podcast Network (tsfpn.com), most podcast listeners create their own programming lineup by way of their subscription lists.

The Niche Shall Inherit the Podcast

All the specialty and niche content shows that are currently beating themselves up and doing everything they can to get that 4:00 a.m. time slot will discover and embrace podcasting by the end of 2006. We're not saying they'll stop airing their programs over the radio, but they will find a bigger and more dedicated audience via podcasting. Sure, you can likely still catch the show at 4:00, but on the very good chance you're catching some shut-eye, you'll be able to listen to it later, as time-shifted content.

Producing an independent syndicated radio program is hard work — especially a quality podcast. But the latter has some benefits. The first is freedom — freedom from the FCC, freedom from a preset format clock that tells you exactly how long your show can be, and even freedom from the real clock and calendar in the time-shifted world.

Podcasters also don't have to worry about keeping stations happy, nor do they have to spend countless hours on the phone trying to convince new stations to carry their programming. We know more than one independently produced syndicated program that has ceased all attempts at gaining new stations simply because its listenership expands greater with podcasting. At least one has taken it a step further and canceled its relationship with its previous network of stations. And why not, when it allows you to dump those burdens and focus on building the best show you can? Sounds like a good plan to us.

Welcome to Your Own Reality

All of us live in our own customized versions of reality, even though you may not be conscious of it. Every day, you make choices that reinforce that reality. You select one particular grocery store as the best even though you could likely choose from five different stores. You choose a particular model of car to buy based on who you want to be as much as any other choice. Your hair style, the clothes you buy . . . it's human nature.

Whether you do it for status, frugality, or to be good to the environment doesn't matter — just as whether it's a good or bad choice doesn't matter. Unless you behave in a completely random pattern, you are reinforcing your own reality with the choices you make.

Podcasting gives you one more thing to add to the inventory of *you* and who you project yourself to be. We're sci-fi fans, and we listen to lots of sci-fi podcasts. Sure we like them, but they also help to reaffirm who we consider ourselves to be. Evo is into holistic health, thinks of himself as environmentally responsible, and digs trippy world music with lots of freaky drums and weird time signatures. Guess what sorts of shows are in his playlist? Tee loves his anime, his sushi, and his martial arts. It is no surprise that his soundseeing tours tend to be centered around the Land of the Rising Sun.

Radio can't do this. Oh sure, you can make the assumption that all NPR listeners are democrats, and everyone who tunes in to the local classic rock station used to have a mullet. While that may be true in some cases, it's likely not true in all, simply due to the complexity of the human psyche. We're complicated guys, and we haven't found a station that gets anywhere near summing us up. But take a listen to some of the podcasts in our playlists, and you're a few steps closer to understanding where we're coming from. Caution: The view from here is a tad bit scary.

You Bought This Book, Didn't You?

We end on the number-one reason podcasting will put a dent in radio: *you.* We're betting you have listened to the radio at least once in your life. We'll go out on a limb and say it was even more than that — a lot more. Yet here you are, reading a book that shows you how to podcast. Even if you are just curious about this phenomenon, your actions speak volumes.

Hey, don't get us wrong. We're not assuming this book has some magical power, or that you're so stunned by the stellar quality of the writing that you'll rip the radio out of your car. But you must be looking for something that radio is not, or by your perception, cannot provide you personally.

Maybe it's one of the reasons outlined in this chapter. Perhaps podcasting just sounds really fun, and you'd love to try it out. You sure can't do that in radio. But whatever the reason is, we hope you enjoy the journey of finding your own voice in podcasting.

Index

• J •

• K •

• *M* •

INESS, CAREERS & PERSONAL FINANCE

0-7645-5307-0

0-7645-5331-3 *†

Also available:
- Accounting For Dummies †
  0-7645-5314-3
- Business Plans Kit For Dummies †
  0-7645-5365-8
- Cover Letters For Dummies
  0-7645-5224-4
- Frugal Living For Dummies
  0-7645-5403-4
- Leadership For Dummies
  0-7645-5176-0
- Managing For Dummies
  0-7645-1771-6

- Marketing For Dummies
  0-7645-5600-2
- Personal Finance For Dummies *
  0-7645-2590-5
- Project Management For Dummies
  0-7645-5283-X
- Resumes For Dummies †
  0-7645-5471-9
- Selling For Dummies
  0-7645-5363-1
- Small Business Kit For Dummies *†
  0-7645-5093-4

ME & BUSINESS COMPUTER BASICS

0-7645-4074-2

0-7645-3758-X

Also available:
- ACT! 6 For Dummies
  0-7645-2645-6
- iLife '04 All-in-One Desk Reference
  For Dummies
  0-7645-7347-0
- iPAQ For Dummies
  0-7645-6769-1
- Mac OS X Panther Timesaving
  Techniques For Dummies
  0-7645-5812-9
- Macs For Dummies
  0-7645-5656-8

- Microsoft Money 2004 For Dummies
  0-7645-4195-1
- Office 2003 All-in-One Desk Reference
  For Dummies
  0-7645-3883-7
- Outlook 2003 For Dummies
  0-7645-3759-8
- PCs For Dummies
  0-7645-4074-2
- TiVo For Dummies
  0-7645-6923-6
- Upgrading and Fixing PCs For Dummies
  0-7645-1665-5
- Windows XP Timesaving Techniques
  For Dummies
  0-7645-3748-2

OD, HOME, GARDEN, HOBBIES, MUSIC & PETS

0-7645-5295-3

0-7645-5232-5

Also available:
- Bass Guitar For Dummies
  0-7645-2487-9
- Diabetes Cookbook For Dummies
  0-7645-5230-9
- Gardening For Dummies *
  0-7645-5130-2
- Guitar For Dummies
  0-7645-5106-X
- Holiday Decorating For Dummies
  0-7645-2570-0
- Home Improvement All-in-One
  For Dummies
  0-7645-5680-0

- Knitting For Dummies
  0-7645-5395-X
- Piano For Dummies
  0-7645-5105-1
- Puppies For Dummies
  0-7645-5255-4
- Scrapbooking For Dummies
  0-7645-7208-3
- Senior Dogs For Dummies
  0-7645-5818-8
- Singing For Dummies
  0-7645-2475-5
- 30-Minute Meals For Dummies
  0-7645-2589-1

TERNET & DIGITAL MEDIA

0-7645-1664-7

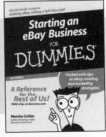

0-7645-6924-4

Also available:
- 2005 Online Shopping Directory
  For Dummies
  0-7645-7495-7
- CD & DVD Recording For Dummies
  0-7645-5956-7
- eBay For Dummies
  0-7645-5654-1
- Fighting Spam For Dummies
  0-7645-5965-6
- Genealogy Online For Dummies
  0-7645-5964-8
- Google For Dummies
  0-7645-4420-9

- Home Recording For Musicians
  For Dummies
  0-7645-1634-5
- The Internet For Dummies
  0-7645-4173-0
- iPod & iTunes For Dummies
  0-7645-7772-7
- Preventing Identity Theft For Dummies
  0-7645-7336-5
- Pro Tools All-in-One Desk Reference
  For Dummies
  0-7645-5714-9
- Roxio Easy Media Creator For Dummies
  0-7645-7131-1

SPORTS, FITNESS, PARENTING, RELIGION & SPIRITUALITY

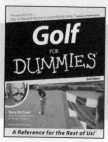

0-7645-5146-9

0-7645-5418-2

Also available:
- Adoption For Dummies
  0-7645-5488-3
- Basketball For Dummies
  0-7645-5248-1
- The Bible For Dummies
  0-7645-5296-1
- Buddhism For Dummies
  0-7645-5359-3
- Catholicism For Dummies
  0-7645-5391-7
- Hockey For Dummies
  0-7645-5228-7

- Judaism For Dummies
  0-7645-5299-6
- Martial Arts For Dummies
  0-7645-5358-5
- Pilates For Dummies
  0-7645-5397-6
- Religion For Dummies
  0-7645-5264-3
- Teaching Kids to Read For Dummie
  0-7645-4043-2
- Weight Training For Dummies
  0-7645-5168-X
- Yoga For Dummies
  0-7645-5117-5

TRAVEL

0-7645-5438-7

0-7645-5453-0

Also available:
- Alaska For Dummies
  0-7645-1761-9
- Arizona For Dummies
  0-7645-6938-4
- Cancún and the Yucatán For Dummies
  0-7645-2437-2
- Cruise Vacations For Dummies
  0-7645-6941-4
- Europe For Dummies
  0-7645-5456-5
- Ireland For Dummies
  0-7645-5455-7

- Las Vegas For Dummies
  0-7645-5448-4
- London For Dummies
  0-7645-4277-X
- New York City For Dummies
  0-7645-6945-7
- Paris For Dummies
  0-7645-5494-8
- RV Vacations For Dummies
  0-7645-5443-3
- Walt Disney World & Orlando For Dumm
  0-7645-6943-0

GRAPHICS, DESIGN & WEB DEVELOPMENT

0-7645-4345-8

0-7645-5589-8

Also available:
- Adobe Acrobat 6 PDF For Dummies
  0-7645-3760-1
- Building a Web Site For Dummies
  0-7645-7144-3
- Dreamweaver MX 2004 For Dummies
  0-7645-4342-3
- FrontPage 2003 For Dummies
  0-7645-3882-9
- HTML 4 For Dummies
  0-7645-1995-6
- Illustrator CS For Dummies
  0-7645-4084-X

- Macromedia Flash MX 2004 For Dumm
  0-7645-4358-X
- Photoshop 7 All-in-One Desk
  Reference For Dummies
  0-7645-1667-1
- Photoshop CS Timesaving Technique
  For Dummies
  0-7645-6782-9
- PHP 5 For Dummies
  0-7645-4166-8
- PowerPoint 2003 For Dummies
  0-7645-3908-6
- QuarkXPress 6 For Dummies
  0-7645-2593-X

NETWORKING, SECURITY, PROGRAMMING & DATABASES

0-7645-6852-3

0-7645-5784-X

Also available:
- A+ Certification For Dummies
  0-7645-4187-0
- Access 2003 All-in-One Desk
  Reference For Dummies
  0-7645-3988-4
- Beginning Programming For Dummies
  0-7645-4997-9
- C For Dummies
  0-7645-7068-4
- Firewalls For Dummies
  0-7645-4048-3
- Home Networking For Dummies
  0-7645-42796

- Network Security For Dummies
  0-7645-1679-5
- Networking For Dummies
  0-7645-1677-9
- TCP/IP For Dummies
  0-7645-1760-0
- VBA For Dummies
  0-7645-3989-2
- Wireless All In-One Desk Reference
  For Dummies
  0-7645-7496-5
- Wireless Home Networking For Dummie
  0-7645-3910-8